POWERFUL

VEGAN

MESSAGES

for a compassionate world
-Anne

D1367325

"*Powerful Vegan Messages* is a delightful and profound blend of advocacy, history, and philosophy in the posthumous work of H. Jay Dinshah edited and updated by his daughter Anne. Leaders in the vegan community provide loving tribute in heartwarming recollections about this activist and pioneer. The stories are at once galvanizing for seasoned advocates, and relatable and encouraging to new vegans and the vegan-curious. Everyone is empowered with Jay's ethical vision and method to live in a way that is courageous and kind."

—Dawn Moncrief
Founder of A Well-Fed World

POWERFUL VEGAN MESSAGES

Out of the Jungle
For the Next Generation

H. Jay Dinshah and Anne Dinshah

American Vegan Society
Malaga, New Jersey

POWERFUL VEGAN MESSAGES
Out of the Jungle for the Next Generation
© 2014 Anne Dinshah

Published by:
American Vegan Society
56 Dinshah Lane, PO Box 369
Malaga NJ 08328 U.S.A.
phone: (856) 694-2887, AmericanVegan.org

Printed in the United States on recycled paper with vegetable-based inks.

Cover designed by Carolyn Githens and Victoria Hart. Front cover photos: Jay and Anne 1971 by Rhoda Elovitz. Anne, Clint, and Harish 2012 by Helga Tacreiter. Back cover photos: Jay and Anne 1976. Anne and Clint 2013 by Darren Dinshah.

The opinions expressed throughout this book are held by the individual contributors, not necessarily those of H. Jay Dinshah, Anne Dinshah, or the American Vegan Society. Jay never would have written an autobiography. Anne directs the Powerful Vegan Messages project which includes the book, e-book, archival and new videos, speaking engagements, and a campaign.

ISBN print: 978-0-942401-24-0, e-book: 978-0-942401-25-7

This book is intended for educational purposes only. It espouses the benefits of a vegan lifestyle primarily for the ethical reasons. For specific questions regarding health, please consult a doctor who is knowledgeable about the benefits of the vegan lifestyle, a vegan registered dietician, and/or other health professionals.

Dedicated to Freya who has cheerfully shared the joyous burdens on the path since 1960.

—Jay

Now also dedicated to Clint who reminds us to continue working to inspire the next generation to embrace the values of compassionate living.

Additionally dedicated to an anonymous person who will pick up this book and be forever changed by its contents.

—Anne

How many vegans does it take to screw in a light bulb?
Just one. Any vegan can light the way for many other people.

Ahimsa lights the way.

Go vegan! Glow vegan!

Be a beacon. No more bacon.

All animals deserve respect including human animals.

CONTENTS

Preface 11

Foreword with the Campbell, Dinshah, Esselstyn, and
    Robbins Families 13

Acknowledgments 21

Introduction from Anne 23

Introduction about Jay 25

Ethical Reasons to Be Vegan: Anne Dinshah 27

The Golden Rule 33

Reverence for Life and The Golden Rule: H. Jay Dinshah 35

A Crank Is Forged: Roshan Dinshah 42

Early Memories: Zinnia Konviser 47

A Joy to Be Vegan: Joy Gross 49

Let's Talk about Ahimsa: H. Jay Dinshah 52

Little Veggie: Dr. Tosca Haag 56

Pen Pals and Ducks: Freya Dinshah 58

Vegan Voice Heard around the World: Jay and Anne
    Dinshah 62

The Three Bs: H. Jay Dinshah 66

Lighting Up Main Street: Victoria Moran 68

Ahimsa Is Dynamic Harmlessness: Nathaniel Altman 71

Let's Talk about Veganism: H. Jay Dinshah 74

Plant Based, Plant Sourced, Plant Strong™, Total Vegetarian,
    or Vegan?: Anne Dinshah 80

Luminaries Love Animals: Sun and Light 83

Graff-itational Forces for Veganism: Brian and Sharon Graff 85

Getting the Veggie Bus Rolling in DC: Madge Darneille 89

F.A.R.M.—It All Began with Jay: Alex Hershaft 91

The Step of Veganism: Jay and Anne Dinshah 93

Vegetarian Societies Unite: Dixie Mahy 107

Setting the Stage for Veganism: Tom Regan 109

He Pushed Me: Lorene Cox 111

Average Amer-I-Can—The Power of One: Robert Amer 114

The Pillars of Ahimsa: H. Jay Dinshah 116

Wisdom and Compassion: H. Jay Dinshah 134

The Next Generation's Pillars of Ahimsa: Anne Dinshah 138

Foxes and Rabbits: Heidi Fox 144

Fashion with Compassion®: Marcia Claire Pearson 146

From Trout to Sprouts: Jane Sirignano 148

The Voice of Rajahimsa: H. Jay Dinshah 150

Our Summer to Remember: Art and Carole Baral 152

Compassionate Co-operation: Bob LeRoy 154

Multiplying One of a Kind Activism: Charles Stahler 157

Into the Sunshine: H. Jay Dinshah 160

Science and Humor: Dr. Joel Fuhrman 164

Seeds of Truth: M. "Butterflies" Katz 166

Believe with Me: Richard Schwartz 168

Transition to Veganism: H. Jay Dinshah 170

Transition to Veganism—A Second Opinion: Anne Dinshah 179

Owning My Decisions: Anne Dinshah 185

Lifelong Vegan Is Not Vegan Enough: Anne Dinshah 191

Healing Lessons: Dr. Michael Klaper 193

Complete Dedication: George Eisman 196

Victories for Humanity and Health: Mark Huberman 198

Humane Meat and Harmless Leather: H. Jay Dinshah 201

Inspiring the Original VegFest: Peter McQueen 204

Conference Organizing and Our Cat: Keith Akers 209

Vote for a Plant-based Hero: Jim Oswald 212

Abolitionist Vegans: H. Jay Dinshah 215

For Butter or Worse: Anne Dinshah 218

Helping the Next Generation Go Vegan: Andy Mars 220

The Mad Cowboy's Advisor: Howard Lyman 223

Awakening a Vegan Hart: Victoria Hart 226

Ethical Dilemmas: H. Jay Dinshah 229

Ethical Dilemmas Discussion with Jay, Anne, and Friends ... 231

Becky's Dilemma: Anne Dinshah 248

Victoria's Ethical Insights: Victoria Hart 252

Convinced Canadian: Dennis Bayomi 257

Vegan Advocacy—A Global Imperative and Personal
      Declarative: Saurabh Dalal 258

Becoming Vegan: Vesanto Melina 262

Of Figs and Thistles: Anne and Jay Dinshah 263

Berry Inspirational: Rynn Berry 267

Strong Vegan Pillars: John Pierre 269

Professional Vegan Cooking: Ken Bergeron 271

To Tell the Truth: H. Jay Dinshah 273

A Side We Didn't See or Hear: Maynard Clark 276

Remember to Relax: Anne Dinshah 279

Vegan and Sharing: Jackie and Jay Steinberg 282

Shine the Light on the Environment: Dr. Michael Klaper 284

Buy the Books: Robert Cohen.. 289

Nourishing Wildflower: Eric Nyman..................................... 291

Priorities: H. Jay Dinshah 293

Let's All Be Bright Luminaries: Rae Sikora.......................... 302

Closing Words: Anne Dinshah... 304

Afterword with the Campbell, Dinshah, Esselstyn, and
 Robbins Families.. 307

About the Authors... 340

American Vegan Society... 342

Books Published by AVS.. 343

Chapters by Jay contain the main concepts he taught in lectures and writings. Updates and edits from Anne are not necessarily noted, although many additions and comments are. All chapters from people other than Jay and Anne are credited at their stories. Anne compiled the stories, edited or wrote the biographies, and developed the catalyst questions for each chapter.

Preface

This book was originally published in print editions as *Out of the Jungle: The Way of Dynamic Harmlessness* by my father, H. Jay Dinshah, the first edition in 1967 through the fifth edition in 1995. This sixth edition has evolved into *Powerful Vegan Messages* and has been substantially edited, revised, and expanded with new chapters and contributors. Additional writings by Jay are mostly from the books *Here's Harmlessness* and *Song of India* and from the archives of *Ahimsa* magazine.

Out of the Jungle encouraged us not to live by the jungle law of "kill or be killed"—living at the expense of others—but to live in harmony and cooperation. Let's get completely out of the jungle line of thinking. Instead of taking, let's try giving, helping, and sharing.

Despite the brilliance of the original title, it doesn't resonate with the current population. The title change to *Powerful Vegan Messages* recognizes the huge advances in veganism. Vegan is now a household word throughout most of America and is even considered cool or sexy in many circles. In 1967 most people had never heard of vegan, ahimsa, or dynamic harmlessness, but they had heard of a jungle, and it was a place to start the discussion. In disseminating a message, pick what works for the times.

Since Dad's death in 2000 numerous people have contacted our family or American Vegan Society to share how he impacted their lives with his delivery of the vegan message. These stories became an integral part of this project because it's one thing to read his words and agree with him; it's another to put words into actions as so many people have done brilliantly. Interspersed chronologically through the book, they tell his biography, and provide perspective, inspiration, and reflection.

There are many reasons to read this book. *Powerful Vegan*

Messages is for everyone vegan-curious who wishes to discover the power within oneself to try something new. You will gain fortitude to make personal changes that have a positive effect on people, the animals, and our world. I admire your courage on this journey.

Whether you purchased this book yourself or received it as a present, someone believes you make an important difference. If you weren't interested in veganism and somehow find yourself with this book, I respectfully hope you find logical, positive information that encourages you to explore your choices. I admire your open-mindedness.

It is also for the person who feels lonely in the new vegan lifestyle and wonders what to do next. May you never feel alone again after meeting new friends in this book who offer realistic, positive solutions for frustrations, energies, and ideals.

This book is for people who have "discovered veganism" after the turn of this century and never heard of H. Jay Dinshah or his work. It's for people who have come to veganism for health, environmental, or other reasons to now add ethical reasons. It is also for all those who love and miss Jay, as well as those who barely knew him, to reconnect and know him better.

If you ever wished to have a mentor, a vegan parent, or a true friend, let me share with you my father: his words, his mission, and his passion to improve the world.

I have three main goals: to help people understand the reasons not to use animals, to encourage people to believe their choices can change the world, and to deliver Dad's urgent message. His message is especially for everyone who has never tried veganism. I hope you enjoy unwrapping his gift page by page, find it useful every day, and share it with others.

—Anne Dinshah

July 2014

Foreword with the Campbell, Dinshah, Esselstyn, and Robbins Families

Joining Anne's family to celebrate the release of *Powerful Vegan Messages* are members of three families. From the family famous for *The China Study*, Thomas "Tom" M. Campbell II, MD, and LeAnne Campbell, PhD, are brother and sister who further the philosophy of their father, T. Colin Campbell, PhD, Tom in nutrition and LeAnne in humanitarian work. Rip Esselstyn and Jane Esselstyn, R.N., are a brother-sister duo finding their own ways to further the work of their father, surgeon Caldwell B. Esselstyn, Jr., MD, utilizing science, health, and athletics to promote a plant-strong™ diet. John and Deo Robbins and their son Ocean Robbins are the family working together in The Food Revolution providing environmental and health reasons to eat plants instead of animals. Freya Dinshah and her grandson Clint Dinshah work with Anne at American Vegan Society (AVS) and are best at explaining ethical and social reasons, but promote all aspects of the vegan lifestyle. Bios follow the foreword.

The foreword captures the sentiments of this group and is based on quotes from actual interviews. The involved parties edited and approved the liberties taken in creating the flow of conversation for publication.

Anne: Thank you all for sharing in this celebration. People come to veganism for health, environmental, ethical, social, and an assortment of other reasons; the families represented travel in parallel paths. Everyone here promotes a journey towards veganism using whatever words work for the audience, but also practices daily the most valuable aspect of veganism that is often overlooked: ahimsa, not just nonharming, but the positive action Dad promoted as dynamic harmlessness. The families I've invited are some of the finest examples of aligning our work with our values. We all have a multi-generational focus of action towards improving our world.

We share a common goal to inspire people to eat plants instead of animals. Recognizing the value in collaboration, each family is endorsing *Powerful Vegan Messages*. We're a minority trying to change the world; we will succeed.

LeAnne: With cooperation and collaboration! There's so much optimism and energy in this room I know we can succeed in making a huge difference in the world. I hope readers choose to live a vegan lifestyle and feel like they are part of something great by joining us!

Jane: Knowledge is power and can change the world. No matter what angle of this movement—health, environment, or ethics—everyone can grab a foothold and get aboard.

We all have to have hope for the next generation. My kids are athletes; my husband Brian and I educate them that what they eat helps them perform. For my day-job, I teach sex ed. I tell the students why they won't need Viagra® if they stay clear of meat and cheese. Eat more grains, beans, fruits, and veggies. They get the message.

It's the same for everyone of any age; information is what arms us and protects us.

Tom: The best reason for the next generation to carry the torch is the severity of the problems we face. We may not have the peace and prosperity our parents had. We're getting to the point that the shape of the world is changing; diet/nutrition is so much more important. We have to consider the use of resources including land, fresh water, and energy.

LeAnne: And this is especially important for the next generation who will have to preserve the planet. We are at a point ethically that each person must think of our position as part of a larger group. We need to get children engaged to think beyond themselves. Knowledge is never neutral; it's political. It can be used to damage or to help the environment and human dignity. Everyone needs to reflect and be thoughtful.

Ocean: Young people have an immense stake in the future. Young people will be here long enough to experience the consequences and benefits of humanity's present actions. Young people have more of life in front, more opportunities, and a broader palette of colors with which to paint. It's my hope that growing up can cease to be equated with giving up on our ideals and can instead become an opportunity to live our values in the world.

Clint: Be like kids. Ask 'Why?' a lot. Why do people hurt animals? Why? Animals don't like it when somebody eats them. Why do people do that? Why?

Tom: Good question, Clint! Rip's book *My Beef with Meat* makes it easy to be armed with useful facts as people transition to veganism. Anne gives great stories and anecdotes from real people in *Dating Vegans*, which helps vegans and nonvegans interact. Yet, I believe it's a difficult personal change to become vegan.

Rip: You and your dad inspired a lot of people with all the science behind *The China Study*. John enlightened the country with *Diet for a New America* and more recently *The Food Revolution* by introducing the public to the enormous impact our food choices have on our health and the environment. There is so much more work to do; Tom, how do you encourage personal change?

Tom: I tell people allow yourself the freedom to consider this an experiment. Do the best you can. You don't have to become 100 percent this or that for the rest of your life. Instead of fearful, be intuitive; give it a try for two, three, or four weeks after which you give yourself the freedom to reevaluate.

Books such as this one encourage personal action. I also like Rip's twenty-eight-day challenge presented in *The Engine 2*

Diet. Many organizations encourage vegan pledges for a week or a month. Different options work for different people.

LeAnne: *Powerful Vegan Messages* presents examples from real people sharing how they persevered when society didn't know anything about veganism. These people planted seeds to grow into a grassroots movement. Looking back, they share the value in becoming vegan, how they have applied this to their life's work, and encourage a continuation of their positive impact on humanity.

For many people, it will be inspiring to know how some leaders in the vegan movement struggled before finding their way forward. Jay knew that mentors, friends, time, conferences, and community were all important to success, but that knowledge holds the most power. Although resources today abound for those looking for the vegan answer, we also should reach out to those not looking.

Freya: We can all reach out by being friendly and social. Share vegan food and meals with friends.

John: Human beings have always eaten what they needed to survive. We've adapted to wildly varying conditions and circumstances in order to survive. Now what we must do, to adapt to a world with the human population expected to reach ten billion and increasingly limited resources, is to eat a plant-based diet. We do not have enough land or water or any of the other inputs that make food production possible to feed ourselves anything like the amount of meat and other animal products that have become common in the Western diet.

Ocean: Everyone has their own part to play and unique contributions to make. There are more than seven billion parts to play. Whatever our history is—struggles and pains, gifts and opportunities we've known—we've been uniquely prepared to make a difference. It's one of the imperatives of the human journey that each of us is called to inquire why we are on this planet and what we can do to be instruments of change and leave it better for having been here.

LeAnne: I relish the opportunity to further this meaningful discussion tonight at the dinner party. Perhaps it's time to let the readers feed their minds.

Rip: Let's invite everyone reading this book to join us again. There we can all chew on information and discuss the bigger picture of promoting eating plants instead of animals. The afterword can be a big celebration with the readers at the end.

Jane: By then the readers will have greatly increased their vegan knowledge.

LeAnne: And then they will also understand the ethical dimensions of the diet we choose to eat. This book is helpful for everyone who is not vegan yet, as well as for aspiring vegans, new vegans, and even those of us who have been vegan for years.

Freya: And it's not just a diet, all the readers will then understand why veganism is a compassionate lifestyle.

Thomas: Readers will know where to go to learn more about health aspects of veganism and gain more understanding of environmental issues.

Ocean: The journey from caring to action starts with a single step. Every step you take on behalf of your values will help you build more momentum. In an increasingly-interdependent and globally-connected world, I don't believe it's possible to be deeply happy or fulfilled without knowing your life is a contribution to the world you want to create.

Rip: What advice do we have for people about to embark on reading *Powerful Vegan Messages*?

Ocean: Personal happiness and positive impact are inextricably interlinked. If you want to live a fulfilling life you've got to find ways to make a difference. Food is one place where the personal and the political meet. What's good for you is good for the planet.

Clint: And good for the animals!

Rip: If people examine their values, killing isn't high on the list. We kill over nine billion animals in the United States each year, and in turn they kill us slowly with our poor health. The ripple effect is profound and everlasting. I like the Gandhi quote, "True happiness is when what you think, what you say, and what you do are all in complete alignment."

Jane: Knowledge is power. Read on.

LeAnne: And read with a critical eye. Don't accept an answer without understanding the question behind it and the alternative answers to this question. Come to your own conclusions because the impact of this knowledge on your life will be far more powerful.

*   *   *

Thomas "Tom" M. Campbell II, MD, and LeAnne Campbell, PhD, further the philosophy of their father, T. Colin Campbell, PhD. The elder Dr. Campbell is known worldwide for his research that provided much of the science validation for a plant-based diet, and he was featured in the documentary *Forks over Knives*.

Tom coauthored the landmark book *The China Study* with his father and they run the T. Colin Campbell Center for Nutrition Studies in collaboration with eCornell offering online plant-based nutrition certification. Tom is a board-certified family physician in an active primary care practice. He is also the author of *The Campbell Plan*, a how-to book to follow up *The China Study*.

LeAnne is the executive director of the Global Leadership Institute which provides opportunities for teachers and students to engage in real world issues, focused on globalization—the flow of culture, power, and resources—and its impact on humanity. She is the author of *The China Study Cookbook*. Her sons, Steven and Nelson, are lifelong vegans, good athletes, and strong in academics.

For more about the Campbells' work: TheChinaStudy.com, NutritionStudies.org, TranscendBorders.com.

Rip Esselstyn and Jane Esselstyn, RN This brother-sister duo find their own ways to further the work of their father, Caldwell B Esselstyn Jr MD, who advocates a whole-food, plant-based diet instead of heart surgery at The Cleveland Clinic. The Esselstyns utilize science, health, and athletics to convey their message offering Engine 2 Retreats—vacations designed to increase plant-based knowledge. Dr. Esselstyn and Rip were also in *Forks over Knives*.

Jane is a wellness instructor, plant-strong™ presenter, and cook. She has been a sex-education teacher for over two decades. Jane developed recipes for Rip's second book and with their mother, Ann Crile Esselstyn, has another cookbook of plant-based, oil-free delicious and appealing recipes, *The Prevent and Reverse Heart Disease Cookbook*. Jane is married to Brian Hart, and they have three vegetarian kids.

Rip saved countless lives as a firefighter; now he is saving millions more with his *New York Times* bestselling books *The Engine 2 Diet* and *My Beef with Meat*. He was a three-time All-American swimmer at the University of Texas and spent a decade as a world-class triathlete. Now he partners with Whole Foods Markets to raise awareness about benefits of a plant-strong diet. He and his wife Jill have three plant-strong children Kole, Sophie, and Hope. More information from the Esselstyns can be found at: Engine2Retreats.com, Engine2Diet.com, Heartattackproof.com, and ForksoverKnives.com.

John Robbins, Deo Robbins, and Ocean Robbins. The Robbins family works together in The Food Revolution, building from the success of John's books *Diet for a New America* and *The*

Food Revolution. The Robbins represent environmental and health reasons to eat plants instead of animals.

Ocean at age sixteen cofounded Youth for Environmental Sanity (YES!) in 1990 to educate young people about the environment, which includes food choices. Through YES! success Ocean learned how to bring people together across boundaries—traditional sources of separation and violence—of race, class, gender, nationality, and religion. His wife Michele continues working with YES! They are raising twin boys, Bodhi and River, in a plant-based lifestyle.

John and Ocean team up their expertise as co-hosts of The Food Revolution Network with Ocean as CEO maintaining online connections to reach people. Their mission is to inform, inspire, and empower people toward action for healthy, sustainable, humane, and conscious food for all.

Deo is an integral part of nurturing The Food Revolution success with her love, organizational skills, and cooking. She is a singer, a therapist for children with autism, and a movement workshop facilitator. She also supports John's work by coordinating his speaking engagements, editing his books, and trying, as best she can, to keep him out of trouble. More about the Robbins family is at FoodRevolution.org and JohnRobbins.info.

Anne Dinshah, Freya Dinshah, and Clint Dinshah. The Dinshahs work together at American Vegan Society (AVS). They are best at explaining ethical and social reasons for veganism, but also they promote all other aspects of the vegan lifestyle. Freya is Anne's mother, Jay's widow, Clint's grandmother, and president of AVS. Freya's longer bio follows her chapter (page 58). Anne's bio is at the end of the book (page 341).

Clint loves happy people and animals. Born December 7 2010, he reminds everyone to do their part to improve the world and to do fun things!

Acknowledgments

Thank you to all the vegan luminaries who share their stories as collaborators for the new chapters: Alex Hershaft, Andy Mars, Art and Carole Baral, Bob LeRoy, Brian and Sharon Graff, Charles Stahler, Dennis Bayomi, Dixie Mahy, Eric Nyman, George Eisman, Heidi Fox, Howard Lyman, Jane Sirignano, Jay and Jackie Steinberg, Jim Oswald, Joel Fuhrman, John Pierre, Joy Gross, Keith Akers, Ken Bergeron, Lorene Cox, M. Butterflies Katz, Madge Darneille, Marcia Claire Pearson, Mark Huberman, Maynard Clark, Michael Klaper, Nathaniel Altman, Peter McQueen, Rae Sikora, Richard Schwartz, Robert Amer, Robert Cohen, Roshan Dinshah, Rynn Berry, Saurabh Dalal, Sun and Light, Tom Regan, Tosca Haag, Vesanto Melina, Victoria Hart, Victoria Moran, and Zinnia Konviser. We are honored and blessed with wonderful friends.

Thank you to the family examples of ahimsa in daily life who joined together with our family to create an inspirational foreword and entertaining afterword: LeAnne and Tom Campbell, Jane and Rip Esselstyn, and Deo, John, and Ocean Robbins.

Thank you to Janelle Davidson, Leandra Brixey, Wenona Dege, Darren Dinshah, Sarina Farb, Vincent Kelley, Sebastian Mitchell, Eric Nyman, and Marya Torrez for editing and comments.

Jal J. Dinshah enthusiastically shared in the task of searching family photograph archives. Carol Githens magically restored photos; she and Victoria Hart demonstrated patience throughout numerous revisions on cover designs.

Thank you for the generous support of *Powerful Vegan Messages* from Todd Alexander, Art and Carole Baral, Patti Breitman, Glendora Buell, Craig and Cherie Cline, Jim Corcoran and Rae Sikora, Climate Healers, Francis and Carol Sue Janes,

Larry and Jeanne Kaiser, Victoria Moran, Edward Moss, NALITH, London Yves Renusson, Janine Silverberg, Anne and Angus Watkins, and Anonymous People.

Thank you to Clint Dinshah for his patience when I was hiding behind the computer and his insistence on our daily fun runs so I have energy to advocate for the animals.

And the biggest thank you with hugs—and it's my turn to cook dinner—for Freya Dinshah whose guidance, encouragement, memory, editing, and wisdom made this project come together.

Introduction from Anne

What began as a simple sixth edition of *Out of the Jungle* has exploded into a big, powerful project with book, e-book, videos, and speaking engagements.

It is often said that we all inevitably become our parents. I always strived to be myself and chose a different career. Instead of running a vegan nonprofit organization, I became a rowing coach. I know too well the toll of devoting oneself to helping the animals every day, internalizing their suffering. I didn't have the desire or strength to suffer with them, although I have always quietly expressed vegan values in my personal choices. After chasing the American dream, falling on my face a few times, taking jobs in various locations, and building my own little cabin, I realized that it's not important where you are or what you have. As long as basic needs are met, life is about what you give and with whom you share time.

Recently I more closely aligned my work with my ingrained vegan values, while maintaining my day job for income. I know the vegan movement needs vibrant, helpful humans who care to do the very best they can every day to help the world. I have chosen to be not just vegan but to be an approachable ambassador for veganism. The main goal of *Powerful Vegan Messages* is to encourage people to do all they can to help animals and people without sacrificing themselves in the process.

A tremendous number of people have shared wonderful stories with our family about how Dad changed their lives. Because of hearing him speak and/or reading his words, many people became vegan and/or aligned themselves and their work more closely with their values. Stories on the following pages are meant to inspire you to live a vegan lifestyle and do your best to change your part of the world. Maybe you too will find yourself changing to a vocation that shines with your values.

After writing *Apples, Bean Dip, and Carrot Cake: Kids! Teach Yourself to Cook* with Mom (Freya), I secretly wished I could also write a book with Dad. I would have preferred to do it together, in person, to go back in time and have the opportunity to appreciate him again, but that unfortunately can never happen. One wintery day in late 2012, Mom and I were in the warehouse getting books to restock the American Vegan Society shelves. She noticed we were down to the last two cases of *Out of the Jungle*. I took one copy for myself, thinking perhaps I would finally read it.

Not only did I read it, I devoured it. I recognized and treasured many lines of the book. Dad had lots of phrases that he used in daily life, such as "Ice, Ice!" at any opportunity drinking a beverage with ice. He was retelling his favorite line of the horse story you will read in later pages. As a kid I half-laughed while rolling my eyes and wondering why I got stuck with the strange father, but he made it easy for me to understand his basic message. Whereas I find his anecdotes in my childhood memories, you'll find them in this book to help with life's decisions.

Through the years I received plenty of personal lectures from Dad on a variety of topics. I attended numerous lectures for large audiences; he often took me with him to sell the books. As a young child I remember scribbling his lecture notes on index cards as we drove to events. Often he never even took the cards out of his pocket during the lecture. Just knowing he had them if needed was enough.

That's how I've treated the wisdom he shared with me. I kept it in my pocket knowing it would be there if I ever needed it. Now it's time to share his wisdom with you.

Introduction about Jay

H. Jay Dinshah's choices throughout his life and the passion with which he shared his thoughts are best understood with this story as his introduction. One thing may change your path forever.

Jay's parents raised their family as lacto-vegetarians. His father, Colonel Dinshah P. Ghadiali, told his seven sons how animals are slaughtered for food. They thought he exaggerated, and they questioned him, "Was it really so horrible?"

Colonel Dinshah, who had visited Armour's slaughterhouse in Chicago in the 1920s, replied, "Go and see."

It was 1957. Jay and his younger brother Noshervan were twenty-three and twenty years old respectively. Together they went to Cross Brothers on Front Street in Philadelphia where cows were slaughtered. The whole atmosphere caused them to shudder. They were assailed by a smell so terrible that Jay felt like vomiting and wanted to leave. Noshervan insisted they see the whole process through to the end, by which time he too wanted to vomit.

Jay said, "Upon emerging from that windowless house of horrors, I disposed of my blood-saturated shoes. I threw every stitch of clothing into the wash. I bathed profusely in an effort to remove the clinging fragrance of that charnel house. Even so, it seemed I could not rid my nostrils of the awful stench for weeks thereafter. Decades have passed since that melancholy day, but the repugnance of those sights and smells is still well etched in memory.

"While clothes and skin can be washed clean in time, what soaps can we use to cleanse the conscience? Which superfortified detergent shall we use to scrub the soul pure and clean?"

Jay made a vow that day: "I will work every day until all the slaughterhouses are closed!" He kept that vow. His supremely workaholic devotion and internalization of all the suffering of animals led him to a life of service that came to a surprising halt by his death on June 8 2000.

He did all he could. Now it's our turn to collectively do our part to accomplish the mission together. Let's work to close the slaughterhouses—nonviolently with our knowledge.

Ethical Reasons to Be Vegan

Anne Dinshah

I have grown to love Dad's words and wish to share them with you, but only recently have I been truly able to learn and understand their full meaning. I recognize we all travel at our own pace, and our journeys through life are a great example. Think of this book as an information booth at a welcome center. Ask questions and take the information you need.

The ethical basics of veganism can be put very simply in plain English. Be kind to all beings. Eat plants instead of animals. Your decision will help people, the planet, and the animals. We go on to more complex explanations from there.

I looked for another simple way to begin to explain what Dad wrote. Sometimes kids amaze us with their answers, so I asked my son Clint to help me. He's three years old and vegan by choice, admittedly still a parentally guided choice at this time. It's my job to teach him my values, to arm him with knowledge so he can make informed decisions as he goes through life. We talk often. He knows his mom's jobs are some days to teach people "how to help animals" and other days "rowing."

Our conversation just before bedtime went like this:

Anne: Clint, what is ahimsa?

Clint: I don't know what ahimsa is because I don't.

Anne: Do you want to know?

Clint: No. This is a backhoe. This is a dump truck. This is an excavator. This is a tow truck. (He went on to name all the trucks on the puzzle he was doing on the bed. I'm sure I didn't want to know the word ahimsa at his age, either, so we did the puzzle together before I continued.)

Anne: The word ahimsa means to be nice to people and animals. What do you think?

Clint: That's better because I don't like animals to die for people to eat.

Anne: What does vegan mean?

Clint: Our food comes from plants. Some people eat animals and some don't.

Anne: Why don't we eat animals?

Clint: We don't want to.

Anne: Is it our choice?

Clint: No, the animals don't want us to. If people eat them, they are dead. The animals need to live so they can play.

I don't like people eating animals, and I don't want that to happen. If we don't want to eat them, they will be happy, and if we want to eat them, they will be dead. If we eat them all, then they will all be dead. The animals should be able to do fun things.

Anne: Wow. Thank you, Clint. You said it better than I could.

Clint: I told you a short story. Now go to bed.

Anne: Thank you for your help. (I kissed him goodnight with a big hug.)

I want to make it easy for people who are not vegan yet to understand Dad's lessons. I lived with Dad for seventeen years, worked with him, and knew him better than most people. It still took many years and my own faraway experiences before I really grasped what he meant in his lectures, not just about being vegan but knowing it deep in my heart.

I remember when Dad tried to sit down with my brother Daniel and me on the sofa and read to us from *The Dhammapada* and *Out of the Jungle*. Those were the longest Sundays of my life. I just wasn't ready for it.

My role is to make this book even more enjoyable to read, especially if you are new to the idea of veganism. I hope the hours or days you spend with us are beneficial to many aspects of your life in today's world. The beauty of electing to read *Powerful Vegan Messages* is that you can close it at any time or flip to a different page. Learn what you want at your own pace. Each chapter is different. Have patience with yourself.

Dad's favorite lectures included words and phrases such as The Golden Rule, reverence for life, ahimsa, dynamic harmlessness, vegan, Schweitzer, and Gandhi. I thought back to my understanding of each at different ages, at let's say, ages five, ten, twenty, thirty, and forty. It's not necessarily anything to do with age, but I picked this as a way to mark my personal understanding of these key concepts. Perhaps numbers indicate ages or stages of interest in information or percent of understanding. We each follow our own progression. Mine went something like this:

The Golden Rule

5   Be kind.

10 Do unto others as you would have them do unto you—as memorized from a church I visited.

20 Do to others as you want them to do to you.

30 Respect everyone and hope they do likewise.

40 The foundation of Dad's book *Out of the Jungle* as he applies it to being kind to all humans and animals.

Reverence for Life

5   Be good.

10 Don't kill.

20 Don't kill unless you have to.

30 Think about the value of life.

40 Respect all animals, human or nonhuman, and take conscious responsibility for any harm I cause.

Ahimsa

5   That's the name of Dad's magazine.

10 It's the name of the magazine of American Vegan Society, maybe a word Dad brought back from a trip to India.

20 It means nonviolence like Gandhi promoted.

30 Dad talked about it as pillars; each letter stands for something important. They are still listed in the magazine, with the slogan "Ahimsa lights the way." Now we have changed the name of the magazine to *American Vegan* which is more appealing to the general public. Almost no one knew either the word vegan or ahimsa in 1960, but vegan is becoming popular.

40 Nonharming and more importantly the positive action side Dad promoted, utilizing the pillars of ahimsa, which encourages people to do something good in the world.

Dynamic Harmlessness

5   Dad needs a hug.

10 I'll go find Dad and help him with a project.

20 Part of the subtitle of Dad's book *Out of the Jungle*

30 Don't harm.

40 Do the least harm and the most good.

Vegan

5   I don't eat animals.

10 We shouldn't eat animals.

20 I choose to eat plants instead of animals.

30 I'd like people to choose to eat plants instead of animals.

40 I need to help everyone understand why we should choose to eat plants instead of animals and not exploit animals at all.

Albert Schweitzer

5 Is he a new co-op/intern coming to work here and to play with me?

10 He's a painting Dad did; not Gandhi, the other guy.

20 He's the bust in the display case that someone sold to Dad as Mark Twain so he bought two.

30 He's credited with coining the phrase reverence for life.

40 I'm re-reading *Reverence for Life* by Schweitzer.

Mahatma Gandhi

5 Is he coming to dinner tonight?

10 A wise Indian man who wears a funny outfit.

20 That three-hour movie Dad went to over and over again like thirty times at the theater before videos became popular.

30 He's an inspiring leader who promoted nonviolent action for change.

40 I'm halfway done reading *An Autobiography: The Story of My Experiments with Truth* by Gandhi

What I said to people who inquired what I'm eating:

5 I don't eat animals.

10 I don't eat animals.

20 I'm vegetarian. I choose not to eat animals.

30 I'm vegan. Would you like to come to dinner?

40 I'm vegan. Would you like to come to dinner? What are your three favorite vegetables?

At age five, I was surrounded by loving, caring people. In addition to my parents, we had numerous interns, then called co-ops, working at American Vegan Society and North American

Vegetarian Society. It was exciting, and 1975 was the year we put on the World Vegetarian Congress.

By age ten I was firmly in place as a volunteer working at vegan and vegetarian conferences. I remember the first day of one conference when Dad put me in charge of registration, then went to take care of other things. Someone came to lodge a complaint. She asked for the supervisor, and all the adults pointed to me. She didn't bother complaining; Dad knew it.

At twenty I was in the midst of my undergraduate years at Notre Dame as the only vegan I knew on campus. I was doing my own thing hundreds of miles away from Dad, not what or where he would have chosen. I'll never forget the time Dad gave me "The Mousetraps of Life" lecture a couple years later on the way to graduate school. It was a long drive from New Jersey to Texas.

I was thirty, living in cheese-country Wisconsin, and chasing the American dream when Dad died; I was "the girl next door" who just happens to be vegan. I was almost forty when I started writing *Dating Vegans* and began exploring veganism as something valuable I had to share.

*   *   *

It is human to have thoughts that evolve, opinions that change, actions that realign with our new values. If you understand the basic concepts involved in the ethical reasons for veganism, can you explain them to someone? How about to a young child? Are you ready for a more in-depth explanation?

The Golden Rule

The Golden Rule is expressed variously as famous quotes throughout the world, especially in religious texts. Historical quotes may have variations depending on the translator; the essence remains as The Golden Rule. We selected some famous examples to get us started:

Do to others what you want them to do to you.
>—Jesus of Nazareth, *Matthew 7:12*, Christianity

Treat not others in ways that you yourself would find hurtful.
>—Buddha, *Udana-Varga 5:18*

It has been shown that to injure anyone is never just anywhere.
>—Socrates, *Plato's Republic*, Classic Greek

Never impose on others what you would not choose for yourself.
>—Confucius, *Analects 15:23*, Ancient China

One going to take a pointed stick to pinch a baby bird should first try it on himself to feel how it hurts.   —Yoruba proverb, Nigeria

Respect for all life is the foundation.
>—The Great Law of Peace, Native American Spirituality

This is the sum of dharma (duty): do naught onto others what you would not have them do unto you.
>—*Mahabharata, 5:1517*, Hinduism

No one of you is a believer until he wishes for his brother what he wishes for himself.
>—Muhammad, *An-Nawawi's Forty Hadiths 13*, Islam

What is hateful to you, do not to your fellow man. This is the whole Torah; all the rest is commentary.

—Talmud, *Shabbat 31a*, Judaism

And if thine eyes be turned towards justice, choose thou for thy neighbor that which thou choosest for thyself.

— Bahá'u'lláh, *Tablets*, Bahà'í Faith

Treat all creatures in the world as one would like to be treated.

—*Sutrakritanga, 1:11:33*, Jainism

Don't do things you wouldn't want to have done to you.

—British Humanist Society, Humanism

Regard your neighbor's gain as your own gain, and regard your neighbor's loss as your own loss.

—T'ai Shang Kan Yin P'ien, Taoism, Ancient China

That nature alone is good which refrains from doing to another whatsoever is not good for itself.

—Dadisten-I-dinik 94:5, Zoroastrianism

*   *   *

In every religion I am aware of, there is a variation of The Golden Rule. And even for the nonreligious, it is a tenet of people who believe in humanistic principles.   —Hillary Clinton

Reverence for Life
and The Golden Rule

H. Jay Dinshah

Although many people in the western world may have heard the phrase "reverence for life," there are probably few who understand the deep meanings and implications of it; and undoubtedly fewer still practice it to a very great degree. Yet there is nothing very mysterious about it. An understanding of the idea can go a long way in helping one to simplify and clarify one's whole attitude and manner of living, thinking, and acting.

The phrase "reverence for life" was originated by Dr. Albert Schweitzer (French theologian, philosopher, and missionary physician, 1875-1965) to describe his belief that life has value. Life can be a worthwhile experience of development for all who partake of it; there is no such thing as worthless life. Still, in some situations we may be faced with having to choose and weigh the relative value of two forms of life. Schweitzer said, "To the truly ethical man, all life is holy, even that which appears to us from the human standard as the lowest. He makes distinctions only under the force of necessity, namely, when he finds himself in situations where he must choose which life he must sacrifice in order to preserve the other. He knows that he must bear the responsibility for the sacrificed life."

Dr. Schweitzer thus assures us that reverence for life is not some fanatical form of absolutism but really a highly ethical scale with which to balance any given situation, a yardstick against which to measure our daily activities. Similarly such means of measurement have been given in the major religious and philosophical teachings in all parts of the world throughout the ages. Probably the greatest and most universal is The Golden

Rule: that we should act toward others as we would wish them to act toward us.

Other luminaries have expressed similar sentiments through the ages. It is written that Plutarch (Greek historian, biographer, and essayist, 46-120) observed "Though boys throw stones at frogs in sport, the frogs do not die in sport but in earnest."

Sir Roger L'Estrange (English journalist and translator, 1616-1704) expresses the frogs' viewpoint, "Though this may be play to you, 'tis death to us." Children do some cruel things because they do not think how they would feel at the other end of the barrage. Adults show them by poor example that The Golden Rule is a paper platitude, not to be actually applied to daily life. Why should we not take it seriously, measuring our every thought, word, and deed against its timeless and benevolent message?

Many people—and the authors are definitely among them—believe that we generally plant what we will harvest and that we can expect to reap what we have sown in life. In eastern philosophies this natural phenomenon is known by the term "the law of karma." Karma literally means action, but in this sense it means a natural law of action and reaction, that for every action there is a corresponding reaction. This does not necessarily mean a system of "crime and punishment" such as the human mind might devise to mete out justice or vengeance. Karma is more of an automatic working of cosmic equity, to afford each individual the opportunity to learn the lessons in life that one must learn for one's own progress and development and perhaps to get closer to ultimate perfection.

Its workings are not difficult to understand. If you have a radio tuned to a certain channel, it will receive only a station broadcasting on that frequency. If you change the setting, it will receive another program and play a different tune. Those people who go through life with their mentalities tuned in to hatred, friction, strife, and discord will experience these unpleasant factors in life and in whatever there may be beyond—we will leave such speculations about the future to the reader's sense of theology or agnosticism.

Such people have a knack of bringing into their lives the oddest calamities by their own attitudes to life. It is a vale of tears, and so they are tearful. It is a jungle, so they act like the worst of beasts. And in so doing, they influence others around them to act in a similar manner. We broadcast by words, deeds, and examples until everyone so influenced or tuned in on a pattern of thought and action turns that part of the world where they live into a jungle worse than any ever devised by nature.

Then they lament that only the "law of the jungle" can apply to life, that civilization is governed only by jungle law. Kill or be killed, rob or be robbed, and exploit or be exploited are the valid rules that one must have to get by in this life. They make a miserable world for themselves and others who fall for this line of reasoning. They never seem to understand that it is of their own making.

However, we also see people who go their way through life in a relatively calm manner, helping others, not asking for reward or applause, doing good because it needs to be done. I want to emphasize that this is the right motive for right actions: performing good work for its own sake and not out of fear of punishment or expectation of any reward.

The Golden Rule does not set up a system of favors granted for goods delivered or works performed. It lights the path for us; it guides us to a superior way of acting. This is enough. Good that is done for the sake of self-gain defeats its own purpose insofar as the doer is concerned: good done for its own sake should be the rule, rather than the exception in life.

The person who has a mind that is controlled and serene, a pleasant and calm disposition, and a ready and sincere smile for others will find others smiling right back. To such a person, the world is a school in which all manner of great lessons are to be learned, and one accepts the education willingly, eagerly. We should recognize several advantages in good actions:

1. They help those to whom they are directed.
2. They help to improve the world outlook of those to whom they are directed.
3. They help to improve the world in general as a place to live.
4. They help to improve the doer, not by prospective self-gain but by the improvement of one's own character.

Thus we may easily understand that the practicing of The Golden Rule helps to bring about harmony and happiness in others and in oneself. Altruistic service in life helps those at both ends of the actions.

Every act of conscious self-denial for the sake of others ennobles the doer. Each act of kindness to others advances that person's moral and spiritual level.

It is not by drifting downstream with the current of popular thought that we attain what is really worthwhile in life. It is by swimming upstream against the rush of current opinion, when such current leads in the wrong direction such as over the falls of selfishness, greed, or injustice. Whatever others may wish to do, we must resolve in our own hearts that we will persevere in doing the right thing even if we stand alone in doing it.

But we are not alone. In between the two extremes of conduct, we may note that the vast majority of humanity is to be found. In selfishness, goodness, attitude toward the rest of life, daily actions, "neither sinner nor saint" completely, the average person plods along on some mediocre sort of ethical middle ground.

The majority of humanity is capable of behavior much more noble than we realize or would think by examining our daily habits. It may take only a nudge in the right direction to start us off on a new set of values and a new way of living.

This is not to say that all one has to do to make the truth known to the world is to set it forth by putting up a few posters or gathering some followers on a hillside. We are not so naïve as to think the great mass of humanity will come swarming to receive it, believe it, practice it, and live ethically and happily ever after.

In this modern age of cheap mass communication a numbness has developed in many minds. This forms a defense mechanism against the over-stimulation of senses by visual and auditory gimmicks. We see so much and hear so much, but so much of what we see and hear is commercial blather from someone with a great big ax to grind. So much just isn't so. So much is tinsel, tinplate, and trickery.

There is so much artificiality and puffery and sham on every side that even if the real thing comes along, it may well be lost in the shuffle, overwhelmed by the blare of neon, newsprint, and nightlife.

The Golden Rule is the real thing. It gives us a firm foundation on which to build a solid structure of ethical living and moral behavior. It immediately sweeps away the cynical "What's in it for me?" attitude, "do anything to get ahead" philosophy, and cheating, lying, and hurtful behaviors.

When I (Anne) was a child, Dad told me this story. It illustrates the difference between the way humans think of some animals as acquaintances—as feeling, intelligent, loving companions worthy of compassion, understanding and friendship—and the impersonal way some of us may dismiss the suffering of animals to whom we simply haven't been properly introduced, as we squeeze the last smidgeon of profit out of them.

Mike was out walking in Brooklyn one day, when he heard someone trying to get his attention: "Psst! Mike!" He turned around, but he didn't see any humans nearby, only a sorry-looking horse harnessed to a big ice wagon parked at the curb. This was in the late 1930s when many American homes still had no refrigerators and depended on routine ice delivery.

Then he heard the voice again and was astounded to see that it was the horse talking to him:

"Mike! Don't you know me? I'm your old friend, Joe. We used to be such fine buddies. Then I had a heart attack and died, and now I've come back as a horse."

"Why, Joe! I didn't recognize you. It's wonderful to see you again. But how is life as a horse? Are you happy? Does your owner treat you all right?"

"Mike, it's just awful. He doesn't feed me enough, and I have to pull this heavy wagon all day long. Then he beats me if I can't go fast enough, but this cheap old collar is rubbing me raw."

Mike was deeply moved by his old friend's miserable plight. "Why, Joe, that's terrible! I tell you what, I'll go and have a talk with your master. Then maybe he'll treat you better."

At this suggestion, the horse was positively terrified. "No, no, Mike you don't understand. You don't know this guy. If he ever finds out I can talk, he'll also have me yelling 'ICE! ICE!'"

A friend asked me if I was going to remove or update some of Dad's antiquated anecdotes, which I have done in various places throughout this book. I said, "Oh, you mean like the horse with the ice wagon?"

"Yes, ICE! ICE!" she said.

"Ah hah! So you remember the story. Then the horse will have to stay. He gallantly serves to illustrate a point and will not be sent to slaughter just because he's older than a refrigerator!"

Although technology has changed so we don't need to exploit horses to deliver ice, humans have devised plenty of other more horrible ways to torture animals. Joe the Horse gives a typical example of Dad's style of making a point. Think of Joe next time you see ice cubes in your glass. Then look at what's on your plate.

The Golden Rule and its obvious corollary reverence for life give you and every other thoughtful human being the basic ethical tools with which to build a new, brighter, and better world. Not all at once—you start in your own little corner of the world. You begin today to brighten this area, to sweep out the cobwebs of wrong thought, wrong words, wrong actions, and habit patterns.

You are well equipped to do this by yourself. You do not have to wait until the next-door neighbor starts in on it. You don't have to get a charter from the state or a loan from the bank or a grant from the government. You can begin it all right away and go along just as far as you like at your own pace.

It may save you money; it is not expensive.

It can be a pleasant and fulfilling experience; it is not painful.

It is outlined in steps, and others have gone before you to guide you. It is not difficult to understand. However, you do have to make the effort for yourself.

People progress one step before another; some skip steps and return to them later. You can tailor your rate of progress according to your present individual limitations. It is not identical for everyone.

It is likely to be the most exciting and rewarding thing in your life!

*   *   *

Translated from a letter to Jay, February 5 1965:

I read your magazine with great interest. In our time did we come across the idea of reverence for life...We have to do it. Because it belongs to the characteristics of man to be kind and compassionate to all animals, even to the tiniest ones. The idea of ahimsa contains the idea of reverence for life.

I thank you for sending your magazine regularly. I am convinced that the destiny of man is to become more and more humane...   With kindest thoughts,
                                                 Albert Schweitzer

A Crank Is Forged

Roshan Dinshah

I'm seven years and four months older than Jay. I'm second oldest; he was second youngest of the seven boys, and we also have a younger sister. Jay was born November 2 1933, appropriately a day after what is now World Vegan Day and during World Vegan Month.

Jay traveled the country spreading his message of veganism. "People call me a crank, but you need a crank to get things going," Jay said.

I remember the first time Jay was on stage around age two. We had a phonograph, put on a record, and he danced. We older kids gave small talks. I can't remember Jay ever had any elocution practice, but he definitely followed in Father's footsteps trying to convince people of a better way of life.

Our father Colonel Dinshah P. Ghadiali (1873-1966) was a vegetarian whose pioneering work in the field of color therapy brought him both praise and scorn as "The Wizard of Colored Light." Father lectured on taking care of oneself for disease prevention through vegetarianism, not just trying to heal with color therapy after a problem. We kids sometimes attended Father's classes on his Spectro-Chrome System, a very well-thought-out system of healing with the use of colored lights projected on the body.

Father was born in India, a Parsee (or Parsi) of the Zoroastrian religion. Parsee people are Persians living in India who escaped Iranian rule under the Muslim conquerors at the end of the seventh century. The biggest migration was around the tenth century when they settled in and around Bombay (now called Mumbai). Hindu rulers of India welcomed them, but they would not be allowed to eat cows. Father became vegetarian at age eighteen, introduced to it by his best friend, a Hindu in Bombay.

Father lectured on the same platform with Mahatma Gandhi and became his personal friend. When he first visited the United States in 1896, he became friends with Thomas Edison, and the *New York Times* hailed Father as the "Parsee Edison."

He returned to the United States in 1911 and became a citizen in 1917. He married Mother, Irene Grace Hoger of German descent, and they raised their eight children as lacto-vegetarians from birth, all in Malaga, New Jersey.

Father had the grandiose idea of one son for each continent to continue his work. I don't know how it would be split up or who he was planning to cover Antarctica. All of us children worked actively in the office and the production of color-light machines.

The medical profession denied the validity of Father's work with color therapy even though many licensed practitioners were using the system with good results. The U.S. Food and Drug Administration determined that his machines fell under its jurisdiction and prosecuted him in federal court. Despite 172 witnesses who swore that the projectors had remedied various disease conditions, he was fined and ordered to cease selling projectors and related books in interstate commerce.

Father was never known as Ghadiali in this country. He was always introduced as Colonel Dinshah; so it was assumed that the kids' names were Dinshah. An Indian tradition is to put the father's name as the sons' middle names with the addition of "ji" if the person is living, indicating who is the head of household. Then "ji" is dropped when the person dies.

In 1953 we had our names changed because it was more convenient for legal reasons to align with the way we were known as a family. My brother Sarosh didn't change; he was in the marines so it would be inconvenient to change when all his clothes said Ghadiali.

H. stands for Jay's Persian given name Hom, meaning a sacred plant of the Parsees or a conference in the woods. Jay is a much more American-sounding name, meaning loud bird; he was meant to be heard. He never used any titles and disliked even so much as Mr. in front of his name. "Just call me Jay. I'm not an elitist," he replied in a letter to one person who tried to bestow a title on him. Jay was a man for the people and the animals.

The name Dinshah means king of duty and responsibility. Our parents homeschooled us to ensure we received enough education in ethics and morality.

Jay learned to follow in Father's footsteps literally onto the stage, speaking after him on many occasions as a teen. Jay always had skill with words. He imitated Father's speaking style with some Geoffrey Rudd influence thrown in. Geoffrey was editor of *The Vegetarian* magazine (U.K.) and author of the book *Why Kill for Food?* Jay corresponded with Rudd, calling him Uncle Geoff.

When Jay and our youngest brother Noshervan went to the slaughterhouse in 1957, Jay was struck by the callous nature of the slaughtering. He came home and talked about it. He resolved to be vegan and devoted his life to encouraging people to do likewise. I had been considering veganism, but had other interests at the time. When Jay said what his feelings were, I thought it would be a good idea to become vegan too, and so it has been.

Father was not very happy when he heard; he said we had to have some animal food, meaning dairy products. Veganism was the main disagreement I had with Father who called vegetarian "the rational food of man." One size, one type fits all.

It was not easy to become vegan, but I did it with a will and never really looked back on it. I didn't like doing without strawberry ice cream. It was a long time before Tofutti® came along. For a year or two I was buying sherbet instead; I didn't realize there was whey in it. Sorbet does not contain dairy.

I think I understood better than Jay how difficult it was for many people to make the change to vegan. I'm aware how difficult it is for people to leave off certain things, particularly when they have been so indoctrinated by "health authorities." I knew the political and economic struggle that veganism faces particularly in a country like the United States so economically driven by the capitalist system.

In 1958 and 1959 Jay was going around talking and putting out news notes. It seemed prudent not to pay taxes on income funneled into the American Vegan Society (AVS), which became a nonprofit organization in February 1960.

Jay thought he would be able to convince everyone to become vegan in his lifetime. He was very confident; without that confidence he might have given up a long time before his life ended.

*   *   *

Roshan Dinshah is retired from being an appliance technician and the owner of Bluebird Appliances sales and service. He is an AVS life member and one of the signers of the AVS certificate of incorporation. Roshan has worked for AVS since 1960. From the late 1960s on, he did building repair and things of a mechanical nature for AVS. When he retired from the appliance business at age sixty-two, Roshan was able to take a more active part in conventions and outreach of AVS. He has served off and on numerous times for the AVS council of trustees and is currently vice president emeritus.

Roshan's spiritual aspect of his life is the most important to him. He was thirteen when he was inducted into the Zoroastrian religion, the ancient faith of the Maji. Roshan studied all the major world religions. He joined the Methodist church in 1965, was granted a license to preach in 1974, and served as a lay-pastor from 1975 to 1977. He joined the Society of Friends in 1981. In 1988 he became a volunteer assistant chaplain at a New Jersey medium-security prison, which he continues to do to this day.

*　　*　　*

Books available for purchase from AVS can further your knowledge piqued by these pages. AmericanVegan.org

The Life of a Karma-Yogi is the fascinating biography of Colonel Dinshah P. Ghadiali who was an inventor, scientist, and humanitarian.

Let There Be Light by Jay's brother Darius Dinshah has information on color-light therapy. DinshahHealth.org

What are you doing to celebrate World Vegan Day? Celebrate Jay's birthday by giving gifts of *Powerful Vegan Messages*!

"Many people say, 'Animals were created on earth to serve humanity.' But I believe that animals are our brothers and sisters, that they have a divine right to enjoy pursuit of happiness, and that they should not be harmed, but loved." —Noshervan Dinshah

Early Memories

Zinnia Konviser

My early memory of Jay was at a hotel on Upper Broadway in New York City where the New York Vegetarian Society was having a dinner, possibly Thanksgiving, in 1950. They were talking about the new American Natural Hygiene Society.

His father spoke, then Jay. I remember Jay hopping up to speak, with all his energy and enthusiasm. Jay was all wound up, eager to empower others. I was eighteen, and it was great to meet another lifetime vegetarian about my age.

*　　*　　*

Zinnia Konviser, a lifetime vegetarian born in 1932, recalled this story in 2013 about seventeen-year-old Jay. Her two brothers have vegetarian grandchildren who are fourth-generation vegetarians. Zinnia's parents ran (Fannie Shaffer's) The Vegetarian Hotel in the Catskill Mountains of New York for sixty -seven years. She has been on the North American Vegetarian Society (NAVS) board of trustees since 1992.

American Natural Hygiene Society (ANHS) is now National Health Association (NHA), the oldest vegetarian-based national health organization in America. While it was founded in 1948, many of the principles upon which the NHA is based were devised as long ago as the 1800s: advantages of following a plant -based diet, importance of avoiding unnecessary drugs and surgery, self-healing powers of the human body, exercise and rest, a healthy environment, psychological well-being, and the role that responsible fasting can play in the recovery of health.

*   *   *

Have you seen or heard anyone who has inspired you? Think about how they inspired you and what you can learn from them. How might you apply that in your own life?

If you are doing vegan outreach, including speaking in public, have enthusiasm for delivering your powerful vegan message. The audience may remember the day they heard it sixty or more years later!

"I have no doubt that it is a part of the destiny of the human race, in its gradual improvement, to leave off eating animals."
—Henry David Thoreau

A Joy to Be Vegan

Joy Gross

I first met Jay at an ANHS conference. I took the train from St. Louis for three days to Los Angeles in 1956. After the conference I was invited to the home of a couple who were vegan. Jay was there too, so that's really where we got to talking about veganism. A bunch of us hung out as friends, just people getting to know each other. At that time it was still unknown that dairy products are bad for our health; it was assumed they were good and necessary.

Although most of us natural hygienists followed the ideas of eating predominantly raw plant foods and utilizing food-combining principles, some of us liked to include dairy products. Jay had been lacto-vegetarian and questioned what happens in the dairy industry. His trip to a slaughterhouse the following year in 1957 made him become vegan. He could no longer drink milk after knowing, seeing, and smelling spent dairy cows being slaughtered just like those raised for meat.

Jay was one of the first people who was into the vegan aspect of things; he worked towards getting the ethical side into our movement. He was a big presence at the natural hygiene conferences. Jay always had something to say and contributions to make, especially on the management end of things. Jay was always a very positive influence on me as well as the other board members.

I began as ANHS secretary-treasurer from 1955 to 1959 and continued on the ANHS board until circa 1982. My food demos at conferences were popular, and I became known as the "Solid Gold Cadillac Girl" of the movement.

Jay was always part of our discussions and decisions about the society as we grew. He was on the board from 1963 to 1967, serving as expansion director or press director because he was very passionate about educating people. He served again from 1982 to 1985 including as acting executive director from 1983 to 1984. He definitely was a powerful force in the natural hygiene society and the world.

When I was six, my mom had latched onto a system of health care that included vegetarianism, fasting, food combining, and exercise. According to her new gurus—William Hay, Arnold Ehret, Herbert Shelton, and Bernarr Macfadden—it was the way to keep fit and well and not need doctors. I ran the other way, towards as many chocolates and sodas as I could get. When I was nine, I developed psoriasis, a wicked skin disease which the doctor said had no known cause nor cure. My scalp was covered with flaky lesions that itched. I tried my mother's way of healthful eating and my skin cleared up. When I veered off track and went on an occasional cheese or ice cream binge, the lesions would pop back out.

I knew the basic principles of veganism since I was a teen, although I had a hard time being different. I also appreciated the wisdom I read in *Dr Shelton's Hygenic Review* and from my many friends through natural hygiene. Jay's explanations helped me share the ethical reasons as an adult.

Reverence for life was always part of my thinking and living. It was part of my philosophy for most of the time that I have been vegan. I went a little off for a while so my children wouldn't be made fun of in school; we were so far ahead of the times. My son Louis is sixty-five, and he's a lifelong vegan.

My favorite quotation was attributed to me in the bestselling health book of all time, *Fit for Life* by Harvey and Marilyn Diamond. It comes from a chapter I wrote in *Positive Power People*, "Life is based on awesome immutable laws. Ignorance of those laws does not excuse anyone from the consequences of their nonapplication of or the breaking of those laws." When we hurt other living beings, it will always come back to hurt us. A simple way to say it is "As you sow, so shall you reap." Eating animals comes back to hurt you and the planet. That's a powerful vegan message!

*   *   *

Joy Gross, born in 1928, looks radiant. She writes a health blog liveyoungerlonger.wordpress.com integrating her experience with her advice.

One of her best blogs is "Sowing and Reaping," which was reprinted in the *American Vegan* winter 2012 issue and contains her favorite quote.

Joy and her husband, physiologist Bob Gross, ran a fasting and healthy-living retreat, Pawling Health Manor, in Hyde Park, near Rhinecliff, New York, which was usually filled to capacity from its opening in 1959 until its closing in 1992.

She has influenced thousands of people, beginning with her lectures at the manor; then people wanted her to write it down so they could take it home with them. Her book *The 30-Day Way to a Born Again Body*, published in 1978, advocated vegetarianism with a vegan goal. She wrote *Raising Your Family Naturally* in 1983.

Joy is also the author of the book *Joy's Recipes for Living Younger Longer*, with color photos of all-vegan recipes. She leads the very active life of a great-grandmother who paints and gardens. She celebrated her eighty-first birthday by going skydiving.

*   *   *

Being vegan is great, regardless of your age. Joy shows how youthful older vegans can be. If you are coming to veganism later in life, we also recommend the book *Never Too Late to Go Vegan* by Carol J. Adams, Patti Breitman, and Virginia Messina.

Let's Talk about Ahimsa

H. Jay Dinshah

"Well, I'm still with you. Where do we go from here?" This may be your thought at this moment. To continue, I will introduce you to ahimsa. Ahimsa is a concept that can make a great difference in your life.

Ahimsa is a Sanskrit term that literally means nonharming. Until the twentieth century it was considered mainly, if not entirely, in its negative, or "thou shalt not," aspect. Mahatma Gandhi stressed the positive aspect of constructive loving action. Today we consider it in its fullest positive aspects as well as negative and explain it as "dynamic harmlessness." It means to go through life doing the least amount of harm, hurting, killing, as possible; and it means to do the most amount of helping, assisting, and benefiting of others as possible. So you see that ahimsa has two sides to it, one negative and one positive, to be understood and practiced together, in balance. This can help us determine what we should not do and what we should.

The concept of ahimsa does not mean that we should just retire to a cave in the mountains and do nothing, or sit on the curb and watch the world go by. On the contrary, Gandhi was a great karma-yogi, an enlightened soul who believed in active service and work to help relieve the suffering of the world. It must be service and work done in the right way through the methods of nonviolence and with patient understanding. Whatever we are to do, we must always use the powers of love and compassion never the negative forces of hatred and selfishness.

We can never really know ahimsa unless we are willing to face the truth about ourselves: our thoughts, our ways of acting and living, our habits, and our hopes. Gandhi called ahimsa "the only means for the realization of truth (satya)." So we cannot have the full truth about ourselves and about life if we do not attain an understanding and practice of ahimsa, nor can we have a full understanding and practice of ahimsa unless we know the truth about ourselves and about life. As we learn more and practice more of each truth, we attain a higher degree of truth about ourselves and about life.

"All right, so we resolve to learn the truth and to live by it. We will also try to be harmless. What's so great or lofty about that?" This may be the first reaction.

Do you realize the vast implications of living up to truth? It means that we cannot color our dealings with others—our friends, family, business acquaintances, other races, other nations, people of other religions and beliefs—according to our own prejudices and then liberally sprinkle the same with a big dash of self-gain.

We have to step outside of ourselves and view any situation impartially, not merely from our viewpoint but also from the other person's. If the judgment is left to us, we must exercise the fairness of King Solomon even if we fall a little short of his wisdom. Is this not fair to your mind? After all, in law, if one person sues another, neither litigant can sit in judgment, nor a relative, nor anyone with a stake in the outcome, nor anyone else who is prejudiced. Don't you agree that is a wise and fair rule?

How is it that in the dealings of nations each side judges the other with the predictable consequences that each sees itself as one hundred percent right and the other wholly in the wrong, then proceeds to act as executioner and to gobble up the spoils of war? This would seem like a judge who is personally involved in a case, yet is sitting on the bench, trying and finding a defendant guilty, pronouncing sentence, carrying out the execution, and then confiscating the victim's property for the judge's personal use.

How is it that we humans declare ourselves the sole authority and arbiter of what is due all other creatures and what we may expect of them? These creatures are considered lower in nature's scale of life, but it is a scale created by humans. Is this not again a case of stark, ruthless use of brute force and power for self-gain at the unjust expense of other creatures?

How is it that we claim to be the highest type of creature, yet act in a barbaric manner that would shame any reasonably decent denizen of the jungle? Do we not make our civilized world a more terribly cruel and unjust place than any natural jungle?

It is easily demonstrated that some aggressive traits serve certain jungle animals well in their constant drama of survival. But we like to boast that we have become better than these beasts who act largely out of habit and instinct and mainly out of necessity. Some people think humans represent the one creature that has been endowed with a mental and moral capacity to plan and build a better world for future generations. We consciously think about and set about to improve our way of life. We weigh, judge, and choose one path or another in life and imagine long-range consequences, abstractions, and ideas.

Humanity is not the exclusive owner of personality and sensations. We are not the only creature with feelings and emotions, family ties, a sense of right and wrong, or thinking ability. We should always bear this in mind when we talk about "dumb animals," many of whom have sensory development that puts us to shame.

If humanity does possess some capabilities in a higher degree, then it is our duty to use them for world betterment. How great the crime if instead we turn our capabilities to world domination and to looting and plundering of every creature who falls within our grasp.

Dominion over the Earth was never meant to imply the delivery of everything under the sun into greedy hands, to be despoiled, ruined, enslaved, slaughtered, or cast aside when we can no longer wring another penny's profit from it. Even leaving aside any such thing as karmic law, it must be obvious that our human greed and selfishness have brought us perilously close to

54

the brink of disaster and even extinction.

One way humans flirt with extinction is through warfare. We humans go our merry murderous way as if we were fooling around with bows and arrows and stone clubs instead of technologically-advanced weapons that can obliterate life wholesale.

Another dismal possibility of self-wrought destruction is our much-trumpeted "conquest of nature." This has many aspects such as denuding the land of forest and field cover, dousing it with toxic materials to create a bugless and perhaps eventually lifeless world, and habitually using poisons for everything from setting hair curls to killing weeds. What a pity we don't put so much effort into learning our own inner nature and conquering our lower, selfish brute nature instead. And if we were to start on all the foolish things we thoughtlessly do to ourselves in the areas of health and food, we wouldn't have enough pages to list them all.

Dr. Schweitzer said, "Whenever I injure any kind of life, I must be quite certain that it is necessary. I must never go beyond the unavoidable, not even in apparently insignificant things. That man is truly ethical who shatters no ice crystal as it sparkles in the sun, tears no leaf from a tree...." Others have spoken about "walking lightly upon the Earth," to leave the "shallowest footprints possible" insofar as damage is concerned.

From the beginner's standpoint, such advanced degrees of ahimsa may seem highly exaggerated or overly idealistic. But one must first learn the lessons in grade school before going to college. We are nothing if we do not have ideals and aspire to live up to them, however imperfectly as yet. It is said that practice makes perfect. Perhaps a whole lifetime may be insufficient to attain such a degree of perfection in harmlessness. That is all the more reason to at least get started on this path *right now*.

Little Veggie

Dr. Tosca Haag

I was eight years old when I first met Jay Dinshah at the annual American Natural Hygiene Society (ANHS, now National Health Association NHA) convention in 1958. He was an intriguing young man with loads of energy. Jay was very kind to us kids at the convention. What I remember the most from hanging around him and hearing him speak to others was this particular word he used: vegan. I understood the word vegetarian because I was one. I was raised without eating any meat, eggs, or fish, and so my little eight-year-old head just thought vegan was another word for vegetarian.

I grew up telling people I didn't eat meat because I didn't want to bury dead animals in my stomach. Basically what Jay was saying with respect to being vegan was that he not only didn't eat meat for the same reason, but he also didn't wear any part of the animal on any part of his body. He didn't wear leather shoes or leather belts and pointed out to me that vegan women didn't even use leather purses, and of course that extended to leather and fur coats. And he went one step further: as a vegan you also didn't drink milk or eat butter. This was huge to me back then.

It was the first time I had heard that you left animals alone because they were living, breathing, creatures of God. This was a moral issue I had never encountered in my teachings from Dr. Herbert M. Shelton and my mother, Dr. Vivian Vetrano. I always thought we didn't eat animals because it was bad for our health.

Over the years I have thought a lot about how gentle and patient Jay was to sit and teach an eight-year-old about his beliefs. He told me I should read *Little Tyke*, the story of a vegetarian lioness. I remember reading this book several times and eventually passed it on to each of my four children.

I saw Jay at the hygienic conventions for a few more years, and then he disappeared from our events. He was busy with his own society called the American Vegan Society.

While I missed seeing him after that, I never lost sight of his vegan message. He gave me the insight to understand the morality and humility of the human being who does no harm to any animal for any reason. I made use of vegan practices throughout my natural hygiene practice.

* * *

Tosca Haag, MD specializes in the field of natural hygiene. She started her career more than forty years ago after deciding to follow in the footsteps of her mother, Dr. Vivian Vetrano, who is world renowned for her teachings of health and natural hygiene.

Tosca and her husband, Dr. Gregory Haag, ran a health retreat in Texas for thirty years where they taught people how to regain their health through natural healing and a diverse vegan diet consisting primarily of fruits, vegetables, and nuts. Though they have since retired from their health retreat, they continue to teach and educate others in the field of health. Tosca especially enjoys children's health promotion and family consulting.

* * *

Think back to yourself as a child. Was there ever something simple regarding compassion or kindness that you heard, and it made intuitive sense to you? Reconnect with your inner child, and follow your heart to do what is right.

Pen Pals and Ducks

Freya Dinshah

Jay and his brothers played in a saxophone quartet, but Jay grew tired of meeting women in smoky bars. He took dance lessons to improve his chances, becoming a very good ballroom dancer, who excelled at jitterbugging. Then he took out a personal ad in *Peace News*, a pacifist weekly newspaper published in London with airmail copies distributed in the United States.

"Young man, American pacifist vegetarian, age 25, desires correspondence with young lady with view to marriage."

Amused by the unusual ad, my mother felt sorry for Jay and suggested I write him so he would not think he was the only pacifist vegetarian out there. He sent me a dollar for stamps so I'd write him back. I was in England and had to go to the bank to get the dollar exchanged.

He was writing articles for the newsletter of the British Vegetarian Youth Movement and sent me a subscription. An early leaflet Jay wrote was in a long version and a short version called "The Case for Eating Food" or "Pass the Pills Please"— pills went right into the trash can. Another leaflet was titled "Why Settle for Half a Loaf?" explaining to vegetarians that it does not matter whether an animal product is eaten or worn—the animal is just as dead.

By this time Jay was clear in his views, but I was skeptical about veganism. It was 1958. The letters got more frequent and longer and longer; some were typed but more often handwritten. The longest was over a hundred pages! I would come home from school and twice a week there would be a letter waiting for me. I read the letter before doing my homework.

Jay always put the time of day he was writing not just the date. He wrote about his life, living in New Jersey, then in California, and back to New Jersey. In New Jersey he was working as manager of a jewelry store where he did window displays and engraving on trophies for the Garden State Racetrack. He was good at engraving, but he questioned the ethics involved in a racetrack. He bought a Doodlebug, a three-wheeled tiny bubble of a car, and commuted to work at a hardware store in Atlantic City, but it was an hour-long bouncy ride, so that didn't last long. He took a job doing accounts receivable for a local oil delivery company. Jay wrote a lot about the reasons for veganism, his father's color therapy business, and his family.

He established a pattern of quitting work to go on a lecture tour, then getting another job when he returned. Although his jobs weren't big careers, at each he learned something valuable to use for American Vegan Society. In one job he did proofreading and layout for the local newspaper.

His writings persuaded me of the ethical reasons to be vegan, but I was still unsure about the practical aspects and the health effects. Jay proposed marriage via airmail, and I came to visit him in the United States. He met me at the airport in a '57 Chrysler DeSoto, blue with fins. Soon after, we were married on August 1 1960. We agreed on so many things in life, and there were not a lot of vegetarians in those days. If we didn't get married, we might regret missing the opportunity.

Jay enjoyed listening to political speakers and liked election campaigns. He must have learned a lot of his speaking skills from them. In his opinion, "It doesn't matter what your politics are. What does matter is that you are an ethical caring person."

We arranged to tour the country in 1961 and spoke to vegetarian societies in Washington DC, Detroit, Chicago, Los Angeles, and San Francisco; animal welfare groups; theosophical groups; health groups such as the natural hygiene groups; organic gardening clubs; and anyone else who would listen. Jay spoke mostly about health and the horrors of the slaughterhouse. He'd just get up and start talking. Where his mind led him was what he said—with somewhat of the flavor of a sermon, a call to righteousness. He was a motivational speaker convincing people to change their ways. Every group received a slightly different version of the same concept.

His views on women were typical of the era, but changed over time due to necessity—my influence. We moved to California in 1962, a new environment, where I got a job before Jay, and it flipped his views to equality.

We worked side by side at AVS but each took on our own roles that went with our strengths. He was happiest being the voice and the face of the organization as president. He also worked every task as a jack-of-all-trades: journalist, writer, speaker, accountant, mason, carpenter, plumber, electrician, whatever was needed.

I was happy to be in more of a support role from 1960 to 2000. In the early years, I took the lead when it came to anything with food such as writing *The Vegan Kitchen* or negotiating with food-service personnel regarding conference catering.

Jay was editor of *Ahimsa* magazine, which began as a mimeograph newsletter in 1960 to convey knowledge, enlightenment, and information to interested people—to reach new and other vegans, and expand vegan awareness in the United States. He was always eager to share his thoughts with the public.

"My father was labeled a quack. I followed his teachings, so I'm a quack too," Jay said, believing things other than the medical and pharmaceutical standards. That's how we began referring to each other as Duck and Duckie for pet names. Duckie stuck. There's a special ceramic duck in the family room at AVS headquarters as a memory of those early days.

*　　*　　*

Freya Dinshah has been president of AVS since Jay's passing in 2000. She is the editor of *American Vegan* magazine, formerly *Ahimsa* magazine. Freya is the author of *The Vegan Kitchen*, the first cookbook in the United States to use the word vegan in the title (first edition 1965, twelfth edition 1996).

She coauthored with her daughter Anne *Apples, Bean Dip, and Carrot Cake: Kids! Teach Yourself to Cook* which is now a book and ebook with gluten-free options and a YouTube channel *Kids! Teach Yourself to Cook.*

Freya has taught cooking classes to people of all ages for over forty years. For several years Freya has volunteered at a local afterschool program where she is currently serving as nutrition educator and teaching basic cooking skills to children ages six to eighteen. She has been a key organizer for local and national events to encourage compassionate, healthful living.

Freya and Jay were the first inductees into the Vegetarian Hall of Fame in 1993. *Powerful Vegan Messages* is dedicated to Freya and her grandson Clint, whom she enjoys teaching how to cook and sharing everyday delights with such as hiking or puzzles. Jay's original book *Out of the Jungle* was dedicated to Freya.

*   *   *

Anne: It's a common misconception that AVS was founded by Jay and Freya, but it was incorporated by Jay alone in February 1960. Freya joined his dream later in the year and has been with AVS since 1960. Now I phone her on August 1, their anniversary, and wish her happy anniversary of the day she married American Vegan Society. For more on Jay and Freya's story, see "The Great Persuader and the Gentle Decider" in the book *Dating Vegans.*

*   *   *

Perhaps you have nonprofit management or administrative skills and want to volunteer for American Vegan Society. Contact AmericanVegan.org or 856-694-2887.

Vegan Voice Heard around the World

Jay and Anne Dinshah

Jay lectured on his "Coast-to-Coast Crusade" across North America in 1961. His second crusade was the "North Atlantic Lecture Tour" in Iceland, Britain, and mainland Europe. During this second tour, Jay and Freya went to the 1965 International Vegetarian Union (IVU) World Vegetarian Congress in Swanick, England. Jay delivered his presentations with an enthusiasm that enthralled the audiences—quite a contrast to many monotone speakers who read their material.

Delegates of the Indian Vegetarian Congress organization successfully pleaded with IVU to hold the next World Vegetarian Congress in India two years later. The Indian vegetarians needed help to counter the pressures and the avalanche of propaganda from various sources that were pushing India ever further from their historic culture and principles exemplified by such great modern sources as Mahatma Gandhi. Pressures included the desertion of the traditional practices of ahimsa and vegetarianism. Pressures mounted for the commercial exploitation of agriculture with the increasing use of harmful chemical fertilizers and pesticides and the refining of natural foods into nutritionally disastrous empty-calorie nonfoods widely consumed in the more affluent nations.

Rising to meet the challenge, the IVU scheduled the 1967 congress to be held in four major Indian cities: New Delhi, Calcutta, Madras, and Bombay (Mumbai). The Indian host group invited Jay to come to India well in advance of the congress to travel the country and carry his message to cities and villages, ashrams, and schools while at the same time helping to publicize and arouse interest in the forthcoming vegetarian congress.

Jay was planning his next lecture tour, but Freya said it was time to have a baby. They negotiated an agreement. Daniel was born on May 22 1967, and Jay began his journey the first week of August.

Jay's "Around the World" lecture tour took him completely around the world, lecturing in eight nations on four continents, and visiting five more countries along the way. This third crusade occupied his energies and talents for eight months, nearly half of the time was spent in India covering the sub-continent twice by a variety of means of transport, lecturing and learning, taking the trouble to listen as well as the time to teach.

Over 10,000 heard his message in person in India; countless others also heard him on radio and on television in other countries. He lectured on ahimsa, veganism, simple natural living, diet reform, natural farming, and more.

To finance the crusade AVS summoned up all its resources about as substantial as a shoestring split lengthwise. It took a full two years to raise the cost of the air ticket that was the main expense. This being accomplished, Jay took leave of his wife, Freya, at that time AVS secretary entrusted with keeping the ball rolling in his absence, and his newborn son, Daniel, and set off on the long path ahead. Thus, the report usually took the form of a letter to his infant son, and this was printed in *Ahimsa* magazine along with the numerous photos he took. The nearly four-month period in India was later chronicled in his book *Song of India*. Jay describes his tour in such a way that the reader feels absorbed in his adventures as if there with him.

It proved to be a truly remarkable adventure including one journey around the country for talks and publicizing the congress and a second trip around with the congress delegates. Numerous special side trips for specific purposes, such as heavily covering the western Indian state of Gujarat twice and a thousand-mile detour for a personal meeting with Gandhi's spiritual successor, Vinoba Bhave, made it veritably as long and arduous as a typical

American political campaign, as bizarre and exotic at times as a chapter from *The Arabian Nights*.

Jay loved sharing his powerful vegan messages in Gandhi's country and even considered moving to India. Sadly, in a generation's time most of India had missed learning about Gandhi's teachings. Here was Jay the American to teach them about ahimsa. He was well received. Jay especially loved speaking to young people.

Jay wrote in *Song of India*:

I spoke to some seventy-five schoolboys and a dozen or so adults at a Jain school. This was an extra meeting arranged two nights before at the first lecture. I always outdo myself at such a meeting. I gave them a strong talk on ahimsa, self-betterment, and character—national and individual. I felt it was the best talk I gave in Surat and perhaps the most enthusiastically received. It also probably did more for the future of India than all the rest put together.

I believe in such young people. I believe they can be reached and that they take to a noble cause even quicker and better than their more cynical and "worldly-wise" elders. And I'm glad I'm still young enough to reach them as a brother and equal, not merely a hypocritical sort of preacher from the fossilized generations.

The Gandhian sort of message I have been delivering strikes a responsive chord with them: a better individual to make a better world. It is fair and just, not "one rule for you and another for me." It is the antidote to the hypocrisy they see around them in adult life. It is a pattern of living they can grasp in its pristine simplicity and follow even if everyone else chooses to go a different way. It provides the real impetus to live a life of goodness and universal love.

School and university students are the quickest people to adopt new thoughts, ideas, and ways of living.

Unfortunately for India, the only "advanced" way of life most are exposed to is western ultramaterialism. In this, they are aping the errors of their elders following discredited, disastrous paths like a pack of lemmings rushing into the sea.

The struggle for vegetarianism and what may loosely be termed the Indian heritage and way of life will be won or lost in the schools—but it can be lost by default, by adult corruption, apathy, inactivity, ignorance, and hypocrisy. It is not our youngsters in any country who are failing us—we have already failed them by leaving them without a strong example of personal integrity and altruism.

The seeds of corruption and degeneration bear bitter fruit, and in a very real sense "the sins of the fathers are visited upon the sons." Give me the schools and colleges, and you can keep your country; I'll win it for Gandhism and ahimsa in a single generation's time!

*   *   *

Have patience with everyone learning about veganism, especially children. Children often understand the meaning of ahimsa more easily than adults.

In 2007 the United Nations General Assembly declared October 2 (Gandhi's birthday) as International Day of Nonviolence. How will you celebrate the day?

"Remember that all through history the ways of truth and love have always won. There have been tyrants and murderers, and for a time they can seem invincible, but in the end they always fall. Think of it—always."   —Mahatma Gandhi

The Three Bs

H. Jay Dinshah

One of my fakir (mystic) friends at Connaught Circus, who had never seen me before in his life, gave me an interesting prophecy to digest. It concerned various "Bs" in my life, including Business, Building, and Baby.

He told me I was not the type of person to ever be content with working for a boss and would instead create a new business. I would also be building a building in connection with the business. And my wife was supposed to have a new baby. All of this he said he saw in the works in the following year 1968.

Now, I knew we were stone broke and in debt up to our ears as always, had various problems that showed no signs of clearing up in the foreseeable future, and that having another baby was about the furthest thing from our minds. American Vegan Society (AVS) seemed business enough insofar as occupying our full time. When he asserted that Freya was due for another child in 1968, I chuckled and told him, "She had better not—I'm not due home 'til April!" But he was most emphatic in his forecasts, and I was duly impressed...

The new "B" for Business forecast in Delhi came about with a "B" for Bang, when in late 1968, my beloved mother, Irene Grace Dinshah, donated her huge family home to AVS to be used as our new headquarters and "educreational" center known as SunCrest...

Almost at once upon moving into the new quarters, extensive alterations were begun, and a new wing to enlarge the office space and provide further guest accommodations. Thus the second "B" for Building was right on schedule!

For many years of our marriage, Freya and I considered AVS our "baby"—and no baby ever demanded more time and loving care—so Daniel was in a sense our "second baby." We therefore thought that perhaps the old fakir had meant the SunCrest project as the "new baby" until New Baby Anne put in her appearance on the last day of 1969. We can forgive the old boy for being a bit off in his timetable.

*   *   *

Welcome Jay's coauthor for *Powerful Vegan Messages*, his daughter Anne.

*   *   *

If fakirs aren't your thing, perhaps you prefer to receive news via email newsletters. Sign up with a number of sources including AmericanVegan.org, DoctorKlaper.com, FoodRevolution.org, MercyForAnimals.org, PETA.org, and VegSource.com.

If you prefer to read magazines, try *American Vegan* (AVS), *VegNews*, *Vegan Health and Fitness*, *Vegetarian Voice* (NAVS), *Good Medicine* (Physicians Committee for Responsible Medicine), *Health Science* (NHA), and *The Vegan* which is the original vegan magazine from the first vegan society in the world, The Vegan Society, founded in 1944 in England.

Lighting Up Main Street

Victoria Moran

I was twenty, newly vegetarian, intrigued by the spiritual and ethical promise of veganism, but I was a practicing compulsive overeater who couldn't stay vegan more than a few days at most. I read everything vegan I could get. At that time, just about everything was written by H. Jay Dinshah. I inhaled *Out of the Jungle*, all of his other books, and every issue of *Ahimsa*. Jay was my mentor at large.

When I learned he'd be touring the country, I arranged for him to speak at my place of employment, the headquarters of the Theosophical Society in America, located in the Chicago suburb of Wheaton, Illinois. Jay arrived in full regalia: a little white car with the backseat made into a bed, books in the trunk, and a passion for this strange word that started with "v" that most people couldn't pronounce.

The theosophical crowd gave him a mixed welcome. Our semi-volunteer staff was comprised of retirees and a contingent of under-twenty-fivers. The elders were threatened: being vegetarian was quite enough for them—but we young ones were thrilled with Jay. I hung on his every word: "The purpose of life is to do the most good and the least harm possible. ...Pity the poor animals whose best hope is us!" I didn't ponder his ideas; I swallowed them whole. If he said it, I believed it, and that settled it.

Two years later in 1973, I was back in Kansas City, living in an ancient rooming house full of hippies and eccentrics, and hosted Jay to speak in the third-floor ballroom of the rumble-tumble Victorian. The electricity gave out during his visit—hot water, too—and I apologized by saying, "Maybe you can think of this as more like Europe," to which the ever deadpan Jay replied:

"Europe? This is worse than India." Even so, we got him an audience of forty-seven souls, and he answered their questions until late into the night before he took off for St. Louis.

When I watched the white car turn the corner, I knew I had been in the presence of an extraordinary man. He seemed like a modern-day John the Baptist—before his time but not too much.

I still did periodic binge eating, and it would be another ten years before I graduated from vegan at home to vegan for certain. Jay never gave up on me. That meant everything.

We all have a handful of people whose lives changed ours. Jay changed me profoundly, as he did so many others. He and Freya fueled the spark of veganism so that today it's a household word—infinitely pronounceable. I am healthy today and at peace with myself largely because Jay invited me to come "out of the jungle" and into the most fulfilling life possible. Thanks, Jay, you're one bright light.

*   *   *

Victoria Moran is now one of the most brilliant lights herself, an engaging speaker with a vibrant energy, enthusiasm, and great physique. She astounds audiences that she is over age sixty with a radiance admired by people of every age. She is on the AVS speakers bureau and an AVS life member.

Victoria's first book was *Compassion: The Ultimate Ethic*, her college thesis originally serialized in *Ahimsa* magazine and then published by a major publisher. When this book on vegan philosophy and practice went out of print AVS took over the publication. Her subsequent books include the international bestseller *Creating a Charmed Life*, the vegan weight-loss classic *The Love-Powered Diet*, and *Main Street Vegan: Everything You Need to Know to Eat Healthfully and Live Compassionately in the Real World*, coauthored with her daughter, Adair Moran, a lifelong vegan.

With *Main Street Vegan*, Victoria has found new ways to further align her values with her work. She has a wonderful weekly *Main Street Vegan* radio show on Unity.fm, and she founded Main Street Vegan Academy where students earn certification as a vegan lifestyle coach and educator. Information about the academy, Victoria's podcast, the *Main Street Vegan* blog, and more are at MainStreetVegan.net.

*   *   *

You may enjoy reading Victoria's story about dating her husband William Melton, which is the final chapter of the book *Dating Vegans.*

Have you struggled to commit to veganism like young Victoria? Be patient with yourself and reread her story. Then check out some of her many books that will help you along the way.

Do you like to teach? Would you like to be a vegan mentor? Do you aspire to be a vegan lifestyle coach?

"Animals are my friends, and I don't eat my friends."
—George Bernard Shaw

Ahimsa Is Dynamic Harmlessness

Nathaniel Altman

I first "met" Jay Dinshah when I came across a copy of *Out of the Jungle* at a food cooperative in Madison, Wisconsin, in 1970. I had originally viewed ahimsa, long defined in the East as noninjury, as an esoteric, idealistic philosophy practiced mostly by yogis and saints. I was immediately inspired—and challenged—by Jay's compassionate way as encapsulated in his pillars of ahimsa.

Through the artful yet simple use of language, Jay greatly increased the depth and breadth of ahimsa to the world. He also placed it in a holistic and practical, everyday context, calling it "dynamic harmlessness." Although I had a good intellectual understanding of ahimsa, Jay was the first person I met who was aspiring to live ahimsa in his daily life. By his example, he created a blueprint for me to follow, showing me how I could lead a more compassionate life.

Through his books as well as by personal example, Jay taught me the basics of how to apply vegan principles in my diet and how to live a more compassionate lifestyle free of animal products. Yet he also inspired me to embark on my own journey towards ahimsa that is still to be completed.

Adopting a lifestyle that does the least amount of harm possible to other living beings, following a path of right livelihood, practicing enlightened consuming, recycling, helping others, saving energy, and supporting organizations that work for good are essential for achieving personal and planetary healing.

Yet at the same time, the "integrity of thought, word and deed" and the "mastery over oneself" pillars of ahimsa that Jay presented are perhaps more important and even more challenging.

In my own life, I discovered that while I would often present a peaceful image to others, subtle yet unresolved issues of pride, jealousy, and anger lurked within. I saw that my vegan diet, cloth shoes, activism, and especially my scholarly knowledge of ahimsa often made me feel superior to others. I imposed my beliefs in an aggressive, self-righteous way.

Gurudevji Chitrabhanu, founder of the Jain Meditation International Center, best expressed the essence of Jay's legacy to the world shortly after his passing in 2000: "Jay Dinshah made innumerable people aware of violence and exploitation of animals and human beings and made them compassionate. What is not possible to do in five lifetimes for the average person he accomplished in this one life."

While people such as Jay may be destined to achieve great things during their lifetimes, I am convinced that our daily, simple, and often unrecognized thoughts and actions can create our own personal legacy. Every day we may have contact with between fifty and one hundred people, whether at school, work, shopping, or visiting with friends and family. This provides enormous opportunity for either promoting discord or peace.

Every one of our daily thoughts, words, and actions adds to the storehouse of human activities on our planet every single day. Through conscious awareness and the practice of compassion, we can help make a difference in the world.

*   *   *

Nathaniel Altman is the author of many books and articles about natural health, metaphysics, and nature. *Eating for Life* (1973) was one of the first vegetarian books AVS sold. Writing the anthology *Ahimsa: Dynamic Harmlessness* (1981) and *The Nonviolent Revolution* (1988) forced him to face personal issues honestly and transform negative currents into more positive ones.

Nathaniel also used this writing process for developing his understanding that one doesn't have to be perfect to make a difference in the world. He is an AVS life member.

*   *   *

Are you overly concerned with trying to be 100 percent vegan? Does it prevent you from trying veganism at all? Just get started and do the best you can.

Veganism is encouraged for everyone. You may be interested in the following websites:

OurHenHouse.org

FoodIsPower.org

VegansofColor.wordpress.com

After Jay lectured in Northern Ireland in 1972:
"...[Jay] went south, and he kissed the blarney stone, which he really didn't need to do. I think the blarney stone probably got a lot from him doing that. He probably empowered it."

—Margaret Gunn-King

Let's Talk about Veganism

H. Jay Dinshah

I am not going to talk to you about ice crystals and the leaves on the trees, nor castles in the air. I am going to tell you about a way that you can take one big step right now, not one that will carry you all the way "out of the jungle" but one that will definitely clear the path for you to find the way out—veganism.

Veganism is a way of living guided by ahimsa and reverence for life. Veganism utilizes a completely plant-sourced diet that is varied and abundant. Vegans are people who choose veganism as a lifestyle. Vegans reject the use of all animal products in food, clothing, and commodities and all other forms of cruelty to the animal kingdom insofar as possible. This includes research, medicine, sport, and entertainment.

There are many reasons why people are vegans. The three most common are health, environmental, and ethical reasons. Some people cite social reasons of relationships or are born into a vegan family. Others have religious beliefs about the matter of killing animals.

Vegans recognize the value of life in all living creatures and extend to them the compassion, kindness, and justice in The Golden Rule. Vegans see animals as free entities in nature, not slaves or vassals, nor as chattel, pieces of goods to be bought and sold.

An animal has feelings, an animal has sensitivity, an animal has a place in life, and the vegan respects this life that is manifest in the animal. Vegans do not wish to harm the animal any more than they would want the animal to harm them. This is an example of The Golden Rule precisely as it should be applied.

Vegans live according to an equitable, ethical relationship between human and nonhuman animals. They recognize that the production of animal-source foods—all of them—and all other animal commodities involves destruction of life. This cruelty and death violates basic laws of humaneness and common decency.

The shocking conditions of animal slavery and slaughter outrage the conscience of any fair-minded person who objectively investigates the matter. These conditions include shortened life span, selective breeding to distort once-natural aspects of animals, profit-oriented diets, various forms of mutilation, deliberate disruption of hormonal balance, taking of the young from their parents, slaughter of "surplus lives" such as those too old, too diseased, or of the wrong sex for profitable production. The deplorable conditions on factory farms have become more widespread as the greed for making money at the animals' expense increases.

Vegans do not use animal flesh, of course, because of the terrible cruelties and abnormal conditions involved in all the stages of the life of the animal in slavery from the moment of conception to the moment of slaughter. We need not go into these details here, as they are well documented in vegetarian and other literature and are readily seen and experienced on the farm or at the slaughterhouse. It is described in books, online videos, and documentaries.

Meat is no miracle food and can easily be eliminated from the diet. This means *all* meat, whether the poor thing lived on the earth or in a tree or in the sea. Meat, fish, and fowl—get rid of the whole foul assortment of slaughter foods. Fish and other aquatic beings advertised as a healthier choice are often the last meat one forgoes. However, they are efficient storehouses of waterborne pollution and waste. Fish are commonly slain by slow suffocation in the course of harvesting.

Vegans take a stand against the whole selfish and ignoble system of enslaving, selective breeding, raising, caging or penning, castrating, branding, doping, disrupting of families, transporting, and of course the final scene in the whole unholy drama, the killing itself. Vegans recognize the impossibility of separating the cruelty and killing from the business of keeping animals or obtaining their products profitably, especially in a modern, competitive society. Thus vegans resolve to root out the whole briar patch of cruelty and suffering, not merely trim a single thorn.

The crime against the animal is just as great whether it is killed for the purpose of food, clothing, drugs, or decorating. Virtually all animals used primarily for nonfood purposes are also killed prematurely at the precise moment in their lives when they pass the point of diminishing returns to the animal raiser or keeper. It means nothing but dollars and cents, pounds and pence, rupees and paise to the animal raiser.

What this means to you and me is that it is worth a great deal in life to have a clear conscience, a pair of hands unstained by blood, a mind that thinks of cleaner and loftier things, and a heart that is pure and beats with the tempo of compassion. We do it by turning our backs on the slaughterhouse and all the brutality supplying it. We send our economic message to all involved; we will no longer support such acts. We refuse to partake of items stolen from the animal kingdom.

The vast carnival of cruelty called animal exploitation goes on and on—and it is all so needless, even counterproductive. There is already an adequate and often superior nonanimal substitute for virtually everything obtained by animal suffering and slaughter. As demand increases for vegan products, it will accelerate still more materials innocent of blood and anguish.

It is easily seen that humanity has imposed a wrongful domination and system of exploitation upon the animals who are used by us for food, clothing, and more. This fosters in us a moral taint, a spiritual bondage, an unconscious guilt complex, and repressed sensitivities, all of which retard and inhibit our higher development. Under these circumstances we cannot hope to see real peace on Earth.

"Let there be peace, and let it begin with me!" There is much wisdom in the song lyrics of "Let There Be Peace on Earth" by Jill Jackson and Sy Miller. Where else can peace begin but in the heart and conscience of the individual?

We dare not hope for peace if we are at war with ourselves, if we have no harmony, no tranquility, and no order in our lives. Let us attain an inner calmness, a sense of duty and purpose, and a certainty of where we are—and where we wish to go—before we look for peace in the world. If we all established these attributes in ourselves, we would not have much else to do to attain peace on a global scale.

Vegans look upon the earth as a great source of food, shelter, and clothing for humanity as well as the provider of sustenance for the animal and plant kingdoms. In regard to feeding the planet's growing human population, a vegetarian diet is several times as efficient as meat production in terms of acreage and water used for growing it, but vegan fare similarly exceeds the lacto-ovo vegetarian diet in production efficiency. As in every reason for basic vegetarianism, veganism lays claim to the same reason and compounds it.

It is readily seen that vegetarianism, which includes milk and eggs in the diet, cannot be counted upon to provide the maximum efficiency in terms of land use and yield per acre, especially if the use of meat is merely replaced by an increase in milk or egg consumption. Only veganism offers the real hope of freeing the land from wasteful animal-food use for the direct growing of human food yields the best possible food quality and quantity.

Feeding farm produce to enslaved animals to convert plants into animal products is the most wasteful and futile way of trying to produce nourishing and wholesome food for humanity. When plants are transported to feed animals instead of directly to feed humans much is wasted, and it takes significantly more energy to produce. Animals use much of the food to keep alive—keep warm, move, and other processes of living—not efficiently changing it to the products humans consume. The wastefulness continues with animal transportation, slaughter, packaging, refrigeration, and more transportation. Production of animal products uses land which was once habitat for wildlife. Biodiversity is threatened as forests are cleared for new pastures.

Health is the most common reason for choosing to discontinue or reduce meat consumption. Many people follow a doctor's orders and try a plant-based diet until a particular condition improves without regard to the big picture of what habits created that condition in the first place.

Health is our normal condition and birthright. Disease is an abnormality, a predictable result of wrong living patterns, including various practices of wrong diet, wrong emotions, wrong thoughts, and/or wrong environmental conditions. Thus, if healthy, we seek correct ways of living to keep us in health; these correct living patterns can help us to rebuild health if we lost it.

The prolonged use of inferior foods, as well as various other factors, increases the risk of degenerative diseases, shown by the high incidence of these in countries having a high consumption of the devitalized and animal-sourced foods. The latter contain quantities of toxins, pathological matter and malignancies, cholesterol, saturated fat, and excessive protein, as well as no fiber. Being dead matter in a state of decomposition, they are not a fruitful source of wholesome raw materials with which to build healthy human bodies and vital energy.

The truth about the harm we do through the eating of animal products is now being adequately researched and publicized. Numerous studies are now published every year on the dangers of consuming animal products and the benefits of plant-based diets.

Many people have gone vegan overnight. When people's eyes open to the horrors of animal production, global concerns, and health tragedies, it is difficult to go back to sleep.

Out of the Jungle for the Next Generation

*   *   *

Dr. Michael Greger at NutritionFacts.org analyzes all the top research data in the areas of health, nutrition, diet, disease, and exercise, and he puts it into understandable presentations and videos often highlighted with his wry and humorous comments.

For health and nutrition books we recommend:

The 21-Day Weight Loss Kickstart: Boost Metabolism, Lower Cholesterol, and Dramatically Improve Your Health by Neal D. Barnard, MD

Becoming Vegan Express Edition: The Everyday Guide to Plant-based Nutrition by Brenda Davis, RD, and Vesanto Melina, RD MS

By Any Greens Necessary: A Revolutionary Guide for Black Women Who Want to Eat Great, Get Healthy, Lose Weight, and Look Phat by Tracye Lynn McQuirter, MPH

The Complete Idiot's Guide to Plant-Based Nutrition by Julieanna Hever, MS RD CPT

The China Study: Startling Implications for Diet, Weight Loss, and Long-term Health by T. Colin Campbell, PhD, with Thomas M. Campbell II, MD

The Food Revolution: How Your Diet Can Help Save Your Life by John Robbins

My Beef with Meat: The Healthiest Argument for Eating a Plant-Strong^{TM} Diet by Rip Esselstyn

The Pillars of Health: Your Foundation for Lifelong Wellness by John Pierre

Prevent and Reverse Heart Disease: The Scientifically Proven, Nutrition-Based Cure by Caldwell B. Esselstyn, Jr., MD

and especially the documentaries encouraging healthful change:

Forks over Knives which features T. Colin Campbell, PhD, and Caldwell B. Esselstyn, Jr, MD

Vegucated from writer-director Marisa Miller Wolfson.

Plant Based, Plant Sourced, Plant Strong™, Total Vegetarian, or Vegan?

Anne Dinshah

Plant-based diet is one based on vegetables, grains, legumes, and fruit, with little or no animal products. It can refer to: 1. a vegan diet. 2. a diet derived predominantly from plant foods with the inclusion of some animal products.

Plant based usually refers to eating plants for health reasons with emphasis on whole, unrefined foods. It sometimes excludes added oil, salt, sugar, and most processed foods. Plant based may mean with or without transitioning to being completely vegan. When one understands the concepts of plant based, it makes no sense to pile a few animals on the plate. People also use terms such as "completely plant based" or "whole-foods, plant-based diet."

Plant-sourced diet could imply that the source is always plants. It is a term less used. Some people use it to mean that plants are one of the sources, and also may use animal sources.

Plant strong™ is Rip Esselstyn's trademark term popular for its athletic sense. It also can mean a diet mostly but not entirely from plants—a good powerful transition to vegan.

Total vegetarian used to be a popular term for people who were vegan in diet but may use animal products in clothing and toiletries.

Why Not Say Vegan?

Here are five top reasons why some people don't call themselves vegan even when they are vegan:

1. Junk food. The health-promoting, plant-based people don't want to endorse those who choose to be junk-food vegans— people who frequently consume unhealthy products such as soda and fries.

2. Radical. The term vegan is sometimes associated by the public with declared vegans who in the name of animal liberation commit violent acts that draw media attention. This is explained further in upcoming chapters, Abolitionist Vegans (page 215) and For Butter or Worse (page 218).

3. Not ready to proclaim. When one departs from the norm of the American way of eating as taught by parents and schools, there may be a fear of being alienated by family and friends. A term such as plant-based may be easier to accept.

4. Unable to be 100 percent. There is a fear that when one announces "I am vegan" that the "vegan police" will swarm down, pat down to the nonanimal-sourced shoes, inspect the car and find tires with a hint of animal products in them (How could one know that yet?) and find two dead bugs on the windshield.

One is hereby pronounced vegan if 99 percent vegan as long as one's heart and conscience are guiding the best possible choices with all available information while one continues to learn. Make responsible choices 100 percent of the time. Enjoy reading about Ethical Dilemmas (page 229).

5. Ethical component. This is the biggest difference between vegan and all the plant-something terms. Vegan implies a lifestyle with ethical reasons that accompany the completely plant-based diet. After reading this book, one should be able to proudly wear the term vegan.

Even if people prefer to describe their food consumption with another term, the animals don't care that people are not eating them to preserve or improve health, sexual stamina, connection with the earth, or any other reason. When the animals are no longer being consumed, tortured, violated, or imprisoned, they will be happy people are vegan.

Ten Reasons Why You Should Call Yourself Vegan

Read, consider, and refer back to list after becoming vegan.

1. Be an ambassador for the true meaning of vegan. Promote a positive impression, not misinformed stereotypes. When you are healthy in mind and body, people ask what you do to look great, fit, young, and happy. Share ahimsa. You keep integrity in the word vegan.

2. Vegan reminds you of ahimsa. Commit to do positive projects to help the world. There are lots of ideas on later pages of this book.

3. You bring delicious food to social gatherings. Everyone wants to know the recipe and you can tell them that it's vegan.

4. You are a normal person. You eat three delicious meals a day and might occasionally swat a mosquito. You interact with people who don't always think like you but all can exhibit mutual respect.

5. You are true to the animals. You can look any animal in the eye and call that animal a friend and not dinner.

6. Vegan is one concise word that means a lot of good. Vegans definitely eat *only* from the plant kingdom. You make conscious, compassionate choices about the products you use.

7. Vegan is healthier. It is economically better, environmentally sound, and ethically unassailable.

8. The pillars of ahimsa are integrated into your daily life, as you will see in that chapter (page 116).

9. You decide to be vegan from reading this book, thinking about the questions, and doing independent thought.

10. Welcome to the vegan generation. You have just increased the number of vegans by one and decreased the number of nonvegans.

Luminaries Love Animals

Sun and Light from Gentle World

We first met Jay in 1973. We had been vegan for three years, not ever having heard the word or the concept and so assumed that we were the only ones. Then, by chance, we met a man who told us that what we were was called vegan and that there were not only others but an American Vegan Society (AVS) in New Jersey, founded by Jay and run by Jay and Freya Dinshah. We hopped into our car and drove to Malaga to be welcomed by the Dinshahs with a vegan lunch and the first assurance and support we had received since making the commitment.

Our next meeting was at our first animal rights convention a few years later. We asked Jay for his advice in publishing *The Cookbook for People Who Love Animals*, which was a complete disarray of wonderful vegan recipes in typewritten form that we had invented over the years. By then, we had read *Out of the Jungle* which we thought—and still think—was one of the greatest books ever written, so he was already a hero to us.

His response to our request was beyond our expectations. He actually volunteered, despite his always-busy schedule, to take the entire project off our hands by getting it into publishable form, something we had no idea how to begin to accomplish. Our esteem for him catapulted when we experienced his expertise and integrity in actually making it happen. We have never forgotten that if it weren't for Jay Dinshah, *The Cookbook for People Who Love Animals*, which has sold over 100,000 copies, would have remained in manuscript form to this day.

Jay Dinshah was and continued to be throughout the years that rare gem in human relationships: a friend in need and indeed.

*   *   *

Light and Sun are founders of Gentle World, a vegan community since 1970 and nonprofit educational organization since 1979. Over the years, Gentle World has evolved into a team of volunteers who maintain two educational centers, one on the Big Island of Hawaii and one in the Far North of New Zealand. People come to experience and learn about the whys and hows of vegan living from people who have been vegan for decades.

In addition to their visitor program, they have sold thousands of copies of their two vegan cookbooks: *The Cookbook for People Who Love Animals*, published in 1981, and *Incredibly Delicious: Recipes for a New Paradigm*, first published in 2000.

They also maintain an informative and inspirational website which attracts hundreds of thousands of visitors every year, accompanied by an educational monthly newsletter *Awakening the Vegan in Everyone*. Visit GentleWorld.org to subscribe. Light and Sun are AVS life members.

*   *   *

Anne: My first paid job, at age eleven, was putting the ring bindings on the early editions of *The Cookbook for People Who Love Animals*. I had been volunteering in the AVS offices approximately since I was born.

*   *   *

Have you purchased a vegan cookbook? They make great gifts. Perhaps you would like your next vacation to be a meaningful trip to Hawaii or New Zealand with a stop at the Gentle World visitors' center. Or save fuel and go online. Take this book with you and re-read it on an airplane or in any public place, and then give it to someone who needs it more than you do.

Graff-itational Forces for Veganism

Brian and Sharon Graff

Brian:

Rewind more than forty years. "Vegetarian" wasn't in my vocabulary. Even though I grew up in a family of animal lovers, mostly for dogs, I never made the meat-animal connection, that is, until Scott (1883-1893) and Helen (1904-1995) Nearing entered my life through their back-to-the-land classic *Living the Good Life*. That book, lent to me by a fellow sailor while we were stationed—of all places—at the Guantanamo Bay Cuba Naval Base, opened the door to a vegan diet. Before departing Gitmo, I learned of the American Vegan Society (AVS) and ordered *The Vegan Kitchen* cookbook and *Ahimsa* magazine (now *American Vegan*).

Upon returning home at the end of my active military duty, I encountered my family's concern about my animal-free diet. To appease them, I consulted a local naturopathic doctor. I tried, with the little knowledge I had at that time, to defend my dietary choice but ultimately was swayed by her strong urging that I include dairy and eggs in my diet. She pointed out that even the famous vegetarian George Bernard Shaw consumed these animal foods.

However, cheese and yogurt weren't going down well physically or mentally, so I decided to learn how to do veganism right by attending an educational program that was being offered by AVS at their SunCrest headquarters.

It was there that I met AVS' leaders Jay and Freya Dinshah, two people who influenced the course of my life in at least three major ways. Jay's persuasive evening lectures for staff and guests brought me back to the vegan path, where I remain to this day. It was here too that I met and married my life partner Sharon, thanks to their work-accommodations exchange program that brought us both to the AVS headquarters. Otherwise, our lives may never have intersected.

And then there's the course of events that led to our life work. A small group of vegetarian activists—including the Nearings—came together in 1973 to create the North American Vegetarian Society (NAVS) which was to host the International Vegetarian Union (IVU)'s first World Vegetarian Congress to be held in North America in 1975 and serve as an ongoing educational organization. Jay with his boundless energy, determination, skills, and plain hard work was, in my estimation, the driving force that ensured both the birth of NAVS and an exceptionally successful world conference. Jay and I worked together very closely in those early years. He was a mentor to me when I was a novice about the functioning of organizations and conferences.

Sharon:

For the first twelve years of my life, I grew up on a dairy farm. I became a vegetarian after realizing that the animals we loved in the barnyard were ending up on our dinner table.

When I was in my late teens, I came across issues of *Ahimsa* magazine. I read an article by Trisha Bell regarding dairy production and the emotional pain and suffering felt by the mother and her calf when being separated. Even after my years growing up on a dairy farm, I was not aware of that suffering. I immediately became vegan after reading her article and have been so ever since. Jay and Freya's outstanding publications provided the support I needed to be able to eliminate animal products. I loved *Ahimsa* and poured over the issues as soon as they arrived in our mailbox.

An advertisement for co-ops (interns) in one issue of their magazine caught my attention. This was an arrangement wherein people worked in exchange for room and board. The idea of doing meaningful work that would help animals appealed to me. I became a co-op for AVS in May of 1974 when I was twenty-two years old.

I met my wonderful husband Brian there. Jay, Brian, and a small group of activists had just formed NAVS. I have been working for the NAVS ever since. Brian and I are especially grateful to Jay and Freya for providing the inspiration, opportunities, and support that set the stage for us to spend our lives as full-time advocates for healthy, compassionate living.

*   *   *

Brian and Sharon Graff:

In 1979 Jay and Freya decided to shift their main focus back to their first love, AVS. Brian and Sharon relocated NAVS to upstate New York where they have been directing its operations ever since. Brian is the president of NAVS and Sharon is the executive director. They are thankful for the good fortune that has allowed them to devote over forty years to NAVS and its goals, doing work in which they truly believe. In 2004 Brian and Sharon were inducted into the Vegetarian Hall of Fame. They are AVS life members.

For four decades NAVS has been educating the general public about the health, animal protection, and environmental benefits of a vegetarian diet. The organization has also provided support to vegetarians that has helped many deepen their commitment to this way of life. NAVS hosts the annual conference Vegetarian Summerfest, coordinates the outreach campaign World Vegetarian Day founded in 1977, and publishes the member magazine *Vegetarian Voice*.

Jay served as president of NAVS from 1974 to 1979 and editor of *Vegetarian Voice* from 1974 to 1980. In his final presidential report he requested the board not reappoint him, citing the great pressures involved in heading both NAVS and AVS and editing two magazines and the difficult and deteriorating financial situation personally and for AVS.

Jay selected terrific people to carry on NAVS in the Graffs. He said, "After more than half a decade of service to NAVS, I am especially gratified to see that at this time—when circumstances finally make it imperative for me to confine and redirect my energy and efforts elsewhere—there are so many dedicated vegetarians of talent, ability, and integrity ready to carry on the good work of NAVS."

*   *   *

Have you wondered about small family farms like the one where Sharon grew up? Are you aware of the suffering that goes on at an animal farm, regardless of size? Consider that the bottom line should be applying ahimsa values to your life and choices.

You can visit the Nearing's last homestead, The Good Life Center at Forest Farm, Harborside Maine (Goodlife.org). The Nearings may inspire you to build a stone house or sun-heated greenhouse or journey into voluntary simplicity with self-sufficient living.

Have you attended Vegetarian Summerfest, the event vegetarians and vegans look forward to all year? Summerfest is like a big family reunion with wonderful speakers, delicious food, and empowering interactions.

NAVS promotes celebrating World Vegetarian Day on October 1st. Have you read *Vegetarian Voice* magazine? Become a member of NAVS and learn more. NAVS-online.org

Getting the Veggie Bus Rolling in DC

Madge Darneille

I was vegetarian for a long time in England; then I came to the United States and looked for other vegetarians. In 1968 I heard about Vegetarian Society of the District of Columbia (VSDC) through a Seventh Day Adventist group. I went to a picnic; the other four people in attendance were all over eighty. Later someone called me, asking if I'd like to be president and get it going. I reluctantly agreed.

I had been running VSDC a short time when I got a telephone call, "My name is Jay Dinshah. I hear you're vegetarian. You sound English; my wife is English." We had a connection. He continued, "We want to put on an international conference in Maine. We can only do it if we have a viable vegetarian society." He proceeded to talk me into being a founding member appointed to the first council of the North American Vegetarian Society (NAVS). Jay was the president.

The 1975 World Vegetarian Congress was billed as "The Greatest Event of the Vegetarian Movement." I was so excited to be around all these vegetarian people. My role was to help with food and to get as many people to come as possible.

I had flown to Bangor, Maine, in February 1974 to help organize the conference. That's where I first met Jay, Brian Graff, Scott and Helen Nearing, and Brian Gunn-King from Ireland. The outcome of that long weekend meeting and a year and a half of working together was the conference in Orono, Maine, which was amazingly successful. It was the birth of a new vegetarian era.

Through the years, American Vegan Society nurtured NAVS and hosted us with our board meetings. At one of those board meetings in Malaga, we developed the concept of a worldwide celebration. Brian Graff and I said simultaneously, "World Vegetarian Day!" And that started it. We selected October 1st and announced it in *Vegetarian Voice*. People celebrated in a variety of ways. In DC there was a bus tour around the city with a big banner on the bus and a huge tethered carrot balloon in the sky.

*   *   *

Madge Darneille has made many important contributions to local, North American, and global vegetarian movements. She helped found the Vegetarian Union of North America (VUNA) in 1987, which served as the North American regional arm of the International Vegetarian Union (IVU). Madge is a fellow of the IVU, served as the assistant honorary general secretary of IVU, and was on its international council for approximately two decades. Madge was honored with the IVU's Mankar Memorial Award in 1996. She is an AVS life member.

She feels her biggest contribution to the vegetarian movement was getting VSDC organized, now over 800 members strong and with an online Meetup membership of well over 2200 and one of the most active United States vegetarian societies. VSDC is the oldest, local-based, extant vegetarian organization in North America. She served as president of VSDC on and off whenever needed from 1972 until 1996. (More about VSDC in Saurabh Dalal's story page 258). Madge loves attending conferences, meeting all the vibrant vegetarian people from around the world.

*   *   *

Will your next visit to Washington DC coincide with a VSDC events and inspire you to create something in your locale?

What are you doing to celebrate World Vegetarian Day on October 1, World Vegetarian Month of October, World Vegan Day on November 1, and World Vegan Month of November? These events broaden knowledge of the vegan message.

F.A.R.M.—It All Began with Jay

Alex Hershaft

In 1975 I had been a closet vegetarian for fourteen years, not quite ready to be teased or questioned about my dietary preferences and a bit put off by the few vegetarians I had met. At a Vegetarian Society of DC picnic, a woman handed me a flier announcing the World Vegetarian Congress later that year in Orono, Maine.

The congress was a mind-blowing, life-changing experience, and I am not given to excitement or hyperbole. Fifteen-hundred people came from all over the globe, with different languages, economic stations, professions, modes of dress, and ages, but they were all vegetarians!

My reaction was swift and natural: "How do I get involved?" My answer came in the person of Jay Dinshah, who promptly appointed me to the board of the North American Vegetarian Society.

I wonder where the vegan movement and I would be today if Jay Dinshah had not provided the inspiration for the most rewarding journey of my life. Somewhere along the way, I became a devout vegan.

*   *   *

Alex Hershaft launched the Vegetarian Information Service in 1976 and founded Farm Animal Rights Movement (FARM) in 1982. His successful international vegan campaigns include World Farm Animals Day begun in 1983 and the Great American Meatout begun in 1985. Annually since 1981 Alex has organized the Animal Rights National Conference. In 1999 he was inducted into the Vegetarian Hall of Fame.

*   *   *

Are you passionate about animal rights? Attend the Animal Rights National Conference to connect with other activists and learn about tactics, organizing, campaigns, and controversial issues. Meet hundreds of compassionate people who are in various stages of learning awareness of animal issues.

Can't afford to go to the conference? You mean you can't afford not to go. Contact FARM about volunteering or ways to make the conference fit your budget.

For more information about animal rights, visit these sites: FarmUSA.org and ARConference.org

"Humanity has always needed ethical ideals to enable it to find the right path, that man may make the right use of the power he possesses. Today his power is increased a thousandfold. A thousandfold greater is now the need for man to possess ethical ideals to point the way."   —Dr. Albert Schweitzer

The Step of Veganism

Jay and Anne Dinshah

Stepping into veganism is a simultaneous three-part process. One part is learning about the gastronomical pleasures available in the plant kingdom, so they can be integrated into daily meals, and finding new sources of clothing, toiletries, and household items. The second part is discontinuing use of all animal products; the first two parts are discussed in this chapter. The third part is utilizing ahimsa; suggestions occur throughout the book.

Food. First it should be emphasized that everybody—even people who are not vegan—should be eating lots of plants in their meals. This idea is supported by the government-advocated MyPlate with fruits, grains, protein, and vegetables making up the quadrants of the plate, with a side of dairy in a glass. Vegans prefer the Physician's Committee for Responsible Medicine's Power Plate with fruits, grains, legumes, and vegetables without dairy. Vegans eat a large variety of wonderful vegetables, legumes, whole grains, fruits, nuts, and seeds. Vegans don't use meat, fish, birds, dairy, eggs, gelatin, lard, honey, foods made with any of these, or any other animal products.

A vegetarian often has an awareness of what must happen to provide people with animal products. The vegetarian has taken the first major step by not using killed animals directly for food and is encouraged to continue to learn and progress. Therefore we begin here with discussing dairy and eggs, providing information for the vegetarian and for those who have not yet started the vegan journey.

Dairy. It is not well realized that the production of milk requires animals to be artificially bred, fattened, and killed. The innocent calves are born to keep their mothers in lactation and are destined for a short and sad life before often becoming platefuls of veal, especially if they are male. The intensive conditions of raising these calves in tiny boxes are so pathetic and disgraceful that it is hard to understand how the human mind can think of such horrible things to inflict upon helpless creatures even for the profit involved. This is the key—always the profit motive—used to excuse a lack of the most elementary compassion and decency.

Artificial methods to make the mother cow give more milk include hormones, overfeeding, and selective breeding. When her overworked body rebels, she is medicated into some semblance of "health." Mastitis and other diseases are common in the modern dairy industry. As in all types of food-animal raising, what no longer turns a profit must go to slaughter, the sooner the better. A veterinarian who once worked in a slaughterhouse and now is vegetarian told us "the slaughterhouse is the farmer's best friend" for the disposing of animals to be used for human food and pet food. If the slaughterhouse makes a person wish to stop eating meat, it is clearly no recommendation for using dairy products.

Milks of various delightful flavors and excellent nutritional value are made from nuts, seeds, grains, or soybeans. Commercial plant milks readily available in supermarkets include soymilk, almond milk, hemp milk, flax milk, oat milk, sunflower seed milk, coconut milk, and rice milk. Many supermarkets are now selling house brands of soymilk, almond milk, and rice milk.

Yogurt comes in soy, almond, and coconut nondairy options. Most supermarkets now carry at least one brand of nondairy ice cream from soy, coconut, or rice. Many now have so many varieties that you can pick a new flavor each week for months. The first nondairy ice cream marketed to the general public came out in the late 1980s. Jay had waited thirty years for commercial nondairy ice cream to arrive. Our family created occasions for banana splits with ice cream.

Nondairy products can be a bit more expensive, so know that

the real price of dairy ice cream is not reflected at the cash register. The dairy industry is government subsidized, and the cruelty is hidden. You can make cheap ice cream at home from peeled-then-frozen bananas and fruit in a food processor. I'll never forget when a friend who was working on his doctorate degree said, "I love the ice cream, but those frozen bananas are awfully hard to peel."

A family favorite is from *The Vegan Kitchen*: whiz bananas and raw cashews in the blender, pour into paper cups with optional mixed-in flavors such as raisins and sunflower seeds, then freeze. We could go on and on about ice cream, assuring you won't be deprived as a vegan. Let's cut to the cheese.

Commercial cheese, though mainly a dairy product, is usually coagulated with rennet taken from a calf's stomach at the time of slaughter; thus it cannot be considered a food suitable even for vegetarian use. Fortunately for cheese lovers, there are numerous ways to make vegan cheeses from soy or nuts. Many people like using hummus instead of cheese. The market is exploding with new ready-to-use cheeses. *The Vegan Kitchen* includes various tasty and nutritious recipes for making nonanimal cheeses at home, and there are entire cookbooks of vegan-cheese recipes. Try *The Uncheese Cookbook* by Jo Stepaniak, *Artisan Vegan Cheese* by Miyoko Schinner, or *The Cheesy Vegan* by John Schlimm.

Vegetable margarine is a more compassionate choice than butter and can be healthier so long as they are made without hydrogenated oils and trans fats. However demand for palm oil is impacting rainforest animals too, so you may opt for other oil or nut products. Margarine and oils should be used sparingly anyway, and many people avoid them for health reasons.

Eggs. Eggs are the furthest things from a wholesome food for humans. One need only apply the test of truth to the precise source of the egg, the anatomical relation to the rest of the hen's body, and the organs producing the material. Unfertilized, the egg is reproductive waste; fertilized, it is the next generation of birds. Eggs are also a source of cholesterol, excess protein, and frequent salmonella.

Most eggs come from factory farms which are efficient to meet demand, but horribly cruel. "Layer hens" are kept in confined conditions, crowded into battery cages, so they cannot do basic things such as stretch their wings. The ammonia waste sears the eyes of anyone entering buildings that often contain thousands of birds. Think what it does to birds in that prison who have committed no crime. As these hens age and become less productive, their bodies are so spent they often are gassed or otherwise destroyed, deemed not worthy enough for food. New chickens must replace them. After a crop of fertilized eggs hatch, baby chicks are sorted by sex. Male chicks are deemed useless and ground up alive or suffocated; this killing is inherent in all egg production.

The compassionate viewpoint that we take toward the cow is just as validly applied to the hen. The spent cow goes to the slaughterhouse; likewise, there is no profit in keeping alive and feeding a menopausal ex-layer hen.

If the test of truth is objectively applied, the result is likely to be an immediate and permanent cessation of the use of eggs. Replace eggs with a variety of plant foods depending on what you are looking for the egg to do. Protein in an egg can be substituted by legumes; fat can be from nut butters. The binding quality might be a starch from corn, potato, or arrowroot; oats or ground flaxseed can bind too. Moisture preserving can happen with applesauce or a mashed banana. Emulsifying can be from soy lecithin. For lightness in baked goods increase the baking powder and add vinegar or an acidic juice such as pineapple, lemon, or orange.

Because eggs are a traditional ingredient in mayonnaise, there are now many vegan varieties available, or you can make your own. There are also numerous ways to enjoy foods substituted for eggs eaten as the main part of a dish, such as making a tofu scramble. With the right amount of turmeric to make the tofu yellow, it even looks similar to eggs.

Meat. The main asset of meat is its excessive protein content. Protein is better provided by nonanimal foods such as nuts, seeds, legumes, whole grains, and various vegetables that have no cholesterol and are easier to digest. Numerous vegan foods rank with meats in amino-acid balance. One should not believe false claims for the biological value of meat over all vegetable proteins.

Beans and nuts are the most typical vegan proteins. Beans take time to cook, and many people choose canned beans for an easier option. Nuts provide good protein and also come in a variety of nut butters. Almond and cashew butters can often be found next to peanut butter. Protein is also found in whole grains and vegetables.

Mushrooms are sometimes used to provide a meaty flavor and texture for people who want a simple, healthful substitute for meat. Portabella mushrooms—readily available at most supermarkets—can be seasoned, cooked, and served as burgers.

Meat analogs have been available in Asian markets of United States cities for decades. Numerous meat analogs are now available at most conventional supermarkets. When one goes to a health-inclined supermarket, the options are impressive for plant-based versions of burgers, hot dogs, sausage, chicken, and many other traditional animal products. Almost any meat can be imitated with plant ingredients nowadays.

The food technology industry has recently received financial backing for plant-based foods from some of the world's wealthiest people, including Bill Gates and Li Ka-Sheng, which will help it to grow exponentially with plant-based options. In "Livestock and Climate Change," Robert Goodland and Jeff Anhang of World Bank Group assessed greenhouse gas attributed to animal agriculture and explained how replacing at least twenty-five percent of animal-based foods with plant alternatives—

whether whole foods or processed ones—could be the only pragmatic way to reverse climate change before it's too late. They advocated that a key change in this reversal can be industry-led or supply-led growth of meat and dairy analogs. Their original article and subsequent writings and citations can be viewed at Chompingclimatechange.org.

Note that authors of *Powerful Vegan Messages* acknowledge the twenty-five percent as a great first goal and from there we should encourage further increase in the world's consumption of plants instead of animals. Those of us who can do more—such as go vegan—should do more. Especially in an influential and affluent country as the United States, we have a moral responsibility to do as much as we can especially because we have access to a great bounty of plant-food choices.

In today's society, analogs provide a valuable link to make it easy to be vegan by providing a direct product substitution. Reading philosophy such as in this book is only half the battle. Experiencing how to happily survive without animal products is crucial to successful transition to veganism. Many vegans don't use any analogs; they don't want to be reminded of animal suffering on their plate with an imitation of it. Veggie burgers exist in two basic categories, meat imitators and vegetable-grain patties. Companies also make numerous additional plant-based meat substitutes that attract people looking for alternatives for their main entrée; some are even featured at the holidays and offered at our local supermarket as a free option instead of turkey for redeeming loyalty bonus points.

With any product, it is good to check the ingredients carefully because some companies produce both vegan and nonvegan items while others are committed to vegan. Companies may change formulas anytime. It's exciting that there are so many vegan products that we can't list them all. If the desired vegan product is not at your local supermarket, ask them to carry it, and contact the company to let them know there is interest in your area.

Additional food items. Gelatin is made from hooves of slaughtered animals. It is easily replaced by agar-agar, a vegetable jelling agent made from seaweed, or kudzu, or tapioca made from cassava root. Various starches from corn, potato, or arrowroot also provide thickening options.

Honey is a stimulating, concentrated sugar obtained by robbing the bees and generally giving them an inferior substitute of sugar water. Honey is easily replaced in the human diet with cane sugar, molasses, dates, raisins, agave syrup, or maple syrup.

Be assured there are plenty of treats for vegans. Packaged cookies, cake mixes, and various other desserts seem to appear as new options each time we go to the store. Completely vegan bakeries are sprouting up throughout the country, and many deliver or ship their products. With the increase in dairy allergies, conventional bakeries are often willing to make a new vegan product to meet demand, if asked. Entire vegan cookbooks are dedicated to desserts while most vegan cookbooks provide some ideas. Anne teaches how to woo anyone with simply the best cookies or a cheesecake in *Dating Vegans*. Robin Asbell's *Sweet & Easy Vegan* lives up to its name, and *Vegan Chocolate* by Fran Costigan is popular with experienced chefs.

Other food issues. Some people mistake gluten for being a vegan issue. Gluten is a protein found in wheat, barley, rye, and sometimes in oats, all of which are plants. It's okay to eat gluten as a vegan. However, some people are sensitive to gluten, and often where people are making gluten-free options one will also find animal-free foods. Always check the list of ingredients because gluten-free may include animal products.

Those looking to avoid gluten will appreciate the information on JoAnn Farb's website Getoffgluten.blogspot.com. JoAnn provided gluten-free options for *Apples, Bean Dip, and Carrot Cake* and has her own cookbook *Get Off Gluten*. Susan O'Brien also creates entire cookbooks geared for gluten-free vegans such as *Gluten-Free Vegan Comfort Food*.

Other terms that may arise as one learns more about food choices include organic, non-GMO, local, fair trade, and sustainable. Organic food is produced without the use of synthetic toxic pesticides and fertilizers that ultimately become part of the food, our bodies, and the environment. Organic also doesn't use genetically modified organisms (GMO) from genetic engineering which often involves manipulating plants with animal genes and animal testing. Locally grown food is good because it supports one's community, is generally fresher and has less preservatives, and requires fewer resources to transport. Items labeled as fair trade ensure that farmers and workers in developing countries are decently compensated, a social-justice issue. Rainforest Alliance certified addresses environmental, social, and economic sustainability. One can technically be vegan without knowing any of these options; we encourage learning more from TheFoodRevolution.org, CenterforFoodSafety.org, FairTradeUSA.org, and Rainforest-Alliance.org.

Clothing. Vegans do not wear or use fur, wool, silk, leather, feathers, down, bones, or any other animal-based attire but instead use either natural or synthetic nonanimal materials. While the term total vegetarian applies only to one's dietary practices, vegan implies much more. Vegans realize that a dollar's worth of leather is just as profitable to the slaughterhouse owner as a dollar of meat. So vegans extend their abstention to nonfood items.

Much has been printed, even by nonvegans, about the extreme cruelties of fur trapping that it should be obvious why you won't see a vegan wearing a fur coat. Vegans also understand that the wool industry and the mutton industry are one, merely representing different products from the same sheep. Much of the wool used in America is "pulled wool," meaning it is taken at slaughter.

Synthetic furs are beautiful and durable and only a fraction of the cost of animal furs. From the environmental standpoint, they use far less fossil fuel to produce than does the raising or trapping, transporting, and processing of animal fur, especially considering the costly and energy-greedy, summertime, refrigerated storage needed to slow the decay of the dead animal matter in real fur coats.

If one feels the need for a fake fur, attach a pin denoting that it is fake fur or in some other way assure people that no animals were used for fashion. Be sure it is truly fake fur, as some real fur is passed off as fake on the label to appease consumers concerned about animals. The easiest way to tell is to look for threadwork backing on fake fur, whereas leather is at the base of the animal fur. Also real fur hairs are tapered at the end unless they have been cut, while fake fur is cut straight across. These tips and more information can be found online at HumaneSociety.org/furfree.

Genuine silk is obtained almost universally by first roasting or boiling the silkworm to death, a process euphemistically known as "stifling" with the little creature still in its cocoon. Vegans do not use silk.

Vegans use popular plant-based sources including cotton, rayon, hemp, linen, and bamboo. Vegans also use mineral-sourced synthetics such as nylon, polyester, and spandex that are readily available. Hemp and bamboo are becoming popular fabrics. Cotton has been made into good garments for centuries; it is best to get organic cotton produced without all the pesticides and bleaching. Cotton is not good for every purpose, such as if it gets wet, so athletes avoid it in winter in favor of synthetic fabrics. Tremendous strides have been made in synthetic fabrics for all seasons. Enjoy examining clothing options such as moisture wicking, breathable, and weatherproof. An online search will bring up numerous sites with everything you could want. Even better is that a simple search now brings up pages of links to vegan items at mainstream outlets, a huge improvement in recent years.

There is an abundance of nonanimal shoe materials both natural and man made and used worldwide. Natural and synthetic rubber, cork, cotton canvas, various natural and synthetic fibers, and many types of plastics are included in the assortment of shoe materials. Some stores carry exclusively vegan shoes—including ones that are poromeric (breathable imitation leather)—either in brick-and-mortar establishments or online.

Vegan coats, shoes, belts, wallets, purses, and jackets are now being labeled as such and advertised as vegan at many traditional stores. Finding the perfect shoe still takes walking around, virtually or in reality, but when the vegan shoe fits, buy it, wear it, and tell all your friends.

Toiletries. Soaps, cosmetics, shampoos, and other toiletries generally contain animal oils or fats such as lanolin which is sheep-wool fat, beeswax, slaughterhouse tallow and its derivatives, and perfume ingredients that involve cruelty and slaughter. Perfumes often contain glandular secretions from animals.

Various lines of products on the market do not contain such substances and are not tested on animals. Verifying suitable products used to require extensive research. Now typically one can check the label for a vegan symbol or for words such as "no animal ingredients" and "not tested on animals."

Unfortunately it is still difficult to find vegan toiletries in supermarkets in many areas of the country. However, health-oriented stores often offer a wide selection of vegan toiletries. Consider stocking up while on a trip if there is not a location near you or look online for your specific item and order directly.

Wherever you go, be sure products are cruelty free and vegan because the former refers to the testing and the latter to the ingredients. Because companies can and do change their formulas at any time, continue to check labels or contact the company directly to get their assurance.

Jewelry. Pearls, shells, teeth, tusks, horns, bones, feet, feathers, and the like usually involve the destruction of animals although they may occasionally be found shed by an animal or from an animal deceased by natural causes. There is no need to wear these items when many ways exist to adorn oneself without hurting animals.

Household goods. Objectionable items here include animal-hair and wool rugs and carpets, down or feather pillows, feather dusters, woolen blankets, and animal-hair brushes and brooms. Animal-free substitutes for all these are in widespread use. Look for nylon carpets, foam-rubber or kapok pillows, cotton or synthetic-fiber quilts, blankets, and comforters, plastic or fiber brushes, and straw brooms. Hemp and bamboo are becoming popular in household goods. Beware of oils, greases, and polishes that include animal fats in the ingredients.

Sports. Hunting, animal fighting, animal racing, and fishing are cruel practices. One should not require a substitute for the devil or a substitute for a blood sport that brings out the worst in humans. Sports of many varieties can be played without any unwilling participation of the animal kingdom. True sport involves fun and fair play, not violence or sadism by getting a thrill out of killing something or bending it to our will.

Amusements. Vegans are opposed to animal circuses and to performing land animals, sea animals, or birds. We are aware of the years of cruel prodding and punishing that lie behind a performance act using animals kidnapped from their natural habitat. The documentary *Blackfish* exposed cruelty rampant in aquatic shows. Some circuses with all human willing participants have been formed and now tour the country offering amazing shows.

Vegans also oppose zoos. Zoos are usually little more than prisons for once free land or sea creatures far from their natural habitat. Despite claims by zookeepers that animals are better off in captivity than in the wild state, animals exhibit neurotic behavior in captivity. Many animals refuse to raise their young in this unnatural condition. National parks, animal sanctuaries, and true wildlife preserves—not preserves set aside for hunting and fishing—are much better and more rewarding for all concerned.

Humans must leave large tracts of land untouched to allow animals to naturally be animals.

Research and medicines. Drugs, vaccines, serums, and hormones are often made from animal matter. An ethical dilemma may be encountered when considering use of an animal product in this category following advice from a health professional.

Millions of animals are used each year to test and develop drugs and techniques to cure disease. There are moral implications in this overwhelming toll of animal suffering, and it has not brought medical science much closer to knowing the actual causes underlying many human diseases. Medical doctors often do not have a substantial nutrition background and frequently opt to prescribe the more convenient pills which people commonly want. We cherish our friends in the medical profession who do understand health and encourage veganism.

Vegans typically choose to use a healthy lifestyle as a defense against disease. Vegans often do not rely on drugs for cures, realizing that nature has provided safer ways of building and maintaining true health with wholesome natural food, pure water, fresh air, sunshine, sufficient rest, ample exercise, and all other factors needed for physical well-being. Vegans reserve most conventional medicine for accidental emergencies. Most vegans have little faith in illusions of health purchased at so-much-a-pound from the drug store but see health as a result of harmonious living in all aspects of our makeup—physical, mental, ethical, emotional, and spiritual. Many vegans also choose to avoid vaccines due to vaccines being tested on animals, having animal content, and introducing disease into the body.

Awakening the conscience. Each person may require a different approach to awakening the conscience. Some people will deny the cruelties in that which they directly contribute with consumption, such as eating eggs. Yet, when the average person is exposed to information such as pets stolen for vivisection, food animals slaughtered in especially brutal ways, or particularly gruesome pictures of baby seals clubbed and skinned for their pelts, their slumbering sense of compassion may begin to awaken.

These first uneasy feelings may lead to the person sweeping the moral dirt under the carpet, joining some movement to mitigate the suffering, or minimizing or changing the type of cruelty. One such example is replacing fur garments made from the clubbing of free creatures with the atrocious cage-farming methods of ranch-grown furs. Another example is lobbying for bigger cages but continuing to eat the products of those animal slaves. When the conscience prods one to inquire about a vegan journey, we provide helpful information for that direction.

The step. By now you should understand how to take the step of veganism. The foundation for veganism is the inner alteration from selfishness to altruism, from *What's in it for me?* to *What can I do for you?* With this change of thinking, what we eat or wear is not burdensome but integral to a compassionate lifestyle. Remember this altruistic concept is the true jewel of veganism.

Your individual actions contribute to the vegan movement. This movement is so strong that some companies are getting into vegan products purely for profit. Many companies are founded by people with plans for a better world. One example is Ethan Brown, founder of Beyond Meat®, who states on the company's website a mission to improve the world's health, the global environment, and respect for animals. Their vision is to reduce the world's consumption of animal meat by twenty-five percent by 2020 which will be achieved by replacing it with "plant meat." Imagine more companies making these types of goals; it is beginning to happen.

The vegan lifestyle is increasing in popularity. Seeing companies commit to goals and make strategic plans encourages the authors—who are committed to closing all slaughterhouses— to persevere in providing information, while businesses make vegan products and consumers commit to compassionate choices. Together we will succeed.

*　　*　　*

Eliminate animal products and simultaneously add plant foods. If you are wondering how to prepare vegan food, start with easy recipes from cookbooks such as:

The 4-Ingredient Vegan: Quick, Easy, and Delicious by Maribeth Abrams with Anne Dinshah

Afro-Vegan: Farm-Fresh African, Caribbean, and Southern Flavors Remixed by Bryant Terry

The China Study Cookbook: Over 120 Whole-Food Plant-Based Recipes by LeAnne Campbell

Healthy Hearty Helpings: The No-Fuss Vegan Cookbook—Quick and Easy Delicious Recipes by Anne Dinshah

The New Favorites: Redesigned Recipes for Your Health by Brook Katz

Vegan Express: Featuring 160 Recipes for Quick, Delicious, and Healthy Meals by Nava Atlas

Virgin Vegan: The Meatless Guide to Pleasing Your Palate by Linda Long

World Vegan Feast: 200 Fabulous Recipes from over 50 Countries by Bryanna Clark Grogan

AmericanVegan.org lists vegan cooking classes throughout the United States. Perhaps you will attend one.

A good resource for checking all those big words on ingredient lists is the book *Veganissimo A to Z: A Comprehensive Guide to Identifying and Avoiding Ingredients of Animal Origin in Everyday Products* by Lars Thomsen and Reuben Proctor.

VeganEssentials.com began business in 1998. The store is at 1701 Pearl Street, Unit 8, Waukesha Wisconsin 53186; phone 262-574-7761. Pangea (VeganStore.com) has provided hard-to-find vegan products since 1995. Pangea Vegan Products, 2381 Lewis Avenue, Rockville Maryland 20851; phone 301-816-9300.

Vegetarian Societies Unite

Dixie Mahy

I consider Jay Dinshah to be the father of the modern American vegetarian-vegan movement. I met him at the 1975 World Vegetarian Congress.

When I heard the congress was to be held in the United States, I was excited to attend and represent our San Francisco Vegetarian Society (SFVS) of which I was vice president. I was pleased and honored that Jay asked me to be an active participant at the congress as an emcee and dancer at the evening plenary session and that he invited me to be a board member of the North American Vegetarian Society (NAVS).

At that congress Jay brought together 1,500 people from all over the world. We were amazed to learn that there were five vegetarian societies in the United States—Washington DC, San Francisco, Detroit, New York, and Los Angeles—yet none of us knew the others existed. There were also Canadian groups in Toronto and Montreal. Because of Jay, we all connected to each other as affiliates to NAVS.

Even more importantly, Jay gave us the opportunity to share our activities with each other, and he encouraged individuals who were in attendance to go home and start a vegetarian group in their communities utilizing our formats. As a result, vegetarian societies started springing up all over our country, and we continued to communicate with each other through NAVS publications.

I remember Jay as a dynamic speaker and organizer. His dedication and enthusiasm was contagious for his audiences and an inspiration for everyone who knew him. Jay was ahead of his time as a vegan and president of the American Vegan Society. I am grateful to him personally for being a vegan example as it encouraged me to become a vegan. I thank Jay for his leadership and friendship.

* * *

Dixie Mahy has been vegetarian since 1959. She has been vegan since 1979 as a result of Jay's influence. Dixie is an exuberant demonstration of vegan action with her activism and dancing. She credits the congress in Maine for influencing many people and providing so much impetus for the vegan as well as vegetarian movement.

SFVS was organized in 1968 by Fred Baldus. Dixie served as vice president of SFVS from 1970 to 1975. She has been president from 1975 to 1996 and from 2000 to the present. SFVS has hosted a World Vegetarian Festival annually since 2000 celebrating World Vegetarian Day. In 2012 SFVS hosted the fortieth IVU World Vegetarian Congress along with the World Vegetarian Festival, which initiated a change for the IVU to prefer festivals over congresses. SFVS.org

* * *

Join forces with others at a conference and focus on getting the world closer to when the animals can dance for joy in freedom.

Has this book or something else recently inspired you to spread the vegan message? Join your local vegetarian or vegan society or vegan Meetup group to find people geographically close to you. If one doesn't exist, you can start one. These groups might do a number of social activities such as host speakers, enjoy potlucks, or dine together at vegan or veg-friendly restaurants.

Setting the Stage for Veganism

Tom Regan

Jay was always ahead of his time. A big canvas was Jay's stage. He painted the picture of a vegan world for everyone to imagine.

The first of his conferences that the Regan family attended was the 1975 World Vegetarian Congress. That was when we learned the difference between "stomach" vegans and "ethical" vegans, the former practicing veganism for reasons of personal health, the latter for altruistic reasons.

One reason to be an ethical vegan is out of concern for world hunger. The simple truth is we could eliminate hunger if we all adopt a vegan diet. How does one make a picture of this idea?

Jay's creative answer was to put hunger in a hearse! The "Funeral for Famine" was staged in a stadium. Thousands were invited to watch from the stands and millions via national network television.

It really was that simple. Veganism was good for the planet, good for the animals, and good for people who were at daily risk of starving to death.

It was Jay's special gift to make abstract ideas meaningful in a way no one could deny because no one could question.

*   *   *

Tom Regan, PhD is best known for writing the book *The Case for Animal Rights*, published in 1983. His book provided a philosophical basis for a growing animal-rights movement also popularized by his booklet *The Philosophy of Animal Rights*.

He is professor emeritus at North Carolina State University (NCSU) where he taught in the department of philosophy since 1967. Tom cites Gandhi as the person whose writings first educated him that the fork is a weapon of violence, helping him question his values and recognize the link between violence and the treatment of animals. He advocates abolition of the use of animals in science, food, and sports.

Tom has written numerous books on animal rights and produced several documentaries. His website TomRegan.info includes a basic informative list, "Ten Reasons for Animal Rights and Their Explanations."

The NCSU Libraries established the Tom Regan Animal Rights Archive to organize, preserve, and provide access to Tom's personal papers and books. It also includes materials from individuals and organizations related to the animal-rights movement in the United States, such as *Ahimsa* and *American Vegan* magazines from AVS. He is an AVS life member.

*   *   *

Are you hungry for more knowledge about these strong reasons for veganism? Examine the efficiency of producing plant foods versus animal products. Then consider the many reasons for animal rights. Can you imagine a vegan world?

He Pushed Me

Lorene M. Cox

In 1975 I had been a vegetarian for three years and was still feeling my way in the world of the vegetable eaters. I had stopped at a health food store and saw the North American Vegetarian Society (NAVS) publication, *Vegetarian Voice*. There was an advertisement for the congress in Maine. Since I needed all the education I could get in the ways of vegetarians, I attended the conference.

That was where I first saw Jay Dinshah. He was the main organizer of the ten-day affair. That conference was also where I first met vegans: the Dinshah family and a group of people from England.

One of the events that impressed me at the end of the conference was Jay's "Funeral for Famine" complete with hearse and flowers. The funeral brought home the message that a vegetarian lifestyle could help feed many more people. At that time, it was said that ten pounds of grain fed to an animal would produce one pound of meat. The grain could be better used to feed more people.

In 1976 at NAVS' national vegetarian conference at a different location, I still felt somewhat lost and had difficulty finding my way through the conference program and around the campus. I spoke with Jay and suggested that someone explain how to use the program and where to get information about navigating the campus. Jay thought it was a good idea and said I should get up on the stage with other presenters that afternoon and explain the program to the attendees. Of course, I told him I couldn't do that, and of course, he told me I could. He would coach me.

We set a time to meet, sat down for ten minutes, and later I took my place on stage to explain it all. That was the beginning of my involvement with NAVS.

Jay knew how to inspire people, although sometimes there was too much inspiration and I had to back away. One thing I learned from being involved in organizations is that when people make suggestions, "the organization should do this..." or "the organization should do that...," the thing to do is to suggest to those offering suggestions that they get involved in the project they would like to see. More often than not, those making the suggestions will back away as I had tried to do. Jay wouldn't have it. He took the time to train me and insisted I could present the information. And so I did. I kept doing it in various ways year after year. I am grateful for that nudge, push, insistence, inspiration, the thing in Jay that got me to act. NAVS is now an integral part of my life.

At the 1976 conference I met more vegans. I said, "Those people are crazy, and I will never be one of them." By 1979 I was one of them—a vegan. Jay Dinshah provided a host of well-educated speakers to present at the annual conferences. Listening to them made a difference. It took four years for me to fully understand the "Funeral for Famine." Thank you, Jay.

*   *   *

Lorene Cox has attended every annual NAVS Vegetarian Summerfest conference since 1975 except one, when she changed jobs, which limited her vacation time. She did something else with her vacation and later wished she had gone to the conference. Through the years she has become more involved with NAVS and has served on their board of trustees since 1988. She is an AVS life member.

More importantly, at the 1975 conference Lorene met Freya Dinshah and a pregnant Sharon Graff who were dispensing food to the registrants. Little did she know that Sharon's baby would someday become her daughter-in-law Heidi and the mother of her granddaughter Eve. Brian and Sharon Graff's powerful vegan story is on page 85; Heidi's is on page 144. Heidi and Daniel Fox's dating story can be read in the book *Dating Vegans*.

Lorene credits Jay for his role in the outcome of her wonderful life. "After all, he pushed me to get involved."

*   *   *

Are you thinking about doing something to help the animals? What are you waiting for? Let Jay's words encourage you. Keep reading and listen to him on YouTube.

Do you have ideas for getting involved and spreading the message of compassion? Follow through on them and make them a reality.

"The question is not, 'Can they reason?' nor, 'Can they talk?' but rather, 'Can they suffer?'"   —Jeremy Bentham

Average Amer-I-Can: The Power of One

Robert Amer

Inspirational and transformative are not words I use very frequently. However, both are very appropriate to describe the two occasions I met Jay Dinshah. In 1975 I was twenty-five years young and a graduate student studying social work at Boston University. I was one of the fortunate 1,500 attendees to ascend onto the University of Maine campus for the congress. It was there that my early experiments with a vegan diet and ahimsa lifestyle philosophy crystallized. The collective energy of that experience was instrumental in shaping the next thirty-nine years—and counting—of dedication to a vegetarian and eventually vegan path.

It was entirely due to Jay, his family, and army of devoted volunteers that this event was made possible. His boundless energy, grass-roots organizing skills, and commitment to the cause were the inspiration behind its success. I met luminaries and advocates from all over the world. We gathered for lectures, workshops, sharing, eating, socializing, and promoting the many benefits that veganism has to offer.

A year later, still glowing from the experience, I hopped in a Volkswagon Bug and with my girlfriend now wife, attended the 1976 NAVS conference at Ithaca College where I met Jay for the second time. Again, his tireless energy and convictions organized what turned out to be another life-affirming experience for me.

Thanks to the influence of Jay, I married a vegetarian and had a 1977 hippie veggie wedding. On our honeymoon we visited Scott and Helen Nearing's homestead. We raised three vegetarian children, all of whom had vegetarian bar mitzvahs, graduations, and birthday parties. I have hosted countless meatless

114

Thanksgivings and holiday gatherings, potluck meals, and veggie social events.

Simply by example and modeling, my lifestyle has influenced countless friends and family members, especially from the next generation of nieces and nephews. What was, years earlier, considered a diet for "oddballs" is now securely quite mainstream and exponentially growing in acceptance and common-sense popularity. Restaurants, supermarkets, college campuses, caterers, etc., all now encompass an ever-expanding vegan consumer market demand. In a short forty years, I went from a "protein-starved, vitamin-B_{12}-anemic weirdo eating rabbit food" to an astute "visionary" and trendsetter. Go figure! When I travel to a new city and search online for vegetarian and vegan restaurants, for each of the many links, I send an imaginary thank you to Jay.

Jay's devotion, deep-rooted convictions, and endless determination to spread the wisdom of ahimsa resulted in countless stories like my own. I think of the impact meeting him has had on my life and then think about the impact I have had on others, who I now notice are further influencing people in their lives. Then I consider that I am but one of the many diverse and countless seeds that Jay has germinated. Do the math. His effect on others was contagious, like the ripples following a stone tossed in a lake. Jay's ripples travel great distances and have touched many lives both close and distant.

*   *   *

Robert Amer is a psychotherapist in the Boston area, vegetarian-vegan for forty years, and "the guy next door." He is an AVS life member.

*   *   *

Gently influence others with your everyday choices. Create ripples today and be part of a vegan wave changing the world.

The Pillars of Ahimsa

H. Jay Dinshah

Ahimsa is the Sanskrit word for nonkilling, noninjuring, and nonharming. Far from mere passiveness, it is a positive method for meeting the dilemmas and decisions of daily life. We term it "dynamic harmlessness," which encourages nonviolent action to create positive changes. Ahimsa is the compassionate way of life.

It was the guiding light of Mahatma Gandhi, which enabled that great soul to marshal the love force necessary to liberate his nation of some four-hundred-million people. Ahimsa was personally advocated by Dr. Albert Schweitzer, who noted that it encompasses the concept of reverence for life.

*   *   *

The six pillars of this dynamic philosophy for living modern life in a more meaningful manner are built on each of the letters of A-H-I-M-S-A:

Abstinence from animal products

Harmlessness with reverence for life

Integrity of thought, word, and deed

Mastery over oneself

Service to humanity, nature, and creation

Advancement of understanding and truth

Abstinence from Animal Products

This is a meaningful, positive, highly practical manifestation of the inward attitude of kinship with all life. It brings positive benefits to the abstainer, the animals, and the fellow humans one contacts.

Harmlessness with Reverence for Life

Humans, being the most powerful creatures on Earth, must use that power ethically and benevolently, not as some mindless creature running amuck, killing and destroying, creating fear and hatred, and leaving degradation and death in its wake. This is another seemingly negative pillar with highly positive results.

Integrity of Thought, Word, and Deed

In ahimsa, we work toward the state wherein there is truth, justice, and kindness in all that we think, say, and do. We should not condone dishonesty, corruption, or hypocrisy in ourselves. We cannot do something that we know to be cruel or wrong merely because it seems expedient or profitable at the moment. This is a pillar of obviously positive values with right thinking and right speaking laying the solid foundation for right action.

Mastery over Oneself

Ahimsa guides us in transcending our egocentric lower brute nature and bringing forth our finer, higher self. Instead of materialism and selfishness, we have enlightenment and understanding. A measure of self-control is necessary for the achievement of every other pillar.

Service to Humanity, Nature, and Creation

The path of ahimsa opens new doors to creative service, to altruistic and unselfish living, and to devoting oneself to helping make this world a better, saner, more harmonious place to live.

Advancement of Understanding and Truth

To know something is not enough; knowledge must be understood. It should not just be swallowed but digested, assimilated, and put to good use. Furthermore, our perception of facts may change in time, as with the good old flat-Earth concept.

We may not know absolute truth about all things. For practical purposes, we can apply Gandhi's measure that truth is for each individual, what one's "small, still voice within" says in guidance, according to the individual's respective development. We also must size it up against the eternal measure of The Golden Rule before translating our relative truth into action.

*　　*　　*

These are the basic tenets of the most effective possible path "out of the jungle" for humanity. Individual or collective efforts to find the way will come to naught if inspired only by selfishness or a base hope of personal gain or reward.

National or international attempts to impose peace are usually made only with an eye to enlightened self-interest for commercial gain or advantage. Our every attempt to find the light, and true peace on Earth, is frustrated because we have not yet had the insight and sincerity to approach life in terms of unselfishness and cooperation, in the age-old context of The Golden Rule. Ahimsa offers a truly comprehensive plan of action in the right direction.

Ahimsa is a balanced program for living, for doing the most

good and the least harm. We concede that we may not be able to attain perfection overnight, if ever; but we must not let this deter us from at least taking the first step, which we can very easily do and should do without delay.

*   *   *

On the next few pages, we will elaborate on the themes suggested by these great pillars of ahimsa.

Abstinence from Animal Products

Perhaps nowhere in the practice of ahimsa is the path "out of the jungle" so clearly defined as in the concept of abstinence from all products of cruelty, exploitation, and slaughter. Think in a sincere and objective manner about the harm and pain caused to the animal world by the use of such materials, and then compare their use with the ideals of compassionate living that mark the practice of ahimsa. The most urgent step on the path becomes crystal clear and obvious.

Further study of the principle of indirect guilt, such as through creating the demand for the harmful actions of others, will also strengthen the resolution to break off all use of such products. It must be understood that the guilt involved in the killing of a creature for food, clothing, decoration, or sport is not merely the metaphoric millstone around the neck of the one who commits the act of cruelty or killing involved while the actual user or consumer remains guiltless. On the contrary, any fair-minded appraisal of the situation, through the full chain of supply-and-demand, must pin the bulk of the blame squarely upon the shoulders of the consumer.

Thus, every act of cruelty, mutilation, abnormal breeding, exploitation, and killing of surplus baby animals and over-age production animals is the responsibility of the people creating the demand for the products involved, not just that of the farmer or animal raiser. And it is, of course, truly immaterial whether the products of this vile traffic in sensitive, feeling creatures is carried out for food, clothing, or any other human profit.

This compassionate way of ahimsa requires us to be straightforward. This is not to say that one who takes a glassful of milk once in a while cannot be practicing ahimsa in other ways or that everyone who abstains from animal foods and other animal products is automatically a saint. What ahimsa demands of us is that we live our own lives in the manner that will do the most good and the least harm to other lives. Certainly under the circumstances attendant to the production of animal products, we must eliminate them if we are to live and practice ahimsa consistently and effectively.

Must We Be 100 Percent Vegan?

Obviously, many great people have done many things for the cause of ahimsa and in the name of ahimsa who could not have been practicing it 100 percent. Even the revered Mahatma Gandhi told the vegetarian movement that he had felt forced to use animal milk to rebuild his body after serious illness or overfasting for political purposes. Although he recognized the moral fault of it, he did not then know how to entirely get away from using it. In 1931, he called this the tragedy of his life, so deeply did he feel about having to depend at times on something in the morality of which he did not believe. He did, of course, express the view that humanity's natural food should be strictly nonanimal. He believed that with further understanding of natural living and nutrition this knowledge would probably come to light eventually as has since happened, enabling people to follow their consciences more consistently.

Dr. Schweitzer was not a consistent vegetarian when he first formulated the concept of reverence for life, although he certainly was later on in his nine decades of life.

It is not the province of anyone who believes in ahimsa to throw stones at another's weaknesses or limitations. Certainly the authors do not claim to be able to practice 100 percent ahimsa in all its most subtle ramifications at all times. But we humans are hardly more than clay if we do not have high ideals and goals to which we can aspire and struggle and, perhaps, one day attain.

We can reach the goal that in this imperfect world may not be complete perfection but doing the best we possibly can. We will not reach the goal if we say, "Well, ahimsa is a very nice ideal, but not very practical or profitable, so I won't bother with it at all until..." And here we may insert, "the world is ready for it" or "next year/month/week/lifetime/world/or you name it" or "I am better able to do so" or "the next fellow does it" or any other convenient and equally spurious excuse for sitting back and doing absolutely nothing.

No, that won't do at all. We must begin now. An intelligently planned, progressive program of nonanimal utilization is a very fine way to begin, not next month or next week but today.

Harmlessness with Reverence for Life

Probably no other part of the practice of ahimsa is so widely known and so little understood as this second pillar. Veganism for ethical reasons is the expression of this pillar.

We should begin by realizing that this harmlessness is not a passive, negative doctrine of nothingness but rather dynamic harmlessness. This does not enjoin us to sit idly by while watching the passing parade of humanity. On the contrary, the fifth pillar later on will tell us how to actively serve. But how shall we act at all?

We must weigh our actions with care. Choose the fork in the road that yields the greatest good and the least harm, preferably for a great amount of good and no harm at all. When we say harmlessness, we are not dreaming that we can exist bottled up in a fool's paradise. If we live in this world, we are bound to harm some plants, certainly some microbes, and even some animals.

Only by living as a complete hermit—not moving or working, in fact not even eating or breathing—could we attain a completely harmless state. And even then, until we died, which would be quite soon, various involuntary physiological processes would keep on working, fostering and killing myriad molecular and cellular types of life within us. We might have to be more like a plant, getting nourishment from dead minerals, a method that is not conducive to highly organized human life. But even as a plant breathes and contains microbial and cellular life, we can easily see how absurd this line of thought can become. We are not preaching an absurd do-nothingness amid a vacuum of activity.

What we are doing in ahimsa is setting up a wonderful goal or ideal and then attempting to live up to it as closely as we can at our present stage of development. All the while we recognize our duty to raise our level of ahimsa as we are able. We do not claim 100 percent perfection in our actions; we do make the effort to raise ourselves from 50 percent to 98 percent. In India, it is said that when you have reduced your himsa, the harm you are doing or causing, to the irreducible minimum, that is called ahimsa.

Harmlessness means that we should speak up for truth and goodness, without malice. It means that we should work for human betterment; indeed, it teaches us how to perform such work meaningfully. If there is oppression, we have a duty to work for justice with amity and not merely against an oppressor. Mahatma Gandhi was never satisfied with outwitting his enemies or vanquishing the oppressors. His goal was always to persuade and convince them and to make friends of them in the end. Where there is darkness, we must spread the light.

The men and women of ahimsa work in the world, all right. We reject the commonplace, crude weapons of the world's struggles, substituting the unquenchable fire of pure love; and the only shield is truth.

In regard to our relationship to others, the second pillar of ahimsa teaches us the practical application of The Golden Rule that marvelous doctrine found in the scriptures of every great religion and major philosophy. We are not the only ones on Earth. There are other humans, and each shares with us the right to life, liberty, and the pursuit of happiness. There are also nonhumans entitled to these rights, and we should respect their rights also, all the more so since they cannot state such claims themselves.

Reverence for life may be misunderstood. It does not mean animal worship. It means having a decent respect for the miracle of life itself, recognizing the same life miracle in varying forms of expression, all with a common bond of universal kinship. Our dynamic harmlessness can well be founded upon this life view. As other lives feel pain, joy, sorrow, and love—as we do—we should extend to them the same courtesy of harmlessness that we would want them to extend to us. As with harmlessness, the idea of reverence for life does not give us an impossible or fanatical dogma that we must never kill or harm anything regardless of circumstance in the animal or plant kingdoms.

What it does is to give us the necessary mental and moral yardstick to measure a particular situation against known values. It cannot make the decision for us, but it gives us the tools with which to do the job intelligently and fairly. Contrary to popular belief, these concepts of dynamic harmlessness and reverence for life are not just emotional or sentimental, but are the result of realistic logic by very practical as well as idealistic people.

These concepts offer a solution to the egocentric moral quagmire in which human folly has placed the modern world in general. They show the way out of the ethical jungle and into the sunshine of a brighter and better world.

Time is running out for the world as we know it, and the widespread adoption of these lofty yet thoroughly practical ideals becomes more imperative and more urgent with each day. We are talking not only of our humanity in relation to animals. Followers of ahimsa are concerned with the whole nasty mess we have made of our relationship to other humans, to other creatures, to our environment, and to ourselves.

We have to do it. We must get our thoughts, emotions, words, and actions out of this vast and dark moral jungle. We don't have to be predators. We are more than merely instinctive killers and selfish brutes. Why take such a dim view of our potentialities and capabilities?

Why settle for so little, when we could be so much? In being selfish, we cheat ourselves of the most noble birthright any creature could desire: humanity, which can be next to divinity. We can make it. And ahimsa will light the way.

Integrity of Thought, Word, and Deed

Integrity means to be complete, undivided, whole. It also means soundness and purity. Finally, it means moral honesty and uprightness. When we refer to this pillar of ahimsa, we mean integrity in all these definitions of the term. Particularly, there are two ways to think of this idea.

First, we should realize that our daily lives are, with ahimsa, built upon the bedrock foundation of right thinking. We must have a sound, wholesome philosophy of life and a compassionate viewpoint of the rest of creation and of how we relate to it.

Right thinking must be the basis, the beginning. Once we have thought things out to a good extent, we may also wish to talk to others about these matters in order to obtain more knowledge or to clarify our own thinking or to help others to gain the point of view we now hold. The obvious result of right thinking and right speaking should always be right action. We should always try to act in the best manner, not just for ourselves but for others as well.

Our thoughts should always be harmonious with the interests of truth, nonviolence, justice, and kindness; and so too should our words. Again, we may not possess absolute truth at any given moment or in regard to some specific subjects, but we should endeavor to know the truth as best we can, to speak only truth to the extent that we do know it, and to learn the truth of what we do not now know.

The cornerstone of tolerance for the views and opinions of others is not only compassion but also the knowledge of one's own imperfections. It is much easier to take an unbiased or clear view of the beliefs or actions of others if we recognize that we may, after all, be misguided or in error in some of our own views, regardless of how cherished and honestly held these may be.

Second, we should endeavor to bring about a state of harmony among our three mentioned faculties of thinking, speaking, and acting. We should try to be consistent. We should not believe in our minds and hearts one thing and even speak out for it, and then do the opposite because it is convenient.

In short, we should have our thoughts, words, and deeds harmonizing as parts of our integral wholeness, each being after all but one facet of our individual character. Ideally, we might attain perfection of such harmony. It is certainly worthwhile to think about it, to speak about it, and to work toward such perfection.

In actual practice, however, it is customary for a person's thoughts to be running in several directions at once, generally a few jumps ahead of one's words and still further ahead of one's actions. This is not a bad sequence of events. It would not do to have words precede conscious thought, though this does occur at times; and hasty actions without prior thought and discussion can be even more hazardous.

We often see people who claim to be "vegan in principle," though their actions tend to indicate that their words are really far in advance of their innermost thoughts and desires, with the actions coming in a sad third place. Encourage the truly sincere person, who is in fact already "in the upward stream," working toward a better way of living, not merely searching for excuses to avoid the stresses of effort of making further progress and advancement. To the truly sincere, veganism and ahimsa are challenges to be joyfully met, not sullenly shirked.

We should be at peace with ourselves, if we wish to find peace in the world about us. Those whose actions are at great variance with their conscience and thought are not at peace; they are in confusion, in an inner turmoil. Many people live in false peace with a slumbering conscience, the pseudo-tranquility of ignorance, and the moral stupor of selfishness. They are to be awakened gently and purposefully at a rate they can handle.

If we ever attain perfection ourselves, perhaps then we will have earned the right to judge others. Until then, it is more mischievous than fruitful to spend one's life and effort criticizing and condemning others. It is much more difficult and more worthwhile to objectively weigh one's own motives and actions. We need not be of the school of thought that claims one must experience everything in life first hand and in a nonjudgmental way. It is not necessary to do stupid, self-destructive, or sadistic things to realize it is better all-around not to do them. A person does not, for example, have to get drunk, drive a car ninety miles an hour, and plow it into a loaded school bus to know that all of these actions are better left undone. They are wrong—to say the least—for any person of conscience.

To "see no evil" is no way to go through life, ignoring the consequences of one's actions that cause pain to others. We cannot achieve wholeness by pretending conscience does not exist. We can only attain wholeness by recognizing its insistent prodding and living up to its guiding light.

Integrity, moral soundness, and harmony of being come only from vigorous activity of conscience, ruled by the human virtues of compassion and love, as well as the practical approach of personal health and well-being, being secondary in importance as motives for action. This is the third pillar of ahimsa.

Mastery over Oneself

The fourth pillar of ahimsa begins with our conquest over our own smallness and pettiness, over the selfish, gross, brute side of our nature that holds us down and retards our progress. As with other pillars of ahimsa, we may examine this from both the positive and negative sides.

Imagine a man in an automobile that is running down a steep mountain road, with the brakes faded out and the steering mechanism broken. Although such a man may be sitting in the driver's seat, he cannot have any real control over what may occur. He is not so much driving the car as the car is driving him, and it will carry him on to physical destruction.

We are like that hapless man if we permit the physical body and its attendant desires of seeking pleasure and avoiding all discomfort to dominate our attention and our actions. When we are preoccupied with the illusory pleasures of materialism and selfishness, when we permit ourselves to be ruled by the runaway forces of such masters as greed, pride, envy, cruelty, hatred, fear, jealousy, prejudice, ignorance, consumerism, and so on—and very hard masters they are—we are no longer master in our own house. We have turned the keys over to the housebreakers, thieves, and arsonists.

There we sit, like a prisoner in our own abode, helpless while these vandals and brigands despoil and plunder all around us: "Look you! There goes one now with a bit of our health. See! There goes another with more of our self-respect. There, out of the open window, fly self-will and self-determination." What will at last be left but the poor empty shell, the ruined hulk of the former structure?

We must take stock of ourselves. We must cast out the spoilers that are wrecking our home. We must fight again the inner battle that was fought by Arjuna, by Gautama Buddha, by Saint Francis of Assisi, by Gandhi, and by so many others. We must fight the battle of life within ourselves. But how does one take up arms against oneself?

One does not. One arms oneself with right thoughts. One begins to see the shape of things as they are in truth instead of how one might wish them to appear. Against envy, covetousness, and greed one arms oneself with compassion, generosity, and simplicity of living patterns and habits. Consider that many consumer products rely on exploitation of human or nonhuman animals as well as on our environmental resources; resources and products should not be squandered.

Against egotism and pride one turns the pure force of true humility that comes from the knowledge of one's true place in the universe as brother or sister to all life. Against the darkness of ignorance one turns the torch of enlightenment and understanding. Against fear, right knowledge and understanding come to the rescue, for we only fear that which we do not understand.

Humanity on Earth acts pretty much as a child in a candy store. We are overwhelmed and tempted by the many attractions, heedless of the stomachache that is the inevitable consequence of our childish indulging. In addition, it may spoil our appetite for the foods that will truly nourish and sustain us. Humanity is far too preoccupied with its physical trinkets and playthings. We are so enthralled by the glittering tinsel of our own making that we sell ourselves woefully short and neglect what we might become if we would apply ourselves.

Our insatiable curiosity has carried us to the conquest of outer space and toward even the stars. In arriving at the Moon, we have found it as dead as our ultramaterialistic heart and soul, as empty as our head in seeking such conquest before we have first made the prime conquest here on Earth. We must master our lower, selfish self before we can realize our higher potential; and we must do both before we are fit to master the Earth, the sea, the skies, and space, let alone claim to be the master of other living beings such as birds, beasts, and fish. Humanity claims absolute dominion over everything that breathes, crawls, runs, flies, swims, or stands still. We have been ill-trained for such a royal position and seem more like a petty tyrant instead.

Without this first and all-important conquest of inner space— the conquest of or at the very least the control of ourselves at the individual level—we are only turning loose a Frankenstein monster with little restraining sense of morality, justice, fairness, and goodness.

We need to utilize the ability to control ourselves by using our sense of morality, justice, fairness, and goodness. Thus we will achieve mastery over oneself and be better able to do the greatest good for other inhabitants of the Earth.

Service to Humanity, Nature, and Creation

The service to humanity, nature, and creation exists where there is one to serve. It does not depend on circumstances or location; where there is a single human being to walk the path, there is a path to be walked.

We are used to the atmosphere of a land of enjoyment; yet we certainly also find more than sufficient opportunities for living up to our duty of service to creation. Human misery, poverty, and despair exist in every city and can be found in the suburbs and country too. The need for gentleness and an ethical, nonviolent way of living and looking at life—ahimsa—is certainly needed as desperately in the United States, in England, and in other "have" nations as it is in India, Ethiopia, or anywhere else. Abundance of wealth has not brought peace of heart and mind or any permanent or worthwhile gratification. We have an urgent need of a fresh new way of looking at life. Opportunities are numerous for those who feel it their duty to help their fellow humans find a more meaningful way of living.

The love is great when it is felt for someone who shares with us only the common membership in the human family or in life itself. The world can be won for love, peace, and harmony if nonviolent individuals who sincerely believe in these ideals will simply stand up and have the courage to live by them, thus being examples to others. Dr. Schweitzer was of the view that example is not just the best way to teach but "It is the only way!" And of course he also knew that there is no value in it if one indulges in egocentric self-righteousness: "Behold! I am setting an example!"

There are so many worthy projects and endeavors that fulfill certain facets of the ahimsa ideal, such as:

A) Helping people to live more naturally and healthfully. This takes in a great deal of territory, including simplification of needs and wants, proper diet, growing of better foods without chemical fertilizers and pesticides—more correctly called "biocides"; the correct use of exercise, rest, sunlight, pure air and water, etc.; civic activity to curb pollution of land, air, and water (including fluoridation a.k.a. compulsory toxic medication); education to natural means of restoring and maintaining health; cultivating and encouraging proper emotional and mental attitudes.

B) Publicizing the benefits of getting out of the rat-race. Meanwhile, provide alternative beneficial outlets for those competitive energies to do more good, such as volunteering to help others, coordinating events with a positive overall ahimsa message, or spreading information about the atrocities of using animals for food.

C) Working for the preservation and protection of wildlife and natural wilderness areas (though not for hunting and fishing purposes) as well as making every attempt to make the cities more livable. Ideas include painting murals over graffiti, picking up litter, planting urban gardens, and organizing neighborhood community activities.

D) Working for the direct benefit of animals. Volunteer at an animal sanctuary either taking care of animals or doing outreach. On an individual basis, care for the various birds and other animals who may come to you for help in one manner or another.

E) Working in any number of ways to persistently teach a more humane attitude toward nonhuman creatures, especially in children, who have not yet been artificially hardened in their viewpoint by the callous and cynical see-no-evil pose of their elders. If you are good at cooking, offer a kids' cooking class at a local community organization. (See the AVS published book, *Apples, Bean Dip, and Carrot Cake: Kids! Teach Yourself to Cook* and ideas for classes at AmericanVegan.org/ABC/ABC.html) If gardening is your passion, offer to teach kids how to connect with their proper food—plants. If hiking is your thing, lead nature walks and remind people how to appreciate the Earth.

F) Working for world peace. Build a foundation of understanding, unity, and empathy, without which there can never be a very successful effort for world peace. Work for understanding and compassion among human beings, including families, states, nations, and races.

G) Working among the poor and unfortunate, to alleviate human misery in general.

There are many other worthwhile causes. Help can be in the form of actual work performed, services rendered in a direct or indirect manner, material goods donated, funds contributed or bequeathed—though it is more meaningful to be a live giver than a dead one—or talents cheerfully offered. Above all, one does not just live and help: ideally one should live to help.

Advancement of Understanding and Truth

To know and to understand are two different concepts. Here is a human example:

Students may neglect their studies in favor of more pleasurable pursuits. Then, they may be obliged to cram facts and figures at the last moment for an exam. With no lasting interest in the subject and no goal in mind but to achieve a passing score and obtain the credit for it, they may seem mathematical wizards or scientific prodigies—for a day. Overstuffed craniums soon dispose of the unwanted material. The following week the same brilliant students can scarcely recall the most elementary part of the material studied so hurriedly and with little real understanding. In further pursuance of this point—the difference between knowing and understanding—ask yourself how many people do you know, and then ask yourself how many of these acquaintances or family members do you really understand.

Today knowledge is at a premium. Millions of animals each year are tortured and slaughtered in research and testing labs, for the purposes of advancing medical knowledge or developing new products. Usually these experiments are either repetitions or outright failures, adding little or nothing of value to any mental fund. Most of them send liberally funded researchers chasing rainbows of questionable value and veracity. All of them add up to the tragically selfish pose humanity takes that humans are the only creatures worth the room they take up on Earth, and that all other living creatures are fair game for us if we can profit from them in some manner. What a difference it would make, if we would only try to understand animals.

If instead of trying to know about animals and life by strapping them down and opening them up to see what makes them tick, what if we tried to understand them in their natural context, as living parts of the whole scheme of things, living parts of the grand mystery of life? Suppose we tried also to understand a little more about the wonderful life force that each of us has in us, instead of concentrating on merely knowing the names of all the muscles and nerves, and so on. What wonders might be wrought in the field of human health alone, not to mention human morality and compassion, if we would stop trying so hard to know and make more effort to understand. If only we could understand that the universe is not malevolent, and that humanity can live in love and compassion without perishing. Indeed it appears more likely that we could perish because we do not practice these virtuous attributes to a sufficient degree.

While gaining understanding of everything heretofore mentioned—veganism, harmlessness, integrity, service, compassion, and more—discuss concerns with others. This will result in an advancement of understanding—the final pillar of ahimsa.

*   *   *

What will you choose to build with the pillars of ahimsa?

"Until he extends his circle of compassion to all living things, man will not himself find peace."   —Dr. Albert Schweitzer

Wisdom and Compassion

H. Jay Dinshah

Far beyond knowledge there is that which transcends understanding, which is wisdom. Wisdom is the ability to put the knowledge we have understood into practice in our daily lives.

We may know that there is intense poverty, cruelty, inhumanity, corruption, and exploitation of human and nonhuman animals in our own country as well as elsewhere. Do we understand it, and are we motivated to do anything about it?

We may know that billions of sensitive, feeling animals are cruelly raised, mutilated, shipped, and butchered annually to feed our cultivated desire for unnatural, harmful foods and savage forms of clothing and shoes. Do we understand the awful implications of all this brutality and the terrible price paid by them—and by us?

*   *   *

To understand the feelings and thoughts of another we need compassion. To adequately assess another's circumstances and be motivated to render meaningful assistance, we should attempt to walk in the shoes, hooves, paws, or fins of another to see things from another angle and viewpoint.

To judge the cruelty to animals, we must see it from their side of the fence, not from the question of cash profits or satisfying our depraved tastes. It is only by claiming that they have no sensitivity or emotions, that they cannot feel pain—as bold a falsehood as the selfish human mind has ever contrived—that we can continue to prey upon them and abuse them in every way.

Contrary to the ill-meaning jests of detractors, this does not mean that one who believes in reverence for life and ahimsa would as soon save the life of a strawberry plant or a stalk of asparagus as the life of a child. It does mean that one understands the underlying bond of all life and recognizes the value of all such life, whatever its manifestation. It may not necessarily be an equal valuation, but it certainly cannot be 100 percent on one side and a big fat zero on the other. It is patently impossible to exist as a human and live by a theory that all life is of exactly equal value, whether it is human, animal, vegetable, microbial, electronic, viral, atomic, or whatever one may wish to include.

It is clearly another matter to hold that, to itself, every life is of equal value. The life of a cat or cow is all the life that she has, and is just as dear and as necessary to her as mine is to me or yours is to you. While the scientific and linguistic complexities of humans may be more developed than those of the wolf or the whale, the natural sensory abilities and sometimes the moral behavior of many animals leave humans behind in the dust.

One need not become embroiled in futile speculation and disputation over irrelevant claims of superiority and inferiority. Learn from the wisdom of President Abraham Lincoln in refusing to be trapped in the loaded questions of nineteenth-century racism. He was concerned not with apparent differences that should not matter under human law and justice. But in the right of his fellow human to enjoy the fruits of one's own labor, Lincoln asserted, "He is my equal."

Masterfully turning the tables on the self-exalted "superior humans" and their racial-inferiority excuse for human enslavement, Lincoln declared that "If God hath given him but little, then let him enjoy what little he hath."

Meanwhile, African-American abolitionist and women's rights activist Sojourner Truth was widely credited with saying, "I'm glad to see that men are getting their rights, but I want women to get theirs, and while the water is stirring I'm stepping into the pool." She was quoted in *The Anti-Slavery Bugle*: "As for intellect, all I can say is, if woman have a pint and man a quart, why can't she have her little pint full? You need not be afraid to give us our rights for fear we will take too much, for we can't take more than our pint'll hold." Certainly she didn't believe women to be inferior in intelligence to men, but she used the oppressors' words to turn the tables. Likewise, animals are not going to take more rights than their "little intellects" can handle, and they need people to speak up for them.

Simple justice demands no less than that advocated by Lincoln and Truth. Justice, of course, can be jimmied, jammed, and junked to suit the wishes of those who have the money and temporal power. With animal oppression, exploitation seeks any excuse and asks, "How much profit can I make from this?" Compassion ever asks, "What's the right thing to do? How can I help?"

In any event, we cannot have it both ways: humanity cannot pretend to be higher in ethics, spirituality, advancement, or civilization than other creatures and at the same time live by a lower standard than the vulture or hyena. The truth of the matter is that it is high time for us humans to leave our lowest brute nature behind and bring our higher self to the fore.

Major social justice movements through the years have advocated rights for all, focusing on race, sex, sexual orientation, and now species. The pillars of ahimsa represent the clearest, surest path "out of the jungle" and toward the attainment of that highly desirable goal.

*   *   *

Good books to read of special interest as one considers veganism as a social justice movement include the following, available from AVS:

The Sexual Politics of Meat: A Feminist-Vegetarian Critical Theory by Carol J. Adams

Sistah Vegan: Black Female Vegans Speak on Food, Identity, Health, and Society by Breeze Harper

The Dreaded Comparison: Human and Animal Slavery by Marjorie Spiegel

Eternal Treblinka: Our Treatment of Animals and the Holocaust by Charles Patterson

Defiant Daughters: 21 Women on Art, Activism, Animals, and the Sexual Politics of Meat by Kara Davis and Wendy Lee, editors

"The time is always right to do what is right."
—Dr. Martin Luther King, Jr.

The Next Generation's Pillars of Ahimsa

Anne Dinshah

I dream that Dad and I tour together, each speaking on our best topics, then collaborating for humorous banter with underlying great meaning. He could "join" me via the magic of technology; yet people will still expect me to talk about any aspect of *Powerful Vegan Messages*—alone.

We're well into concepts Dad taught—the hardest part for me. I'm good at explaining veganism, ethical dilemmas, priorities, and other chapters. My biggest challenge is discussing the pillars of ahimsa. To many people this was Dad's most notable work—a way to go about modern life—back in the 1960s. My present-day interpretation is from the viewpoint of "the girl next door."

Will you close the book and quiz yourself, or shall I go first?

*　　*　　*

Ahimsa means nonharming. More importantly, Dad advocated it as a way to create positive action in the world. Each letter in ahimsa stands for a valuable action in an aspect of our daily lives.

Animals! Be vegan for the animals: the animals need us to make wise decisions.

Harmlessness with reverence for life: weigh actions for the most good and least harm.

Integrity in thought, word, and deed: align these honestly expressing good thoughts in the ways we talk and act.

Mastery over materialism, envy, gluttony, greed, and selfishness: identify and clarify needs and wants.

Service to humanity: find happiness by doing something to benefit people or the environment.

Advancement of understanding *Powerful Vegan Messages*: create ways to share the lessons.

Animals! Be vegan for the animals. The animals need us to make wise decisions. Do not kill or hurt the animals; do not eat or wear them. I could say abstinence from animal products means to be vegan. As soon as I start with the word abstinence, my mind thinks of sex. Sorry, it just does. So I focus the "A" for animals. If you are not vegan, give it a try for the sake of the animals. Try it for a set number of days, or gradually incorporate more and more vegan meals into your life. If you are not sure how to get started, check out easy vegan cookbooks or ask a vegan to be your buddy.

During your initial vegan, vegan-curious, or transition-to-vegan days, watch a video about what really happens to animals in production. Also, go visit a vegetable farm or fruit orchard and connect with what you eat. Then find an animal, preferably one of a species typically in food production such as at a farm animal sanctuary, but a companion animal will do the job if you make the connection. Look the animal in the eye and ask for the strength to stay on the journey.

Learn to enjoy the bounty of plant-based food. Don't just cut out animal products and live on soda and fries. Veganism can be a wonderful, healthy journey that's better for the animals and better for you too. If you are already an experienced vegan, be a happy, approachable, shining example to encourage others.

Harmlessness with reverence for life. Weigh actions for the most good and least harm means to make conscious choices. Extend The Golden Rule to all creatures. In the rare occurrence that one needs to decide whether to take a life—such as a direct threat to a person's or creature's life—weigh the value of each life, choose to preserve the higher life form, and accept responsibility for the action taken.

These days with modern food transportation that brings the bounty of plant foods to stores year-round, there is no reason to eat animal products. We do not need animal products for our survival. Animals definitely suffer needlessly for humanity's tastes. When food shopping, let the conscience overrule habits. Take The Golden Rule and apply it to purchases; this is a logical yardstick with which to measure daily actions.

Most animals are killed for food in faraway slaughterhouses which keeps the consumer from making a conscious connection. I like Paul McCartney's quote, "If slaughterhouses had glass walls, everyone would be a vegetarian." Extend that to veganism.

The most common exception to faraway killing is hunting, a conscious choice to kill creatures, yet hunters' lives were not in any danger. My hunter friends say they love the outdoors, camaraderie, skill, and sighting animals. I agree on those points and hunt with a camera. Some say they like the taste of venison and other wild meats. Some ask, "What if the deer overrun us?" Humans made the problem by moving into the deer's ancestor's territory. Humans killed off natural predators such as wolves and bears and created a landscape where deer thrive so humans can hunt. We need to think about the big picture and have wild lands for wild animals.

We also took away the animals' habitat to make farmland. We grow big crops to feed to animals sent to slaughter for food. I'm oversimplifying it here, but we could feed all the world's people if we fed people plants directly, and we would be able to return some of the farmland to forests. It would improve the environment, upgrade life for the animals, benefit our own health, and be more in line with reverence for life.

Integrity of thought, word, and deed. Align these honestly expressing good thoughts in the ways we talk and act. Make the best decisions possible with all the information available. When conflict in these is eliminated, you will be in harmony with yourself and most likely happier. Gandhi put it succinctly: "True happiness is when what you think, what you say, and what you do are all in complete alignment." Listen to your conscience. Have conviction to do what is right, honest, and ideal. It's easy to explain, harder to do.

Mastery over materialism, envy, gluttony, greed, and selfishness. Identify and clarify needs and wants. This was originally mastery over oneself, Dad's beautiful all-encompassing way to remind people to self-evaluate. I will never forget the time a friend asked if mastery over oneself referred to sex. Therefore I prefer to spell out a few items of this pillar regarding necessities and pleasures.

Since the topic came up, let's first talk about sex. Sex is great in moderation, meaning it can't be the only thing one does, and there are a lot of choices involved, such as with whom, where, and when. Then think about how humans deny animals any choices. Animals are routinely artificially inseminated—raped— to produce the next generation of meat or more milk. Think about how often animals of the "wrong" sex are killed early in life because they are useless to the industry such as male baby layer chicks and male dairy calves. Females in egg and milk production are also killed after a miserable painful life of servitude. All animals in meat production are killed and almost all are the products of rape. Turkeys have been bred to be so distorted for profit they can not have natural sex even if given the opportunity.

Distinguish between needs and wants. Does one need animal products? What price is really on that car with leather seats? Or that steak, omelet, or ice cream? Seek options before selecting a product. Try a vegan alternative.

Mastery over oneself encompasses more than avoiding animal products. It is assessing every aspect of one's actions for pure intentions. Dad listed this pillar to include mastery over greed, pride, envy, cruelty, hatred, fear, jealousy, prejudice, ignorance, and consumerism. That's a tall order, but it is realistically doable. Start with materialism, envy, gluttony, greed, and selfishness, then check back for the rest of his list. I'm not saying these four are any more important than the others, but once these are addressed the others will be easier. Plus this can be remembered as mastery over materialism because I like alliteration and then get rid of e.g.g.s. as you take stock of what is important in life. When needs are countable and wants are fewer, it frees up a lot of time, money, and energy for meaningful endeavors.

To combat materialism, have a budget and shop with a shopping list. If tempted by an impulse purchase, walk away, and if it still beckons to be purchased the next day or month, then get it. With envy, if a friend or neighbor has something admirable, appreciate it for what it is, but think of the time, money, and space saved by not having it. For gluttony, choose to eat food that is nourishing, delicious, and healthy for one's body, without eating to excess or destroying another creature in the process. Have enough money and belongings to be comfortable, but not so much as to be greedy—a standard to be periodically reevaluated. If one has excess money and belongings, think who would benefit most from receiving them.

From personal experience, I know it may take a tragedy in one's life before truly understanding this pillar to its fullest potential. Perhaps it's something of the magnitude of bankruptcy, divorce, surviving a flood or fire, death of loved ones, or severe illness or injury. Maybe a happier event such as the birth of a child, making new friends, or exploring a new career brings clarity to the priorities in life. Embracing this pillar makes the other pillars more achievable.

Service to humanity. Find happiness by doing something to benefit people or the environment. Find ways to involve oneself and other people in meaningful activities to make the world a better place. Instead of another round of a video game, wouldn't it be nice to make and serve vegan soup to people who line up to receive what may be their only meal of the day? Maybe make a big commitment, such as adopting a child who's been waiting for years for a loving home. Or do something smaller, like spending a day picking up trash from along a waterway pretending it's a treasure hunt. Perhaps neighborhood kids who run amuck can be offered cooking classes to channel their energy in positive ways?

Look around and find a calling. Tune out the noise of our technological lives and tune in to the people, the animals, and the planet. Take care of yourself and your family first. This doesn't have to be about sacrifice. We don't have to dress like Gandhi to live up to what he taught.

Advancement of understanding *Powerful Vegan Messages.* Create ways to share the lessons. When you know the importance of what is conveyed here you cannot be silent about the exploitation of animals or any other injustice in the world. Do what you can to help others learn. Continue to learn something new yourself every day. Find your role. This book provides options for how to get involved and personal stories for inspiration. Keep reading. Thank you for sharing this mission.

When new acquaintances find out I'm a writer or motivational speaker, they often ask my topic if they haven't found out about me on the Internet. I politely say, "I speak on compassionate living and healthy recipes." Then frequently they ask, "Are you vegan?" and initiate a good conversation. It's amazing how many people want to be compassionate and healthy. They just don't know they want to be vegan—yet.

*   *   *

If you didn't quiz yourself on the pillars of ahimsa at the beginning of this chapter, are you ready to do so now?

Foxes and Rabbits

Heidi Fox

Before I was born, Jay began to impact my life. My parents met at SunCrest where they were working for American Vegan Society (AVS) and North American Vegetarian Society (NAVS). After a short time, they realized that they had many of the same beliefs about how animals should be treated and the vegan lifestyle. They fell in love. On a cold day in January they were married. Just under a year later, I was born on January 24 1976.

Jay encouraged my love for animals when I was a young girl. He even painted me a mural of a rabbit with a rainbow. I will always feel a special connection with Jay through that rabbit at the AVS office.

When I was nearly four years old, my parents and I moved to upstate New York. My parents brought NAVS with them to continue Jay's work helping animals. When Jay and I would see each other over the years, we would talk about how my rabbit was doing.

My love for animals has continued throughout my life. I have never forgotten the important things Jay believed. Helping animals was very important to him, as it is to me. Jay has done many great things and affected many people. For me, he was always family and will hold a special place in my heart.

*   *   *

Heidi Fox is a lifelong vegan. Every year she works as part of NAVS Vegetarian Summerfest staff team along with her vegan husband Daniel, her parents (page 85), Daniel's mom (page 111), and numerous friends. Heidi is an AVS life member.

Heidi and Daniel are proud to raise their daughter Eve as a vegan. They talk with Eve about why veganism is such an important choice. At age three, when asked why her family is vegan, Eve said, "Because we don't want to hurt the animals."

*   *   *

Are there kids in your life? What are you teaching them? Think about finding ways to introduce them to vegan children such as attending a conference like Vegetarian Summerfest which features a great children's center. Expose them to many of the wonderful children's books about veganism and compassion. Ruby Roth has books that come right out with the facts in *Vegan is Love, That's Why We Don't Eat Animals,* and *V is for Vegan.* *Dave Loves Chickens* by Carlos Patiño is an excellent choice with a more subtle inquisitive message of compassion. Invite kids to take a role in their food preparation with *Apples, Bean Dip, and Carrot Cake: Kids! Teach Yourself to Cook* by Anne and Freya Dinshah.

"If a rabbit defined intelligence the way man does, then the most intelligent animal would be a rabbit, followed by the animal most willing to obey the commands of a rabbit."   —Robert Brault

Fashion with Compassion®

Marcia Claire Pearson

I was vegetarian since 1968 and went to my first vegetarian conference in 1976. By the end of the conference I found out about the whole veal industry: to get milk that humans drink, the calves are shipped off to veal farms. That was it. Milk is just as inhumane as eating the flesh of the animal. I became vegan that week in Ithaca, New York.

I first met Jay in person in 1976 at the conference but had corresponded with him since 1972. I had read about American Vegan Society (AVS) and contacted Jay by phone when I was still in college. I wanted to start a local vegetarian organization in Seattle. He taught me how to run a meeting, get out publicity, not offend people, and not be political; he gave good pointers on how to reach the general public and vegetarians.

I was part of a team popularizing the use of the term cruelty-free in the United States; Lady Dowding had used the phrase since the 1950s in England. Jay and I created the Fashion Compassion show at the vegetarian conference in 1977. The show featured vegan clothes, handbags, shoes, activist t-shirts, and personal-care products. I did everyone up with Beauty Without Cruelty cosmetics. Many people brought their favorite nonanimal items and paraded them on stage. It was educational and fun. We showed you can dress normally and fashionably.

This led me to be hired to create a similar Fashion with Compassion® center-stage entertainment show in 1978 for the Environmental Faire, an exposition of alternative energy and sustainable lifestyles at the Seattle Center Coliseum.

Through Jay I was able to meet incredible leaders and authors. Notables include Dr. Gordon Latto, Nat Altman, Dixie Mahy, Dr.

Michael Klaper, Dr. John McDougall, Dr. Neal Barnard, Helen Nearing, Alex Hershaft, Howard Lyman, Ann Wigmore, Connie Salamone, Tom Regan, Victoria Moran, and especially Dick Gregory. All the big people came to the conferences, often before they became big activists. We all came to learn and be around kindred souls.

*   *   *

Marcia Claire Pearson founded Seattle's first vegetarian group, the Seattle Vegetarian Society, in 1976. In the mid-1980s it merged into the larger Seattle EarthSave group. Now the local group is Vegetarians of Washington, which puts on events.

Marcia's Fashion with Compassion® evolved out of her association with AVS and is now her registered trademark to be used for vegan events. From 1977 until the information became available online around 2000, she provided a comprehensive list of products that were both nonanimal, meaning no animal ingredients, and cruelty free, not tested on animals. Her column in *Ahimsa*, "The Compassionate Consumer," for years told people all the wonderful new products to enhance the vegan lifestyle such as clothes and shoes. She also wrote a question and answer column called "The Glow of Beauty" for almost two decades in *Nutrition Health Review: The Consumer's Medical Journal.*

She was a professional model of only wholesome products and purposes from 1973 until becoming a mother in 1984. Marcia's two daughters, vegan since birth are Tahira, born in 1984 and Karaena, born in 1987, who loved conferences because Jay did the bunny dance with them. Jay put his hands vertically on his head for rabbit ears and hopped which attracted people to dance.

*   *   *

Are you making compassionate choices and using cruelty-free nonanimal products? Are you spreading positive vegan messages with all your actions as best you can?

From Trout to Sprouts

Jane Sirignano

"That's a creature, and I don't want to eat creatures!" I thought at age sixteen when I saw the fish on my plate looking back at me. At our home, you ate what you were served, and there weren't any discussions about choices.

The next year I went to college, and most of my friends were buying their foods at a food co-op. I loved the concept of the whole foods in burlap bags and brown boxes, and I thought about running a food co-op someday. I stopped eating meat, fish, and chicken because I didn't like the idea of eating something with a face, and I didn't care for their taste. I also quit dairy products.

I began reading books about diet and health beginning with Helen and Scott Nearing's *Living the Good Life*. The simple life they described appealed to me as well as being considerate of the animals and the land. The winter of 1976 I was nineteen and living in a cabin in the woods by myself.

Next I read *Be Your Own Doctor* which led me to Hippocrates Institute in Boston where I learned much about raw foods and growing sprouts and greens. A request came to Hippocrates for someone to speak about sprouts at an American Vegan Society (AVS) convention, and I was offered the job.

My talk on sprouts was well-received. Jay and Freya asked me to stay and help at SunCrest, the AVS headquarters, for the summer. As I lived with Jay, Freya, Daniel, and Anne, I was inspired by their commitment, dedication, hard work, humor, knowledge, and self-sacrifice. Some of the foundational information I needed for my new journey with foods and healthy lifestyle, including raising healthy children, I gained from Jay and Freya. Jay needed my help in the office, and Freya taught me about food preparation. Jay and Freya were always a team and supported each other. Seeing a family work together with the goals they had, in helpful ways and in good spirits, was a novelty for me.

For the next four summers I attended the NAVS conference and worked side-by-side with Freya and the food service. I listened to speakers, especially Jay whose knowledge and heartfelt conviction were a big inspiration.

Jay and Freya's simple, hard-working, and intelligent lifestyle influenced me greatly. They were always reading and learning in their field, and I trusted their views. Their goal of helping others rubbed off on me. Their commitment to the vegan lifestyle helped me stay on track. It is my great privilege to still be in touch with Freya and Anne and continue to be inspired by their happy, humble lives of service.

*　　*　　*

Jane Sirignano founded a food co-op and managed a natural foods store. Jane worked seven years with the Coronary Health Improvement Project (CHIP), a community education program that helps people reverse heart disease, type-2 diabetes, obesity, and other such problems. Along with other jobs and training, Jane helped conduct nutrition workshops and helped rewrite the original CHIP instructor's manual. She has a diploma in nutrition. Jane is an AVS life member.

Her dream job of eight years has been teaching nutrition and cooking classes. Topics include cancer, diabetes, wellness, making healthy choices, and classes for kids. Jane has been making presentations and conducting food shopping tours at local supermarkets for twelve years. She is currently pursuing studies in raw foods preparation and teaching certification.

*　　*　　*

Would you enjoy taking or teaching classes in food shopping or preparation?

The Voice of Rajahimsa

H. Jay Dinshah

Every so often we print a philosophical saying or witty comment by Rajahimsa. Raja means king, so he is king of ahimsa. Rajahimsa is not a man but an ideal. Although I named Rajahimsa, I feel I was created to serve "him." I believe everyone has a measure of Rajahimsa within, whether one calls it the meek voice of mercy, the sharp sting of conscience, the gentle guidance of the Holy Spirit, or the finest and noblest ideals one may possess.

I do not believe that a conscience should be treated as the child of the mind, to be properly decorative but not expected to express especially valuable opinions! Rather, it must be a constant guide for our everyday actions, in our meetings with all creatures, human or otherwise.

It is the primary function of this publication to arouse people's thinking processes and encourage alignment of actions with the dictates of each person's fertile and active conscience. It is only when one stops repeating trite excuses and vain half-truths that one can really begin to hear the voice of conscience. Every day, we are faced with many decisions of an ethical, moral nature at every meal and in every business, personal, or social transaction. Why do so many people thoughtlessly forfeit their own rights of conscience, surrendering them to convention or to that monster called "everyone else does it"?

*   *   *

"The next time you are faced with a decision involving the use of animal matter and the exploitation of fellow creatures or the wronging of a fellow man, won't you try to keep silent for a moment and THINK? Then maybe you, too, will hear and heed the voice of Rajahimsa." —Jay

"There is no man so foolish as the one who wrestles against his own conscience and having subdued it cries, 'I have won!' He is LOST!" —Rajahimsa

*　　*　　*

If you are looking for a concise leaflet to read and share with people, go to VeganOutreach.org and ask for one such as "Why Vegan?" Consider volunteering to hand out these leaflets at a college campus near you.

"As long as people will shed the blood of innocent creatures there can be no peace, no liberty, no harmony between people. Slaughter and justice cannot dwell together."
　　　　　　　　　　　　　　　　—Isaac Bashevis Singer

Our Summer to Remember

Art and Carole Baral

The summer of 1976 was one to remember. With our six-year-old son Matthew, we ventured to Ithaca College in New York state to attend our first of over thirty-five vegetarian conventions put on by the newly formed North American Vegetarian Society (NAVS). We joined over 200 people there from many backgrounds and persuasions. It was a new experience to see so many gathered for a unified purpose: to save the animals!

There was a speaker who moved us more than anyone previously had, although we had already been vegetarians for almost five years. That man was H. Jay Dinshah, president of the organization. He possessed an almost evangelical tonal speaking quality obviously expressing total conviction in his beliefs.

Art states, "Physically he was not a big man, but spiritually he walked like a giant!" and "He was the George Washington of the vegan movement" in the United States. We have been inspired by Jay to fight the good fight for the animals who he said he would never stop trying to liberate. He worked tirelessly with indefatigable energy.

An ironic image is the Dinshah family arriving at that summer convention in their huge black hearse. This was the perfect large vehicle to carry all the conference supplies, including books for sale and toys for the children's center. It was such a contrast that this hearse carried life not death, triumph not failure, and compassion not complacency.

Our kids grew up together as they shared veggie summer camp at the children's center at the vegetarian conferences, every year where they would also share their meals and ideals. Matthew, now age forty-three, is still a vegetarian as well as a naturopathic

152

physician, due to, we believe, these early associations with the right way to live.

We still read the book *Here's Harmlessness* with awe and wonder as Jay was the force behind this project and a voice for sanity through this compilation of various essays written by famous ethical people who believed in the vegan principles. These are the real heroes of the day, people with conviction and courage.

Jay's life continues in us as we fight for those who have no voice!

*   *   *

Art and Carole Baral continue to enjoy attending Vegetarian Summerfest celebrations, which now gather over 700 attendees. Carole continues to serve on the NAVS board of trustees as she has since 1991. She has taught classes in yoga, cooking, and philosophy at Summerfest and other locations for three decades. Carole writes a monthly food column "Vegan Delights" online at PawlingPublicRadio.org. Art and Carole are AVS life members.

*   *   *

Maybe Carole will inspire you to relax with some yoga among the accomplishments in your active day or to take time to reflect on what you have read.

Compassionate Co-operation

Bob LeRoy

Part of my never-ending college-years' journey of questioning and self-discovery linked me to twelve other people in sharing a "supper co-op," collectively preparing and enjoying four weekly meals. This venture eventually evolved into a food-buying club, then four linked buying clubs, and a tiny tumbledown storefront co-op that grew into a great natural foods source. Later I founded two food co-ops on my own.

In stark contrast with my extraordinary sense of community around food co-ops, my pathway of reevaluating my own eating choices felt isolated and meandering. Everyone around me who wasn't eating a typical American, junky, greasy diet was pretty much celebrating a diversity that ranged from bacon to homegrown tomatoes and never stressing out over what to eat. In that environment, I agonized alone over what different foods might do to my arteries or my colon; how much money, land, and energy it took to make those different foods; why killing for food was taken for granted; and so much more.

I decided to go to nutrition graduate school, I guess to try to avenge the deaths of my parents from heart disease and cancer when I was sixteen. I became a vegan several months before entering while still not knowing any other vegetarians. Almost immediately, by chance I saw a flyer for the 1976 North American Vegetarian Society (NAVS) conference. Vegetarian society? With people like me? Perhaps I could make the long trip. But, I always resist walking into a room or a community empty-handed. What could I offer, not yet holding any nutrition credentials? I wrote a letter to the NAVS home office proposing that I give a talk at their conference about what I knew well, organizing food co-ops, expecting I'd be laughed at.

In a few days, a reply phone call came in, to my shock, from H. Jay Dinshah, president and cofounder of NAVS. He said, "Great to hear from you, Bob. Come on down. We'd love to have you teach us about organizing food co-ops." He bowled me over with his graciousness and welcoming tone. In later years, I further saw this gift he had as a leader, for seeing the raw potential in people, inviting them to join, and giving them a chance.

I was stunned at what I found at the NAVS conference; it was truly a little "society." There were many hundreds of people from all walks of life discoursing eloquently together about all the very questions I had previously pondered in solitude. They were not only engaged in cerebral pursuits but also playing music, dancing, performing skits, watching the stars at night. I could eat vegan natural foods with them, outside of my own secluded kitchen. There was even an elaborate fashion show displaying clothing made 100 percent without harming any animals.

In the midst of it, there was Jay, the initiator of it all, lightening every casual conversation with witty rejoinders, prompting attendees to let their hair down and dance, and even going on stage to do comedic impersonations of famous historical figures, Bugs Bunny included. You've got to love a president who will risk making a total fool of himself just to bring smiles and laughter to the faces of others, especially of children.

I am extraordinarily indebted to Jay for first introducing vegetarian and vegan community to my life. He opened the doors years later to my own service to the NAVS organization.

Just as far-reaching was his intellectual influence. From his speeches at the first conference onward through his writings in books and magazines, he helped cultivate a conceptual framework for me, via ahimsa values, that retrofitted and matured the vegan lifestyle I had already adopted intuitively before meeting him. He sure helped model a determination never to take a single day off from the highest values you've embraced!

Jay's words that first moved me memorably include these:

"We are likely to concoct some clever little sophistries with which to convince ourselves that we did not, after all, create all the misery and suffering in the world and can hardly be expected to clean it all up by ourselves."

"Whatever knowledge or wisdom we may have acquired, whatever material possessions are needed to sustain our lives, and even the breath of life itself—all of these are but lent to us, given in a kind of conditional loan or stewardship, as it were. If we have been fortunate to be entrusted with a little more, then so much the greater is our responsibility, our bound duty to do the very best that we can to keep faith with the spirit of that trusteeship."

"The concept that life of some type exists in worlds even coarser than the highly ordered animal kingdom is, if anything, an additional motivation for going into veganism. It is by no means a valid excuse for remaining on the very lowest level of selfish brute force and violence in our treatment of the other lives around us."

*   *   *

Bob LeRoy, MS, EdM, RD has been nutrition advisor for NAVS since 1990 and a member of the NAVS board of trustees since 2004. He is the founder of Plant-based Prevention of Disease (P-POD) project. Bob is an AVS life member.

*   *   *

Are you new to vegan food? What if you don't like to cook? Create a vegan supper co-op like Bob's for four nights of fun, friends, and food. Or cook with two friends and each person cooks once a week, planning leftovers for the next night, you could have six nights of meals and go out to eat once.

If you like to buy delicious local and/or organic whole foods maybe you could join or start a food co-op? Are you feeling alone in your choices and need to attend a vegan event?

Multiplying One of a Kind Activism

Charles Stahler

I was volunteering for the United Farm Workers and visiting Houston, Texas, when I picked up a copy of the newspaper *Vegetarian World*, which later merged into *Vegetarian Times*. *Vegetarian World* had an ad for NAVS, which was looking for volunteer interns. So I went there in February 1977 to help promote vegetarianism. At that time, NAVS and AVS shared the same property, resources, and staff.

I was vegetarian but had never heard of veganism before this. Vegetarianism was hardly yet a modern movement in this country. The animal rights movement didn't really take off until several years later, and in the beginning many of those participants weren't vegetarian let alone vegan.

During my four months at AVS I worked mostly in the kitchen and in related duties. One day I made orange juice from concentrate for the little kids. I thought they should develop their skills and taught them how to open the can themselves and make their own orange juice. I probably got in trouble for that although one of those kids, Anne, grew up to coauthor *Apples, Bean Dip, and Carrot Cake: Kids! Teach Yourself to Cook*.

While I was working at AVS, a friend sent me my last nonvegan food—a candy bar. I became vegan before departing AVS as it was an extension of the nonviolent reasons why I became vegetarian.

Next I volunteered with the Vegetarian Society of DC (VSDC) for about four years. Then I moved to Baltimore for graduate school. I looked for a vegetarian group, but when I went to the address listed, it was an abandoned building. Since there wasn't a vegetarian group in Baltimore, five of us in Baltimore who were involved with VSDC started a group in 1982 that became the Vegetarian Resource Group (VRG).

As anyone involved in movements knows, there are people with strong opinions. Certainly Jay was one of them. In my more than thirty-five years of veganism and other types of activism, I have almost never encountered anyone who has said he/she is sorry for some type of action. Most people who knew him could never imagine Jay saying he was wrong. However, years and years after I was at AVS, Jay found me at a conference and apologized for something that had happened and said that I was right. On the one hand, nothing really changed after he apologized. On the other hand, his going out of his way to apologize was something that rarely anyone else in a movement that preaches nonviolence has done. It remains an act that influences me. I'll carry that with me the rest of my life. Jay impacted me in a different way than most of the experts and leaders in the cause.

*   *   *

Charles Stahler is one of five cofounders of the Vegetarian Resource Group (VRG.org), a nonprofit organization dedicated to educating the public on vegetarianism and the interrelated issues of health, nutrition, ecology, ethics, and world hunger. He is VRG codirector and an editor for *Vegetarian Journal* magazine. VRG worked with dietitians to start the Vegetarian Nutrition Dietetic Practice Group within the Academy of Nutrition and Dietetics formerly American Dietetic Association. He is coauthor of *Meatless Meals for Working People* having more than 100,000 copies in print. In 2003, Charles and his wife Debra Wasserman were inducted into the Vegetarian Hall of Fame.

Charles coordinates VRG polls on the number of vegetarians and vegans in the United States. Results are cited by the National Academy of Science in their discussions about the new dietary reference intakes for calcium and vitamin D, and also cited by mainstream media sources such as ABC, CBS, National Public Radio, and *USA Today*.

*   *   *

Have you ever wondered how many vegans there are in the United States? Increase the count by one more today.

Interested in health, nutrition, ecology, ethics, and doing your part to eradicate world hunger? Become a member of VRG and read *Vegetarian Journal* and then take an active role in learning facts so you can help educate the public on veganism.

"You must not lose faith in humanity. Humanity is an ocean; if a few drops of the ocean are dirty, the ocean does not become dirty."   —Mahatma Gandhi

Into the Sunshine

H. Jay Dinshah

The truest test of any philosophy, any way of living, is what sort of person it tends to produce and what sort of world conditions it would help to bring about. It is no idle speculation to think of what it would mean to the world if everyone were practicing veganism and ahimsa.

One very important point usually overlooked by detractors is that veganism and ahimsa are not likely to become the prevailing ideas and practices of humanity overnight, however beneficial or inconvenient this might be. There is no danger of having more peace than we can handle, more good fellowship than is good for us, more selfless love than we can stand right away. In any event, artificially bred animals and caged birds certainly cannot overrun us in the two or three years it could take to phase them out of production, as demand for them gradually evaporates.

Even if we do choose to leave the moral jungle in which we now find ourselves, we do not dream that this world will automatically become a perfect place. We do not claim that the animals who are already predators will necessarily follow our path out of this cruel way of living. We do emphatically declare that humans have the conscience, the intelligence, the reasoning power, and certainly the incentive to develop to a much higher level of ethical action than the low ground we now occupy.

As each level of enlightenment is attained, further doors ahead are seen—further parts of the path that previously escaped our notice due to distance or lack of perception. As we approach these further doors or mileposts, the way to keep going will also be found as our enlightenment continues to expand and grow. There is no point in moaning that we can't all be 100 percent perfect today and trying to excuse our truly inexcusable behavior at perhaps a 10 percent ethical level.

If we make the necessary effort to reach the 50 percent level, we will then see that it is not as difficult as we thought to go on to 90 percent or more. It is the sluggard or ethical slacker who uses impossibility of perfection—whether true or not—as a flimsy excuse for laziness and inaction.

Humanity has been in the jungle too long. As with a mole or owl viewing bright sunshine, we are presently so dazzled by the brilliance of what may lie ahead that we prefer the comfort of our present position. We seem to be possessed by a great inertia; we cling to that which we think we know, rather than attempting that which we do not yet fully understand. We despise something that might be infinitely better for us because we do not bother to learn of its benefits.

If we are to transcend the jungle law with which we so blithely cover our most shameful actions, who knows where the path might lead us? The world is much more than a tangled jungle; we might come out of the darkness into the lovely sunshine and become used to the bright light after a while. We might follow the path farther than we can see from hiding as we do behind the twisted vines and weeds of our own sadly distorted world view.

The path might lead us through lovely gardens and along beautiful brooks, through green meadows and orchards, and by great rivers of real thought and wisdom. We might wend our way up a steep mountainside, or freed from the terrible tangle of our own mental and self-imposed moral shortcomings, we might even find that we can soar in the skies of progress and enlightenment. Let us each make our choice and resolve to choose the path of:

LIFE instead of DEATH;

LOVE instead of HATRED;

PACIFISM instead of MILITARISM;

HARMLESSNESS instead of CRUELTY;

COOPERATION instead of CONFLICT;

FELLOWSHIP instead of JUNGLE LAW;

COMPASSION instead of INDIFFERENCE;

LIVE AND LET LIVE instead of KILL OR BE KILLED.

In a book of this size and scope, it is impossible to more than hint at the finer points of getting out of the health jungle, that is, utilizing natural methods of living for better daily health. However, much has been written about the health effects of a vegan diet. See suggestions at the end of this chapter.

Above all, do not allow yourself to become sidetracked from the path by arguments and excuses of others who have their own axes to grind or who do not understand or believe in the compassionate way of life you wish to lead. They have their own way to go; you have yours. They are responsible for their own actions, as you are for yours.

If you really want only a few reasons for not doing the right thing, remember these gems:

"The cattle will overrun the Earth."

"My social activities preclude veganism."

"I may develop protein/calcium/boron/silicon/molybdenum/zinc/uranium/goose-fat deficiency."

"The sky will fall."

"Gandhi did not stick to veganism; why should I?"

"Dr. Schweitzer was not a vegetarian at all times in his ninety-year lifetime."

"Fine ideals but not really practical."

"The moon is, after all, composed entirely of green cheese."

"I'm not ready yet...maybe next week/month/year."

"Pigs have wings."

Put behind you the irrelevant excuses born of inertia and ignorance. Resolve to discern the best that is to be found in anyone else, and adopt it as your own model in one aspect of living, making whatever adaptations are required for your own individual needs.

Obtain the guidance of others who have gone further along the path than you have as yet, but do not be afraid to sift and sort the advice according to the truth as seen in your own heart and mind. Follow your conscience and inner light; they are the greatest guides on your long but fruitful trek "out of the jungle" and into the brighter light of a new and better tomorrow.

*   *   *

Some great books for general introductory vegan information available from AmericanVegan.org include:

The 30-Day Vegan Challenge: The Ultimate Guide to Eating Cleaner, Getting Leaner, and Living Compassionately by Colleen Patrick-Goudreau

Becoming Vegan Express Edition: The Everyday Guide to Plant-based Nutrition by Brenda Davis, RD, and Vesanto Melina, RD MS

The Complete Idiot's Guide to Vegan Living by Beverly Lynn Bennett and Ray Sammartano

Main Street Vegan: Everything You Need to Know to Eat Healthfully and Live Compassionately in the Real World by Victoria Moran and Adair Moran

The Vegan Cheat Sheet: Your Take-Everywhere Guide to Plant-Based Eating by Amy Cramer and Lisa McComsey

Virgin Vegan: The Meatless Guide to Pleasing Your Palate by Linda Long

Science and Humor

Dr. Joel Fuhrman

After Jay's death I wrote, "Jay was a true American hero. His decisive thought, humor, and commitment touched the lives of thousands of people who are indebted to him for his work. Our children should learn about his work and his life in schoolrooms across America."

When I was just a teenager, from my interest and reading about nutrition, I had already understood the scientific evidence that indicated that a plant-based diet, with minimal animal products was best for our long-term health. However, the thought of removing animal products totally from the diet seemed so radical and unachievable until I met Jay Dinshah around 1978.

With logic and humor Jay made the idea of being a vegan seem right, not radical. Very few people in those days lived their life in parallel to their thoughts and convictions. Jay was far ahead of us all, and he was unwavering at all times. He foresaw that without care for other creatures and as curators of our planet as a whole, we would develop a multitude of problems on the earth that would damage us all exponentially in future generations. I thought back then that he was a little extreme, but it turned out he was right.

His life was an example of devotion to his principles as he extended his principles of kindness to the animals and to the world as a whole. In the midst of a heated argument at a health conference board meeting, Jay would come up with a quick quip or joke, such as, "We are sure lucky that Edison invented the light bulb, otherwise we would have to watch TV by candlelight." No matter how stupid it sounded, it made everyone smile or laugh. I observed how he could argue his point and keep the subject light and friendly simultaneously. No matter what hardships he had in life, he kept his sense of humor. Yes, I learned lots from Jay Dinshah, and it wasn't all just vegan philosophy; it was about being a role model and about life.

Please note: Any reproduction of this chapter must receive permission from Dr. Fuhrman.

*   *   *

Joel Fuhrman, MD, is a board-certified family physician and nutritional researcher specializing in preventing and reversing disease through nutritional and natural methods. His PBS television shows bring nutritional science to American viewers.

He has authored five *New York Times* bestselling books: *Eat To Live, Super Immunity, The End of Diabetes, Eat to Live Cookbook*, and *The End of Dieting*. Dr. Fuhrman has written several other popular books on nutritional science including *Disease Proof Your Child* and *Fasting and Eating for Health*. He is the research director of the Nutritional Research Foundation and has published several times in scientific journal publications. His scientific study on food addiction and human hunger entitled, "The Changing Perception of Hunger on a High Nutrient Density Diet" was published in *Nutrition Journal* in November 2010.

A former world-class pairs figure skater with his sister Gale, he placed second in the 1973 U.S. National Pairs Skating Championship and third in the 1976 World Professional Pairs Skating Championship. He continues to be an enthusiastic participant in multiple sports and lectures to world-class athletes for maximizing performance and preventing injury.

*   *   *

Have you watched Dr. Fuhrman on TV or read his books? Or maybe he inspires you to go exercise. Do you use exercise to improve the way you feel and connect with the world?

Seeds of Truth

M. "Butterflies" Katz

In 1979 I was vegetarian, and somewhere in myself I knew that this was not enough. It seems to me now that I didn't want to know the truth because that would have meant that I would have to change. I felt addicted to dairy products, and there were no alternatives back then.

Someone placed a copy of *Ahimsa* magazine in front of my eyes. I read an article that Jay wrote about the horrible crimes inherent in the dairy industry. Jay's written word was so powerful that I pronounced myself a vegan right then and there.

Immediately after reading his words, I emptied my closet of leather. I stopped my purchases of any products sourced from animal exploitation, including cosmetics and toiletries; which required investigating, phoning companies and learning if ingredients were animal-derived.

Jay's words were compelling and convincing. I was introduced to his books *Out of the Jungle* and *Here's Harmlessness* by the founders of Gentle World, the only other vegans I had heard of in those early years of being vegan. I treasured *Out of the Jungle*.

When Gentle World purchased Shangri-La in New Zealand, a sanctuary and vegan visitor and educational center, I received the sad news that Jay passed away. I planted "The Jay Dinshah Tree" in his honor. Thank you, Jay, for planting the seed that we can try to live without harming others. Many have inspired me since reading Jay's words, but he was the first. He introduced me to the concepts of ahimsa and veganism and will always hold a special place in my heart.

*　　*　　*

M. "Butterflies" Katz co-hosted, catered, and spoke at an event in Florida, "It's Easy to Be Vegan," reported on in *American Vegan*, #12-3 winter 2012. She has helped put on many such events in the last three decades. She was the volunteer head chef at a restaurant called The Vegan on Maui, Hawaii, which inspired many vegans.

Butterflies is coauthor of *Incredibly Delicious: Recipes for a New Paradigm* by Gentle World. Her blog is Veganism: A Truth Whose Time Has Come! TheVeganTruth.blogspot.com often features inspirational stories about vegans around the world.

She authored *Metamorphosis: Poems to Inspire Transformation* and the website VeganPoet.com. Her Facebook page is Facebook.com/ButterfliesVeganAdvocate. Butterflies, along with Sarah Austin, started the Facebook group Vegan Dog Nutrition: Facebook.com/groups/vegandognutrition/ and more recently started the rapidly growing Facebook group: Veganism IS an ethical stance beyond diet: Facebook.com/groups/ VeganismIsEthicalStance.

*　　*　　*

Have you hesitated to find the truth because it would mean you have to change your consumer choices? Are you inspired to try living in alignment with the ethic that we should not unnecessarily harm animals?

Are you willing to join this social justice movement and help make history? Please take this opportunity to open your heart, eyes, and mind to living the path of ahimsa.

Believe with Me

Richard Schwartz

Almost thirty-five years ago when I was first becoming a vegetarian, I was seeking information to reinforce my beliefs and to help convince others of the many benefits of vegetarianism. I read widely on the subject and attended conferences to gain more information. I recall very appreciatively that the work of Jay Dinshah was especially valuable during that period.

I gained much information from his pioneering book *Out of the Jungle*, his many informative and challenging articles in *Ahimsa* magazine, and his inspiring lectures. I also appreciated the many books and other vegetarian material that he brought to sell at vegetarian conferences. This enabled me to build up a library of very helpful books and talks on CDs.

What sticks out in my mind is that he was not interested in just presenting information but in urging others to follow his example of making veganism a holy crusade. This crusade is essential to end the horrendous mistreatment of animals, to reduce the widespread diseases caused by animal-based diets, and to help shift our imperiled planet onto a sustainable path. Also, he was one of the few early activists to stress that eliminating meat from one's diet was not enough but that it was essential to also give up dairy products, eggs, and other animal products.

I am sure that his memory will continue to be a blessing and that his works will continue to inspire people for many years. "To live in the hearts of those we leave behind is not to die," said Thomas Campbell, a Scottish poet.

*   *   *

Richard H. Schwartz, PhD, professor emeritus at the College of Staten Island, is the author of *Judaism and Vegetarianism*. He has over 200 articles and 25 podcasts at JewishVeg.com/schwartz. Richard is president emeritus of Jewish Vegetarians of North America and president of the Society of Ethical and Religious Vegetarians. He was the 2005 inductee into the Vegetarian Hall of Fame.

*   *   *

Join the journey of veganism. It doesn't matter what your religion is. We can all come together for this goal.

"The greatness of a nation can be judged by the way its animals are treated."   — Mahatma Gandhi

Transition to Veganism

H. Jay Dinshah

Newcomers often ask, "I am just becoming a vegan. What do vegans do with the leather shoes, wool items, or fur coat that they may already have?"

There are so many aspects to this question, some rather obvious and some quite subtle, that it merits a thorough examination. The authors are not here to just put forth some dogmatic path for everyone to follow unquestioningly but rather to provide facts and to assist all to choose the wisest and most compassionate course of action.

Vegans refuse both food and clothing from animals because it all involves slavery, suffering, deprivation, exploitation, and killing of the animals. But what is the harm in using up some animal-based clothing or food you already have? We should consider the effects on the user, on others, and on the animals of various choices of actions.

Plan #1) Continue to use the objectionable items until they wear out and are gradually replaced with nonanimal items.

Plan #2) Simply throw the offensive items away.

Plan #3) Dispose of them by giving them to other individuals or needy charitable causes.

Plan #1 offers the advantage of easing what can be a somewhat distressing time of transition for the newcomer. It affords the grace period of a gradual phasing out while finding suitable replacements, and it avoids what could be a fairly expensive outlay for new apparel all at the same time. It is also environmentally destructive to replace existing goods with new goods, which undoubtedly involves resource depletion and in some cases human exploitation.

It might easily be argued that what's done is done, that the animals involved cannot be brought back to life, so one might as well continue to use up the specific items. Most vegans would probably agree that it is better in the long run to ease into veganism gradually at one's own pace and then stick with it than to set an unrealistically difficult plan and then give it up altogether in discouragement.

Those of us who have been in the vegan movement for a long time may tend to forget that not everyone will go "cold Tofurky®" and stay with it. Newcomers may be scared half to death with the old nonsense about juggling amino acids to get complete proteins or worried about their bones dissolving from some imaginary calcium starvation.

In approaching veganism, one may wish to taper off in the matter of wardrobe by using up what one has if the individual requires this to get started toward veganism with the understanding that it is only a transition period. This is consistent with the generally accepted view that it is better to go through a limited transition period such as lacto-vegetarianism, if that is what it takes, and then become a vegan and stay with it, rather than to make the change all at once to veganism and fall back again into meat eating. These are not the only alternatives, and some do fine going all the way in one jump; others find it a lot to undertake at once.

Each animal-sourced item in the closet or refrigerator is something of a reproach, and there can be no thought of going on a binge or stocking up on items of cruelty and death before putting your new ethics into effect. You have a more active and better developed conscience than that or you wouldn't be coming into veganism in the first place. Frankly, in five decades of veganism, we at AVS have never even heard of anyone going out and buying a fur coat because "I'm going to start veganism tomorrow." But knowing of the variety in human nature, it is possible that it has happened in isolated cases involving some little item thought to be difficult to come by as a vegan. We can say that at any time when you buy a product of animal suffering, you do not pay the price, you only pay some money. It is the animal who pays the real cost.

Besides the effect of plan #1 on the prospective vegan's immediate wardrobe concerns, what about its effect on others? If you resolve to be a closet vegan, there may be little influence upon others. Therefore a modification of plan #1 would be to divest oneself of the animal items as fast as reasonable substitutes are found. Plan #1 is the least satisfactory from the immediate ethical standpoint, excusable only as a strictly temporary option for those who seem unable to make a clean break with the past all at once. It is to be seen as a sort of crutch, which can be a marvelous means of getting around for a person who otherwise can't walk at all. A crutch can become an addictive impediment; it is far better to walk without a crutch if able to do so.

Plan #2 is to throw animal products away. The sooner you are rid of them, the sooner you are free of their hold on your conscience. You willingly force yourself to quickly find new products.

Depending on the feelings of the individual, it may not be a benefit to have a transition period at all. Each and every animal-source item may make its tragic little lesson known to the increasingly sensitive user. Any continuation of their use may come to be regarded less as a boon than as a cross of suffering to be borne as a reminder of past thoughtlessness. The very thought of walking around wearing dead animal material brings only repugnance and sadness, not comfort and pride.

Even if one originally chose plan #1, there may come a day that it becomes imperative to change to plan #2. It is bad enough that you know of your new difficulty in wearing these things; but if you have ever discussed your lifestyle choices with friends, relatives, or coworkers, what influence will it have on them?

There was a schoolgirl many years ago who had talked up veganism, to the annoyance of some of her classmates. While seated in class one day, a girl in front of her turned around to deliver what was supposed to be a brilliant put down: "You're wearing leather shoes!" A world of exposed hypocrisy was implied in that loaded remark, saying: "See Miss Smarty, we kill and eat them, and you kill and wear them. What's the difference?" But as it happened the girl had already completed her plan #2 and found suitable replacement. She simply replied, "No, I'm not," and she showed her nonanimal shoes to prove it.

Additionally there is the sad fact that some items of clothing are promoted not only for warmth or utility but as status symbols: emblems of wealth and success. If the prospective vegan has a selfish sense of status or any craving or attachment for such a base possession, it is all the more reason to be rid of the wretched thing as soon as possible. Whether it is a dead fur coat, a pearl necklace, a cashmere goat-fuzz sweater, a pair of designer leather shoes, or a sorry silk scarf, the more desire and craving one feels for it the better off one will be without it, once the proper attitude toward it can be formulated.

Plan #3: From its beginnings in the early 1940s the modern vegan movement has been concerned with animal suffering, not just endangered species but also with humanity and ecology. It has been increasingly seen that veganism is good for all life: human life, animal life, even plant life, and the life of our planet.

This being said, how shall we take and bury a slightly used coat or pair of shoes in a world where so many must go cold and barefoot? How can we throw away a serviceable wool coat when, even in the wealthy country of the United States, hundreds of thousands of unfortunates shiver in the streets?

It is of no use to pass the buck and blame the system or politics or the establishment or economics or whatever and then wash our hands of it or look the other way. Vegans should realize that while they work for a better world they are still obliged to live in the world of today, as it is, warts and all. Though we may do our best for a better day after tomorrow when everyone has at least enough to meet their basic needs, it can be seen as a cop-out—if not an outright obscenity—to destroy, as an act of conscience, the very item that could alleviate the suffering—possibly even save the life—of a much less fortunate human brother or sister.

Almost every community has charitable works run by religious or other organizations. Some provide employment for persons with disabilities. Many welcome donations of used but usable shoes, clothing, furniture, and other household items.

With some charities the items received are distributed free to the needy. In other cases, as with the storefront operations, they are sorted, perhaps repaired, and sold at bargain prices. People with minimal money are much more likely to buy clothing or shoes there because they have to keep warm or dry than to be concerned about the latest chic styles or status symbols. This option can give your animal items another life, not the one they originally had but a small token in the right direction to help the world.

The Law of Supply and Demand

You cannot bring the animals back to life; that is certainly true in a literal sense about the specific animals in a specific article of clothing. But if we understand the marketplace correctly, there may be a way to give new life to a dead animal item: put it back on the market. This cannot wipe out the original crime, but it can spare the taking of the equivalent amount of other animal lives.

It works like this: Everyone should understand that in refusing to buy a chop or roast today, it does not save the life of any single specific animal anywhere in the production pipeline. Nearly every animal that is alive in slavery today will be raised in whatever manner the slaveholder may see fit and ultimately sold for slaughter.

Even a well-meaning but misguided attempt to help the situation by buying a slave animal and setting it free or raising it as a pet is an exercise in futility and self-defeating, creating the demand for a replacement slave to be produced. The creatures at farm animal sanctuaries serve a duty as ambassadors for all animals on death row though none committed any crime. These ambassadors reach people in ways that no speeches, books, or demonstrations ever will. Repeatedly they create instant vegans.

The cumulative effect of a year of abstaining from meat and replacing it with nonanimal products means an actual reduction of one large animal, plus many smaller creatures such as fish and birds, who will never be bred in captivity and born to the slaughter. It is the consumer who creates the demand for the farmer to breed another animal at the beginning of the production pipeline. Farmers will keep on breeding them and raising them in the abominable conditions of slavery, and the packers will keep on killing them so long as we keep on demanding—by accepting and buying—meat and other animal products.

Let us suppose that you have a few hundred pounds of meat in a freezer when you resolve to become a vegan. You decide to get rid of the stuff so you can start to live as a vegan right away. You throw it in the back of a pickup truck and roll down Main Street, tossing it off to the homeless and hungry unfortunates, a chunk here and a haunch there, like feeding time at the zoo.

So you have salved your conscience, but what is the real good in it for the animals? The recipient wasn't planning on dining on steak tonight anyway so may look upon the gift as a real windfall; but the net result for the animals would probably be little better than neutral, a big fat zero.

On the other hand, if you were able to dispose of it at a price near or somewhat under the prevailing market prices, you would be competing against the meat packers in a small but very real way, and each pound of meat returned to the marketplace and sold would be a pound less that they would need to supply. The freezer load might make up the equivalent of a fair-sized animal that now would not have to be bred, raised, and killed. You have put that animal back into the marketplace and have, to this extent, reversed the harm that you did in buying this meat and in creating the demand in the first place. So while you can't literally bring your animal back to life, you can save the life of another who will not have to be born to slavery and suffering.

In the case of the fur coat, the principle is the same. If you give it away to someone who was not planning to buy a fur coat or who couldn't afford one anyway, the net effect for the animals is the same as if you kept it and wore it yourself. If it were advertised and sold at or near the going market value, you have in a sense brought the animals back to life—or undone the original harm by removing the demand for the equivalent amount of animal suffering and death. This is of course proportionate to the amount of useful life left in the coat. If an item is nearly worn out and so tacky that it's almost ready for the ragbag anyway, it is obviously of little value for taking the place of new animal goods in the marketplace.

Also obvious is the fact that you could not try to palm off a fur coat in the way that furriers do by "selling the sizzle," by describing it in glowing and glamorous terms thus convincing Madame Frankenstein that she would look glamorous if she has a lovely bunch of animal carcasses draped on her. You are not helping matters any if you convince someone to buy and wear a fur who wasn't already going to do it. It is only by replacing the supply and not fostering some new demand that you can help matters with the specific item you have on hand.

Is your conscience uneasy about the hungry, shivering, homeless, poor people? You don't even have to personally give them a side of beef or a fur coat. A more useful method might be to take your "ill-gotten gains," whatever money you get from selling off the unwanted items and donating this to a charity to use in a more practical and long-term way of helping them.

We have used the examples of a large quantity of meat and an expensive fur coat. We could just as easily have cited a car with leather seats or furniture with leather or wool upholstery or any other item of considerable value that involves large-scale destruction of animal life. The facts of supply and demand would be the same, though modified to suit the peculiarities of the specific product.

At the opposite extreme of value, small and relatively inexpensive items are not practical to sell or even give away. It is difficult to suppose that someone else might want to use your stub of beeswax lipstick or a bit of sheep-fat lotion at the bottom of the jar. If you are now seeing the incongruity of decorating an animal lover with daubs of such animal matter, you may feel impelled to follow plan #2, throwing a few such remnants and relics of barbarism into the garbage.

Prospective vegans will use Plans 1, 2, or 3 or any combination or variation of them, depending on a variety of individual factors. These may include personal attitude, motives for coming toward veganism, degree of commitment, and financial situation for replacing items. You can choose to emphasize the new lifestyle by making a clean break. Or it is possible to rationalize that what you do in a fairly brief tapering-off period may be of relatively little consequence in comparison to the tremendous suffering, exploitation, and death that you are saving the animals in your many years to come living as a consistent vegan.

Clearly, the sooner you graduate from the transitional stage to full veganism, the sooner that saving can reach its maximum. What is of the greatest importance is that you do resolve to come into veganism and that you then implement the decision, with compassion, knowledge and common sense, as soon and as fully as you are able to bring your physical actions into harmony with the guidance of your conscience.

*　　*　　*

As you think about charities, consider donating money or time to a vegan hunger-relief agency:

You could help Vegfam for whom AVS accepts and transmits such donations in full, or they can receive donations online. This aids people overseas who are much worse off than most of the poor are in the United States and helps them toward nonanimal self-sufficiency. VegfamCharity.org.uk

Or donate to A Well-Fed World which is a hunger relief and animal protection organization promoting the benefits of plant-based eating. They raise funds, partner with, and promote projects in vegan advocacy, vegan feeding, and farm animal rescue and care. AWellFedWorld.org

The next two strive to be vegan, although there may be occasional vegetarian meals in some locations. You can designate your funds for vegan projects only.

Food for Life is a food-relief program with thousands of volunteers providing billions of free vegan meals since 1974. The flagship programs are in India (thus occasional noncommercial dairy), and they serve in over sixty countries. FFL.org

Help Food Not Bombs provide meals or even start a group anywhere in the United States or the world. FoodNotBombs.net

Transition to Veganism—A Second Opinion

Anne Dinshah

Are you now wondering "What did Jay do?" Dad never tried to give back a fur. He never bought one in the first place. There were no haunches of meat to throw from his truck because he was a lifelong vegetarian. When Dad quit eating dairy products there were lacto-vegetarians in his family who continued to use them, which negated any purging of the fridge. If one were to speculate that maybe the shoes he wore the day he visited the slaughterhouse were leather, he left them on the street after the tour. The shoes were blood-saturated, and he didn't want to soil the carpeting in his car. All shoes he wore after that day were vegan even if it meant having only one style of canvas shoes.

Dad explained his suggested plans; they are ideas to inspire thoughtful consideration. In editing his plan 1, 2, 3 for this book, I considered each plan and debated throwing out part of the supply-and-demand argument. Then I saw the fun of including it as he wrote it. Veganism relies on education to reduce the demand, but it's different when discussing how to transition to veganism when animal-sourced items have already been acquired.

Readers should question everything they read. Just because something is in print doesn't make it right. Whether or not you have agreed with much of the book thus far, ultimately you will have to come up with your own scale of right and wrong.

Dad and I had plenty of arguments through the years, but on vegan topics he was untouchable. Now I can possibly win an argument with Dad. You decide.

It's clear that Dad advocated plan #3, so we will start with discussing giving away or selling the animal products. Supply and demand is an important complex concept to understand in the big picture of animal exploitation and one's role in it. However, his supply-and-demand idea here is flawed in at least two cuts of meat and one extra-large furry animal.

First, people would be wary of buying meat from a fly-by-night salesman. With all the known disease connections, even the comfortably unaware want to purchase their meat from a reputable store. If it is found that you are a new vegan-to-be, then the meat is doubly suspect as you might be wishing harm on people who continue to eat meat. They don't know all about your commitment to ahimsa.

The second big flaw is that, as a salesperson, you represent your product. Will you be comfortable convincing someone to buy your meat? In good conscience you know it is not only dead animal that you yourself do not want for ethical reasons but also that eating it carries grave health implications.

For the fur, although I see Dad's point, I make my argument similar to the meat. In selling your coat you are representing a product, endorsing its use. In one regard, putting the coat back on the market might absolve you of the burden of responsibility in your conscience by returning it to the supply chain in equivalent proportion to the useful life of the coat. However, in many circles it has become politically incorrect to be seen wearing a fur coat, and returning it to the marketplace perpetuates its display as a fashionable item. You should not overly punish yourself for making a decision back when you did not know the truth.

Since a fur coat is a status symbol, buying a used one does not have the same status. The person buying a used coat typically needs it for warmth and would be happy with a coat of manmade materials. I believe you must go a step further. Convince someone who would buy a new fur coat, and has the means to buy one, that he or she is more beautiful without the fur. If the person needs a coat, he or she will be well-suited to a coat of obviously vegan materials or one of fake fur with a button stating it's fake.

Realistically, how do you find someone to convince? Do you

stand outside the fur coat store holding a sign until you are asked to leave? Perhaps you talk about your dilemma with a friend who, conveniently, was going to go coat shopping.

How about donating the fur to a wildlife rehabilitator or an animal shelter to be used for bedding? The thought of snuggling to a dead animal sickens me, but I understand animal fur does bring comfort to scared or injured animals when their surroundings are cold and hard or their only interactions are with unfamiliar humans. While there, it might be a good time to apologize to those animals as representatives of the animals killed for the coat; this action may help strengthen your commitment to veganism and make it easier to part with the expensive item.

Plan #1 is what many people use for the reason of not throwing out everything until they use up items while finding replacements. It's a typical tactic if they don't know other vegans to advise them, are tentative in committing to change, or have a very limited budget. It may work for food but not easily for a leather or fur coat which lasts longer. I add to Dad's suggestions on this plan:

Wearing the fur should not feel right. Could it be used instead as a display along with photos of actual animals who gave their life for a coat? Draw lines on the coat indicating shapes of each animal taken. Advertise a screening of the film *The Witness*, a powerful documentary by Tribe of Heart about the realities of fur. Be sure to offer vegan refreshments and other enticements to attract people to attend. Have a discussion after the film.

Perishable food may be easier to use up than the fur. Just because you select the use-it-up option doesn't necessarily mean by yourself. Throw a party. Invite people who are not vegan over for dinner to help you use up the animal products more quickly. Maybe at the end of the meal thank them and announce that you are going vegan. Perhaps you make a mediocre meat dish and an incredibly scrumptious vegan dish so everyone raves about how wonderful your new cuisine will be. Give them gifts of your surplus meat to get them thinking and talking. Technically this is a hybrid of plans #1 and #3, creating a fourth option that maybe your gift will be the last meat they eat. Plant seeds of information and options.

Plan #2 is to simply throw objectionable items away. In an informal poll, I found it is the solution most chosen, especially for food. I believe plan #2 is a solid option for good practical reasons. Nothing will return those animals to life. The number of animals killed for one's stockpile are few compared with the number of animals who will die if one uses plan #1 so long that the transition to vegan becomes overwhelming, feels reliant on animal products, and takes actions so slowly that it is not action.

If Wednesday is trash-collection day, then Tuesday is the best time to declare your commitment to veganism. Get rid of all the animal products at once. Giving things the big heave-ho as an emphatic resolution is therapeutic. The physical act of throwing can release frustrations with a calming result. If you learn about veganism on Thursday, create a big ceremony and take your deposits to the landfill yourself. This purge is a one-time occasion, not an endorsement of being a throwaway society. Dad didn't like plan #2 for the wasteful component, but sometimes time and resolution are more valuable than commodities.

I think of plan #2 like demolition of a destroyed house after flood or fire damage. The sooner it gets torn apart, the sooner it can be rebuilt. The longer one waits, the more disgusting the task becomes with mold, mildew, and decay. Similarly, the nastier the meat, milk, leather, and other animal products will become after one learns about veganism. Address the concern immediately.

My friend Janelle Davidson said, "I got rid of all my animal products in one fell swoop. Once I learned about factory farms, I felt burdened by the products in my refrigerator and clothes closet that had a heavy, sad aura. Getting rid of them made me instantly lighter and happier. I didn't have to cringe when I opened the refrigerator or closet anymore."

There's a new feeling that comes with plan #2, sparking a creative adventure in finding what to eat. It's a great reward to open one's eyes to the plant-based possibilities as it forces an immediate restocking of the fridge. Plan #2 begins retraining your taste buds, not just cutting back the animal products. The longer those addictive animal foods stay in your repertoire, the harder it is to change. Make a clean break.

Janelle shared, "Another reason for plan #2 is to be able to immediately advocate veganism to others without being a hypocrite. I joined an animal rights group and was warned not to show up at a rally wearing any leather because that is the first thing hecklers will point out. They will feel righteous and entirely ignore your message." This reminds us of Dad's story about the girl's shoes, but it works at any age.

Plant-based foods have been sustaining people for millennia and will now sustain you with a new freedom in your conscience. After any of the plans it eventually becomes time to replace the animal products. State your new values with your monetary choices. Maybe you learn voluntary simplicity and decide to be happier with less stuff. The fourth pillar of ahimsa, mastery over oneself, covers the preoccupation with materialism. Minimalism and devoting one's resources to good deeds instead of possessions is admirable.

However, we must be cautious not to equate veganism and compassion for animals with slovenliness. Although for some jobs sloppy clothes are practical, most of us require a successful and polished presence to optimally convey information to other Americans. The point is to get them to want to be more like you. You hold the key to something they want: health, vitality, energy, inner beauty, compassion, success, and even outer beauty. Be sure you also replace your wool suit with a nice vegan one, ready for your next occasion. And if you can find your nonanimal suit used and in good condition, so much the better.

Maybe you have a budget that allows you to buy the most

glamorous vegan coat to make up for the hole in your wardrobe. You gain the envy and attention of others to whom you can then show all the virtues of your new vegan coat. If you can get people's attention and use it to further good, then is it selfish?

I endorse second chances. One shouldn't dwell on the past, especially if all your decisions were made with the best information you had at the time. If you are now a committed vegan, then shine the light for others to see the way. Give the gift of patience and the opportunity to learn to someone who is currently in the dark, as you once were. Start with people who don't know you; friends and family remember your past and often are guarded about learning anything from the "new you." Teach something to someone of the next generation, regardless your age.

*　　*　　*

How will you transition to veganism? If the answer is not clear, it may be helpful to make a list of the facts and your personal concerns, then make a chart of the pros and cons of each plan.

Owning My Decisions

Anne Dinshah

When lifelong vegan kids rebel they might experiment with a bit of the dark side. I (Anne) know some vegan peers from my childhood who went completely nonvegan just to fit in—and still live that way. I share thoughts on this topic because I believe that everyone must question and test their values. The process makes us stronger so that we become vegan by our choice, whether we began life as vegans or not.

In college, I kept my vegan values. I didn't know any other vegans, and I was a quiet one who just avoided animals on my tray in the cafeteria as best I could. I certainly never bought meat, so I can't tell you about coming back to veganism or what to do with a storage full of meat. But I'd like to tell you about some other unacceptable items. Perhaps my faults will help you make the right decision for your items.

I just wanted to be part of the team. I have a wool coat with leather sleeves. It is a symbol of "earning a letter" for Notre Dame's rowing team, on which I competed all four years of college and earned three letters. At that time we were a club, so we purchased everything ourselves. I earned the letter and with it the right to purchase the coat. It was a conscious decision.

I don't wear the coat anymore. I don't need it. But I don't want someone who hasn't earned it to have it either. I earned it through hard work, pulling on an oar at five o'clock in the morning six days a week, plus competition regattas. The coat has sat in a box for many years. This writing is forcing me to think about it. The best solution I can think of may be to give it back to the team, with an explanation that someone else can make good use of it. I hope it will keep someone else from buying one. I should include an explanation of the actual reason why I'm sending it, and maybe the team will consider nonanimal sources for coats in the future. Or would they think I'm some crazy, crackpot alumna? Would I be whispered about at the next Alumni Row, the annual event for former and current team members?

I dug the coat out of the box in which it was stored and looked at it. There it was with my name embroidered discreetly in the pocket, for a true team does not want distinguishing marks on their attire to separate them, yet needs identification when the coats gather in a pile.

I looked at the label. It said "recycled wool." Hmm, not regular wool? Does that make it better? Not really, but maybe a hint. There was mention of manmade materials, but no mention of leather. Perhaps the sleeves were vinyl after all?

I took a sniff. A bit musty, I couldn't send it like that. It will have to be cleaned. I held it up and took a good look. The coat felt lighter than I remembered. Does wool disintegrate? It felt thin, not the heavy winter coat I remembered. Maybe I should figure out from where that recycled wool comes. Can I re-recycle the wool part? Can I cut a new body of the jacket from the wool pattern, sew it in, and have a cruelty-free coat I can proudly wear again? Would my son think I'm cool wearing it, or would he want to wear it someday? How many hours of my time will this take?

I put the coat back into the box, resolved to look at it again soon—or later. I went back to working on this book, a use of my time that will do more good for humanity in the long run than whether that coat sits years in disuse. It may occasionally tug on my conscience but not hard enough to test my strengths as did competing on the team. Rowing on that team laid the foundation by which I have earned a living; coaching rowing supports me so I can afford to also do my vegan efforts.

I saw laying in that same box my fake fur coat also in storage in my basement. Purchased during the same time, it was worn a few times. Once at a dance, my nonvegan date who didn't even know I was vegan, took it out of the coat check and teased me by putting it on his head and making it bark. I was embarrassed; luckily no one else saw him do it. I thought it was obviously fake. I need a big "Fake Fur" button before I wear it again.

Years later in Texas, I needed western boots for dance class and couldn't find a suitable nonleather pair. Shopping with a friend, we found comfortable stylish leather boots at over $100— a huge sum for a graduate student. We discussed my dilemma about costs—to my wallet and to the animals. He offered to not eat meat for a month. A decade later, I put the boots in a charity box; I couldn't wear them in good conscience. Soon after, I recognized the distinctive boots a friend was wearing; she had picked them up at a thrift store and was thrilled. Meanwhile, I had bought nonanimal boots. I neglected to double-check sizes and purchased one boot that is smaller than the other. It bites my foot after an hour, my karmic reminder of those original boots.

Through the years, I've tried to make the best decisions with all the information I have at the time. Someone else might not agree with all my decisions, but I own them and I believe my decisions are improving. To my knowledge, I haven't purchased any more animal products such as coats or boots. When a well-meaning friend gave me a bag of hand-me-down clothes, I simply passed along the silk shirt to a charity box where it would have gone anyway if it hadn't stopped for a minute in my hands.

One friend, new to veganism, said she received a nice, new wool hat from her roommate but didn't know what to do with it. She couldn't wear it, being vegan. She couldn't not wear it, being a gift from a roommate who would notice. She couldn't give it away, for fear of hurting the roommate's feelings. They would be roommates for at least the whole winter season, so I suggested it would be best to address the situation, especially because she did not own a suitable winter hat. If she explains why she cannot accept the gift but appreciates the thought, the roommate could return the hat to the store or choose to give it to someone else. The roommate could opt to buy a vegan hat for the vegan. The dialog may alleviate any future nonvegan gifts from her roommate and their circle of friends. It may serve as a gateway for further discussion, and the roommate may even try veganism.

When there is a possibility of receiving nonvegan gifts from anyone, I try to gently inform them of my values. Occasionally I accept a wrapped box, only to find it is disguising an offensive item. I remember that gifts make the giver feel good, and I am a gracious receiver. It was most likely not given with the purpose of undermining my values. Whenever appropriate, I can take the opportunity to educate: provide hints for future suitable items, give gifts in advance such as a batch of cookies with the vegan recipe, or invite someone over for a delicious vegan meal instead of a wrapped gift. Plant gentle vegan seeds in friends' minds.

I had a problem with gloves. Well-meaning friends brought leather gloves to my cabin while it was under construction, usually for themselves to use but sometimes brought for me or left behind by mistake. I've done a combination of returning gloves to owners, passing them along to charity, and using them on rare occasions when it's freezing out, and all other suitable gloves are wet while yet a task must get completed. I don't believe in getting preventable frostbite or splinters. Then I remember to put vegan gloves on the shopping list again. I frequently smile and tell people "Come visit. I have plenty of work gloves." which they generally take to mean that there's lots of work to do, and they will enjoy an activity. I'm not forwardly saying "Don't bring me leather gloves." but it has reduced the glove problem from people who get to know me, then learn about veganism. For most of my friends, I'm the first vegan they met.

I do buy extra pairs of nonanimal gloves in assorted sizes and styles to have available at my cabin for others. I stop short of insisting friends must use my gloves when they step on the property, just as I won't be checking the tags on their boots and belts. I feed them delicious vegan food in thanks for their time. It's better to begin a positive discussion about veganism than a negative one. "Wow! This is delicious!" Not, "Don't wear your clothes here."

If I have to hire people to get a particular job done, I don't examine their lunchboxes, but I do offer them vegan food. In the course of working with me, the subject of ethics will eventually arise. I admire the stories I've heard about big construction projects who feed all the workers vegan lunches while working on green buildings. Where I live, if I hire only vegans or forced all my values on others, my project would never be completed. When people come over socially, all food brought onto my property is vegan.

Owning one's values is an important process decided for oneself instead of just continuing parents' decisions. This goes in both directions, for vegan and not-vegan-yet, as many people take the time—especially in early adulthood—to explore their options, instead of continuing a path of what their parents chose for food or commodities. It is a fine time to question everything.

*   *   *

Here's an excerpt from *Dating Vegans*, my book about vegan-with-a-nonvegan relationships and a catalyst for thought. This story has been popular with audiences when I am lecturing:

Robert Crane reminds me I am alluring; beauty on the outside deserves to be flaunted. I need to see in myself what he sees in me. One particular shopping excursion Robert compiled a varied stack of clothes for me to try. Robert noticed I neglected an item...the leather halter top. I told him it was leather and I was not going to get it so there was no point in trying. His dejected look convinced me to put it on for a few seconds. The multitude of metal fasteners confused me and I required his assistance in adjusting. Then he turned me toward the mirror where I did not recognize the slutty vixen staring back at me. She had power! He said, "You should get in touch with your inner dominatrix."

For a moment, I was tempted. The top was certainly different from anything I owned and surprisingly it did not smell like raunchy old leather. Despite being at a second-hand store it was new, unworn, with the original tags, and significantly marked down. It could be mine for only twelve dollars, and well worth it. I would receive twelve dollars' worth of drinks from suitors in the first public minute of wearing this thing, if I had the courage to wear it—or if I drank.

But it had been worn before. As I refused to purchase the top, my mind played a video of a cow, hanging upside-down from her hoof, writhing in pain with her throat slit, blood pumping out, terrified in her last living moments. She had worn it before me, proudly, where it belonged. I could not take her hand-me-down clothing since it was not given willingly. Robert was disappointed with my decision, but he expected it. He pointed out that my skin would only touch the satin interior; the leather was on the outside. He did not win this discussion.

Robert reminded me I am beautiful to him. "Your clothes are about bringing the outer packaging up to match the great qualities on the inside."

I thought a lot about the top recently. It does not matter how many dates it might have gotten me. If I am not true to myself, who am I? For one moment I liked the leather-clad woman in the mirror: her look conveyed adventure, confidence, and beauty. However, the compassionate woman who possesses those qualities quickly made the vegan choice. I always try to make the best decisions possible with all the information I have. I confidently concluded I could never parade around in someone else's skin and then expect a man to take me seriously in my own.

* * *

Have your interactions with someone made you re-evaluate your values?

Lifelong Vegan Is Not Vegan Enough

Anne Dinshah

I'm sure by now I've infuriated at least three members of the "vegan police" who will criticize me for not being vegan enough. I can imagine their banter already:

"Anne disgraces Jay's ideals and the Dinshah dynasty."

"She owns an old recycled wool coat in her attic! Let's hang her like the sheep she chose to kill!"

I always ask judgmental vegans, "What were you like a year before you became vegan? Were you not a kind, compassionate person, deserving of being loved?"

They usually respond, "Yes, of course."

"Give someone else that chance!" I say.

Some vegans create blockades instead of welcoming people to get on and stay on the path of veganism. Some are referred to as "vegan police," claiming to be 100 percent vegan yet functioning as self-appointed vigilantes, with animosity not ahimsa. There is no such thing as being 100 percent vegan; 99 percent is the best we can do in this imperfect world; we strive to make the best decisions 100 percent of the time and learn from our failures.

I harbor no ill will toward vegans or people following the cultural norms perpetuating animal exploitation. It will take a multitude of ways to enlighten people. Some will back away from the light of truth while more come closer. I make no apologies for the times I reach into the darkness to lend a hand and give someone a respectful pull in the right direction.

My book *Dating Vegans* was designed to make people think. It's working. People don't have to agree with me but just to think what they would do in any situation. No two people are alike—

that makes us human and fun. I'm a catalyst for thought and discussion. I've been criticized that I once told a man that if he became vegan too quickly, I'd lose interest. I devoted one year to dating only nonvegan men for the book. I want them to be vegan, so it's a conundrum. I wrote a book for the greater good.

There's also the occasional bite of animal products I have done for research. Vegan police attacked in force with the red and blue flashing lights, "How can a lifelong vegan dare to poison herself with something not vegan? What a terrible example!"

I grew up vegan when there were hardly any good vegan products on the market. Vegan desserts tasted more like cardboard than you can imagine, and I had no true frame of reference. I could make something better than cardboard, but how good was it? As a vegan cookbook author, the bites for research gave me the confidence to help many nonvegans devour vegan dishes. My recipes inspire change and open doors for their descendants to be lifelong vegans.

It's about doing the greatest good within reasonable parameters, applying reverence for life, understanding ahimsa, and choosing to do far more good than the minute harm done that enables the good. I build bridges by my tasting someone's food that they "cannot possibly do without" and then creating with them an even better version that is vegan.

Being a lifelong vegan *was* not vegan enough until I found my own ways to bring people into the light. I now understand the enthusiasm Dad had for doing the right thing. I am true to myself. I have not lost any friends due to veganism, but I have gained new ones. I am confident Dad would praise my decisions.

*   *   *

Are you a vegan lending a hand to bring people to the light of veganism?

Top left: The Dinshah boys in birth order in 1946. Back row, left to right: Cyrus, Roshan, Darius, Jal, Sarosh. Front row: Jay and Noshervan.
Top right: Jay at the organ.
Middle: Saxophone quartet of (left to right) Jay, Jal, Noshervan, and Darius.
Bottom left: Jay (left) and Jal (right) on violin with Roshan at piano in 1947.

Above left: Freya on left and Jay on right with their mentor, Dr. Catherine Nimmo "Momma Duck," who led the first vegan society in the United States from 1948 to 1960 in California. When Jay founded the American Vegan Society in 1960, she was the first member. Photo circa 1961. Above right: Freya and Jay collate and bind an early edition of *Out of the Jungle*. Below: Jay and Freya at a picnic in 1961.

Opposite Page
Top left: Jay, 1964 by Olan Mills. Top right: Jay printing *Ahimsa* magazine on an old Multilith offset press in 1967. Bottom: Dinshah family in 1971—Jay and Freya holding Daniel and Anne.

Above and right: Anne and Jay collaborate on projects at AVS. Anne performs cut and paste tasks (photo by Jay) while Jay uses the typewriter (photo by Rhoda Elovitz). Notice the Gandhi portrait Jay painted that hangs on the office wall. Below: Helen and Scott Nearing (holding Anne) and Brian Graff (page 85) in 1974. The Nearings inspired Brian and Anne to each build their own stone houses years later. Brian and Anne also share the New Year's Eve birthday. The Nearings are mentioned in many stories of this book. Photo by Jay.

Above left: Sharon Graff (page 86), Freya, Jay, and Anne enjoy a meal with local press including photographer John Pietros. Above right: Jay and Freya were honored and garlanded at India Night of the 1975 World Vegetarian Congress. Photo by Jack Walas. Below left: Anne and Daniel in 1975. Below right: This copy of a photo from 1977 features six people who wrote chapters, left to right: Brian Graff (page 85), Nathaniel Altman (page 71), Madge Darneille (page 89), Marcia Pearson (page 146), Dixie Mahy (page 107), and Jay.

Top: Jay, Freya, Daniel, and Anne in 1981. Photo by Phil Mancini. Middle left: Jay circa 1986. Middle right: Daniel Fox and Heidi Graff Fox in 1986 (page 144). "Heidi's Rabbit" painting and photo by Jay.
Right: Freya and Jay at the 1998 AVS conference. Photo Ivan King.

Left: Jay takes time to play and pose in a Seattle-area park with vegan kids. Tahira McCormack (left) is a daughter of Marcia Pearson (page 146) who took the photo. Hannah Heathcote (right) is a fourth-generation vegetarian.

Right: When Jay received the 1996 International Vegetarian of Year award from the Indian Vegetarian Society, he was too busy to travel. His brother Roshan (page 42) on left, received the award on Jay's behalf and presented it to him. Photo by Jal Dinshah. Below left: The authors dancing in 1998. Below right: Anne in 2013 by Linda Long.

Above left: Clint and Anne by Linda Long. Above right: Clint and his friend Roderick Rabbit in 2011. Photo by Justin Dinshah. Below: Clint, Anne, and Freya in 2013. Photo by Linda Long.

Healing Lessons

Dr. Michael Klaper

I summarize Jay's character and spirit in two words—consistent and uncompromising. In his vegan beliefs, Jay was the most consistent man I ever met. He was on a level all his own when it came to being vegan through and through to the very fiber of his soul. It was clear that he lived his vegan ideal of dynamic harmlessness in every waking moment (and probably while he slept!), from the food he ate, to the clothes he wore, from the words he used and, most importantly, to the actions he performed. If any aspect of his life did not meet the standard of ahimsa, he had no use for it. In that way he was totally uncompromising, as was evident in our conversations that ranged over many topics.

As a newbie to the vegan life in the early 1980s, I would have many intense conversations with him, and I would probe him for inconsistencies in principle, as well as in living life in real-world situations. In every case, his steadfastness to the vegan ideal vibrated like a taught string on a guitar—a pure, clear tone of integrity that resonated deeply within me. In those moments, try as I might to find some inconsistency in his argument or principles, I had to acknowledge the small voice within me that persistently said, "You know, he's right."

In his fierce defense of the vegan approach to life, Jay set a gold standard for me that to this day is what I try to measure up to in all my decisions and actions. In the early years of the more than thirty years that I have been vegan, I would frequently ask myself, "What would Jay Dinshah do?"

It is a testament to him and his example that I no longer have to ask myself that question because deep in my soul, I *know* what

Jay Dinshah would do. Mahatma Gandhi said, "My life is my religion." In his connection with the divine heart of compassion, Jay manifested that magnificently.

Reflecting back on our intense and ultimately formative and wonderful interactions so long ago, I realize that Jay Dinshah shared with me his greatest gifts: his vision, his example, and his life. Every day, I know that I am blessed to walk in his footsteps as I try to bring peace and healing to this world and to all beings I may encounter.

Since I became a vegan, I watched my body become lean and healthy and witnessed my previous high blood pressure resolve without medications. As a result, my medicine has taken on a decidedly vegan flavor, so to speak, and counseling my patients to adopt a whole-food, plant-based diet is, by far, the most powerful therapeutic tool I have. Most of the maladies that sicken and kill most Americans are from the meat-based, highly-sugared, overly-processed diet they eat. A truly healthy vegan diet is specific and effective therapy for high blood pressure, obesity, diabetes, clogged arteries, and a host of inflammatory diseases. As a result, I have spent much of my past thirty years of medical practice utilizing and teaching the public and other health professionals about plant-based nutrition.

I can truly say that knowing and learning from Jay Dinshah made me a more compassionate physician and a much better man. It is my responsibility and my honor to carry on his example in everything I do for the rest of my days on this planet, and like Jay I will do so with humility, gratitude, and passion. Having the privilege to know Jay has made me a fortunate man, indeed.

*   *   *

Michael Klaper, MD, currently practices nutritional medicine full time as a staff physician at TrueNorth Health Center in Santa Rosa, California, where a truly-healing, vegan diet is the cornerstone of all their therapies. Healthpromoting.com

He is director of the nonprofit Institute of Nutrition Education and Research and in 1995 was inducted into the Vegetarian Hall of Fame. He is an AVS life member.

For eleven years he hosted a radio program, "Sounds of Healing" heard in Washington DC, and Hawaii where the message of healthy diet and lifestyle was broadcast weekly. He conducted the Vegan Health Study utilizing questionnaires and optional medical testing. This generated a picture of the health of vegans on which he reported and made recommendations.

Dr. Klaper has produced numerous valuable health audiotapes and a popular videotape/DVD called *Diet for All Reasons*, encouraging healthy vegan diets to combat the typical American ailments. His books *Vegan Nutrition: Pure and Simple* and *Pregnancy, Children, and the Vegan Diet* were forerunners in their fields and classics, now out of print. His DVDs include: *Fasting: Safe and Effective Use of an Ancient Powerful Healing Therapy* (2011), *Digestion Made Easy* (2011), and *Understanding Your Blood Test Results* (2012). Additional videos can be seen on his website, DoctorKlaper.com.

*   *   *

The world needs more people to be like Dr. Klaper. Perhaps you too are considering being a wise vegan doctor. Or maybe you can gently educate your own doctor about the benefits of veganism.

"The human body has no more need for cows' milk than it does for dogs' milk, horses' milk, or giraffes' milk."
—Dr. Michael Klaper

Complete Dedication

George Eisman

Jay Dinshah inspired me from the moment I first met him at a vegetarian conference in 1982. His work ethic, his energy, and his complete dedication to the vegan way of life gave me the wherewithal to dedicate my professional life to the same noble goal.

I try to spread information to the public each day through my talks, my writing, and my organization's website. This is a collection of my favorite quotes, evidence that substituting plant-based foods instead of animal sources can lower cancer risk:

Meat consumption—including poultry and fish—is associated with a significantly higher breast cancer incidence rate. Each serving eaten per day on average increases risk by about 30 percent. *European Journal of Cancer Prevention* (17:39-47) 2008.

High consumption of dairy products is associated with higher breast cancer incidence. *British Journal of Cancer* (24: 633-43) 1970.

Men who eat the most meat, poultry, and dairy products are the most likely to die from prostate cancer, while those who eat the most unrefined plant foods are the least likely to die from this disease. *Journal of the National Cancer Institute* (20: 1637-1647) 1998.

People who consume two or more servings of dairy products daily have a three times greater risk of developing colon cancer, which kills more Americans than any other type of cancer, compared to people who have consumed little or no dairy products. *American Journal of Clinical Nutrition* (86: 17 22-1729) 2007.

*   *   *

George Eisman, MA, MS, RD is nutrition director for the Coalition for Cancer Prevention through Plant-Based Eating (CoalitionforCancerPrevention.org). George wrote *The Most Noble Diet: Food Selection and Ethics* in 1994, *Basic Course in Vegetarian and Vegan Nutrition* in 1999, and *Don't Let Your Diet Add to Your Cancer Risk* in 2008. He is the 1996 inductee in the Vegetarian Hall of Fame and an AVS life member.

*   *   *

Help protect yourself and loved ones from cancer by going vegan. No creature, human or nonhuman, should have to leave this planet before living a full life.

Do you know any animals who died at the hands of humans? Honor them by going vegan.

If you are already vegan, then invite nonvegans to share a meal with you and gently start a meaningful dialog. Or charm them with copies of *Powerful Vegan Messages* and George's books given in a fruit basket.

Victories for Humanity and Health

Attorney Mark Huberman

My late father, Max Huberman, always loved to quote the great educator, Horace Mann, who set the standard by which we all should live. Mann said, "Be ashamed to die until you have won some victories for humanity." By that standard, there was no shame in Jay Dinshah's passing since he won many victories for humanity and health.

I have been a vegan-type vegetarian for all of my sixty-two years in that I have never partaken of any meat, fish, fowl or dairy products. For virtually my entire adult life, I have also been a leader of the National Health Association (NHA), which has advocated this type of a diet since 1948.

Through my involvement with the NHA, I have had the privilege of crossing paths with a number of remarkable human beings who have broadened my horizons and imprinted my life on a host of important issues of life and health. NHA founders, Drs. Herbert Shelton, Gerald Benesh, William Esser, and others provided the foundation of my diet and health perspective. Scott and Helen Nearing taught me how to find the good life in nature. Professor Barry Commoner taught me about the closing circle of our delicate planet. Cesar Chavez enlightened me to the plight of farmworkers. The Rodales convinced me about the importance of organic farming. Alex Hershaft exposed me to the world of animal rights.

H. Jay Dinshah—I confess to never knowing what the "H" stood for, he was always just "Jay" to me—taught me that veganism meant much more than just being a vegetarian without meat and dairy. It has an ethical component that involved having a reverence for all life—something I probably instinctively had but never fully appreciated in a larger context. Fortunately, I had the opportunity to work and serve directly with Jay for a number of years and feel very fortunate to have had the opportunity to share his wisdom firsthand.

Like many of the truly great men and women of our time, Jay not just "talked the talk" but he "walked the walk." I was always impressed with his uncompromising avoidance of all things animal-based, from the nonleather shoes he wore to the kind of food he ate. During his service on the NHA board, he brought a moral compass to our deliberations, and during a period of great organizational upheaval, he provided a steadying hand and soothing voice.

I admiringly recall Jay being a jack-of-all-trades, especially during his tenure as acting executive director of the NHA in 1983. When the NHA purchased the personal library of Dr. Herbert Shelton, Jay journeyed to San Antonio, Texas, and almost single-handedly packed and shipped not just thousands of precious books but also the five or six large stunningly beautiful mahogany glass-encased bookcases in which they were housed. And when the collection needed a new home at the NHA headquarters in Tampa, Florida, it was the master carpenter in Jay who literally designed and built a new library where the world could view them.

There are not a lot of individuals in this world who can be credited with starting an entire movement that has benefitted humanity. However, as the founder of the American Vegan Society, Jay Dinshah is one of those precious few. He truly won victories for humanity and health and I am just glad that I had the opportunity to cross his path and call him a friend.

*   *   *

Mark Huberman has been an attorney in Youngstown, Ohio, for thirty-seven years. For the past sixteen years, he has served as the chief magistrate of the Mahoning County Domestic Relations Court. He frequently writes engaging interviews for *Health Science*, the magazine of NHA. He began his service to NHA as a board member at age eighteen and has served ever since in various capacities. He was elected NHA's youngest president in 1977, served three additional terms in the mid-1990s and 2004-2005, and returned again to the position in 2012, which he currently holds. He loves sports and is an avid organic gardener. He credits his good health and youthfulness to his natural health choices. Mark is an AVS life member.

*   *   *

Have you explored the principles of the health movement called natural hygiene? Perhaps you are interested in attending their annual conference. Learn more and become a member at HealthScience.org.

Are you a teenager interested in the vegan path? Just like young Jay in the 1950s and Mark in the 1960s who began serving humanity as teens with NHA, you too can be an inspiration and show your peers the ways to a better lifestyle.

Humane Meat and Harmless Leather

H. Jay Dinshah

The latest craze in meat is for humane and organic meat. Perhaps the animals are treated slightly better or have access to a tiny opening to go outside just enough to qualify for the "free-range" certification, larger cages, no growth hormones or antibiotics, or a more humane method of killing. The animals are still unwilling participants in the for-profit food business, destined ultimately to be killed for food. There is nothing humane about any creature's untimely slaughter—with just as much blood, fear, and death. Humane and organic meat are an excuse for slightly enlightened people to stop thinking any further and let their conscience go back to sleep.

Harmless leather shoes are definitely not vegan. The concept is that some cattle in India have died of old age and shoes are made from the hides. Even where cows are kept to die of natural causes, many are hastened to their deaths by short rations and slow starvation. The circumstances of their retirement are often far short of even lacto-vegetarian acceptability. Such conditions of "cow protection" I have seen and reported firsthand when I visited retirement places in India for cows who no longer give milk.

Vegans are not only completely plant-based in diet. Vegans do not sneak off to a forest hoping to stumble across some decomposing furs no longer needed by the dead animal wearing them, nor do they seek a wool sweater knitted by a kindly lady who only kept one slave in her backyard. Vegans do not send off to an exotic area for a pint of milk in the naïve hope that it comes from a mythical bovine paradise and is therefore somehow vegan. We have been at it long enough to know better.

We are reminded of the whimsical old satire—it may be in Erewhon—about the mythical utopian civilization that had progressed to the point where it was forbidden to kill animals for meat. However, the people still yearned for it and somehow there was always enough to meet the demand.

It seems that quite a few individual animals managed to meet with mysterious accidents, and even fair-sized herds were able to go sleepwalking on mountain trails and fall to their doom. Astonishing numbers of cattle, sheep, goats, and pigs in excellent health would simply trip and impale themselves on a conveniently sharp stump. Or a herd might be grazing suspiciously close to the edge of a high cliff, suddenly be seized by an epidemic of the blind staggers, and would in every case stray in the direction of the cliff.

In another ingenious excuse, some of the animals would take to fighting among themselves and were mutually gored, leaving remarkably even wounds in critical parts of the anatomy with invariably fatal results for all the animals concerned. It was not difficult to fill the demand with these careless and hapless animals meeting with such a natural and unaided demise while still in the prime—or perhaps USDA choice, select, or utility grade—of life. After the shedding of suitable tears it was always decided that it would be silly to waste such a windfall, and so it might as well be put to some use and eaten.

Back to reality: humane, organic, free-range, cage-free, harmless, and other tags masquerading as ethical options are animal products. Human beings are still trying to make a buck, rupee, pound, peso, shekel, dinar, drachma, or however the profits are measured in any specific part of the planet. Cruelty knows no geography.

As for truth in advertising, remember that the typical agribusiness factory farmer is happy to proclaim that the slaves on this plantation are treated just fine. They receive the most scientific blend of wholesome feed to mature and fatten them up quickly. All their medical care is seen to, meaning routine doses of antibiotics in the feed or water, and the farmer gives the crowning glory of animal-factory doublespeak: "We can't afford to treat the animals badly because only happy animals give more milk, wool, eggs, honey, or whatever."

Then come various routine indignities and outright cruelties that may depend on the type of slave involved, such as branding, tail-docking, and castrating, which are commonly done without any anesthetic to mitigate even the immediate pain. The prodding, goading, and shocking make the slaves move when and where their masters want. Babies are separated from mothers. All animals are generally deprived of freedom. Animals are killed who are born with the "wrong" sex or have grown too old to be profitable any more. All these crimes against the individual animal and the animal world are seen for the atrocities they are and always have been and will ever be opposed by any knowledgeable vegan.

*   *   *

Were you previously convinced by the myth of humane meat? For more on this topic, check out HumaneMyth.org brought to you by filmmakers Jenny Stein and James LaVeck who produced the documentary *Peaceable Kingdom*. TribeofHeart.org

Do you now understand why veganism is a better option? If you need convincing, Mercy For Animals is well known for doing undercover investigations of animal farms of all types, whether they claim to be humane or standard farms. These videos expose realities of standard practices and egregious abuse that will make any compassionate person lose their appetite, or better yet, change food choices. MercyForAnimals.org

Inspiring the Original VegFest

Peter McQueen

Jay and Freya Dinshah were trailblazers. I like the AVS slogan "Lighting the way since 1960." A lot of people came to the movement as vegetarian, and they introduced us to veganism.

I became vegetarian in 1975 as a teenager with no influence from anyone. It was my own thought processes. I had no knowledge of anything going on such as the big conference in the United States or the Toronto Vegetarian Association (TVA). I attended a meeting of the Canadian Natural Hygiene Society (CNHS) and learned about TVA from them. I was more influenced by the ethical arguments than the health focus of CNHS. I started going to TVA meetings in 1975, then got elected to the board of directors in 1983. I wanted to connect with people and learn more.

I attended my first big vegetarian event in 1984, the North American Vegetarian Society and International Vegetarian Union (NAVS/IVU) conference in Maryland. I was a confirmed lacto-ovo vegetarian. I was somewhat aware of the issues but was exposed at that conference to vegans and vegan food. I saw that and said, "Wow! I can eat this way. And there are reasons for doing this!" I went home and cut way down, I guess about a seventy-five percent reduction on the eggs and dairy, and gradually became vegan. It took me about ten years to completely transition.

I remember coming back home in 1984; I went to my local health food store and looked for soymilk because I didn't want dairy. There was an expensive six-fluid-ounce pack or I could go to Chinatown for a heavily-sweetened soymilk. I wasn't going to make my own, although I had a book about it. Nowadays there are so many choices! That's just one example of what's become so much more convenient about being vegan.

In one way I've been fortunate in making a slow transition because I can be accepting of others who may make a slower transition. It's a bit embarrassing that it took me so long, but I understand when people have roadblocks. It helps me not be frustrated with people.

Then I started going to Vegetarian Summerfest regularly. Each time I kept meeting Jay. I became a member of AVS and received the magazine. I found his writing to be highly influential to myself and others. I remember reading it on a regular basis and always gleaning something new. He was a valuable inspiration.

Having the regular *Ahimsa* (AVS) and *Vegetarian Voice* (NAVS) magazines and conferences made a huge difference to me. I took the information to others. In 1986 I had been so inspired by Vegetarian Summerfest that I thought we should do one in Toronto. I met Keith Akers around then, and he was a big influence too. I was young, a bit naïve, and quite gung ho. In the end we held our own multiday conference in 1987 in Toronto. It was a useful learning experience.

Jay was there; we founded the Vegetarian Union of North America (VUNA) and elected him president. With the Internet now, there's not as much of a need for a regional organization, but back then there was. Jay wanted to hold a conference on the west coast so we (AVS and VUNA) went to Arcata, California, in 1989. I had a fun role chairing some plenary sessions and helping out in general for the 1991 conference in Denver. Keith Akers and his wife Kate did a lot of local promoting, and Maynard Clark organized the conference schedule and speakers. The next co-organized conference was in Portland, Oregon, in 1993 and then the International Vegan Festival in San Diego in 1995.

When I joined the TVA board, my goal was to modernize the organization and get it on a better financial footing. It was also my firm belief that we needed to do outreach beyond potlucks.

We built it up to have the conference and so much more. For example, we publish an annual vegetarian directory—a guide to places to eat and shop around Toronto. We print 50,000 each year, plus it's available online. It's such a handy outreach tool. We also developed the "Veggie Challenge"—an online program of information, recipes, and support to encourage people to go meat-free or vegan for a week or a month. It's kick-started many people into a veggie or vegan life.

To my knowledge we were the first VegFest in 1984. We got the idea from a CNHS health fair. Our first one was a Vegetarian Information Fair. Then we decided "information" sounded dry. Former board member Michèle Brennan and I suggested it be rebranded as the Vegetarian Food Fair with food demos, samples, speakers, live music, and the next year moved to a bigger location at Harbourfront Centre, a great publicly accessible venue—location is so important!

It's now called the Vegetarian Food Festival and is 100 percent vegan. We've grown to 40,000 people attending annually with free admission making us the biggest VegFest in North America if not the world. Well over 100 vendors include free and for-sale food, books, equipment, clothes, and lots of groups represented, such as animal rights and vegan. Many companies launch their new products with us.

It takes over 200 volunteers for the festival alone. A key to success is being very organized. We now hire someone to coordinate our festival, full time about half the year and part time the rest of the year. We also usually get a government grant to hire a couple of students to help over the summer. Our two full-time staff also greatly contribute to its success. It's grown to a three-day festival—Friday afternoon until Sunday evening—in September typically the weekend after Labor Day.

We have buildings and tents so we are partially outdoors; with the music it's a great, festive atmosphere. Special programming enhances the event, like a successful Guinness World Record weightlifting accomplishment on stage, which garnered great press coverage.

Two programs developed more recently by TVA are the annual Totally Fabulous Vegan Bake-off and Veggielicious. The bake-off is a celebration that invites both amateur and professional bakers to bring their most impressive vegan baked goods to be voted on by celebrity judges and audience members. Hundreds of people attend every year, and bakeries proudly display their prize-winning creations year-round.

Veggielicious is a two-week celebration of compassionate cuisine featuring great deals and prix-fixe vegan meals at over forty restaurants, cafés, and bakeries across the greater Toronto area. Modeled after the city-sponsored Winterlicious and Summerlicious, Veggielicious has resulted in great media exposure, more customers for veg- and veg-friendly businesses, and satiated eaters.

TVA's programs have influenced and been adopted by veg and animal rights groups in North America and other parts of the world. In the same way, the inspiration of Jay and Freya has continued to influence me and so many others around the world.

*   *   *

Peter McQueen has been on the TVA board since 1983, except for one year when he attended a university in another city to get his teaching degree, serving in various capacities, twice as president. He was VUNA president from 1991 to 2005. When he became vegetarian, he also founded Canadian Organic Growers— Canada's only national organic organization—a group of farmers, gardeners, and consumers increasing availability of organic foods.

Peter is an elementary school teacher, mostly in special education. He married his wife Jenny at the 2000 World Vegetarian Congress, hosted by TVA and coordinated by Peter;

they met at the previous congress in Thailand. Each aspect of his life he does because he enjoys making a difference.

*   *   *

Are you daunted by the thought of making the transition to veganism? Start on the path and just do your best, like Peter did. Check out a VegFest; you could volunteer too.

"Nonviolence is the greatest force at the disposal of mankind. It is mightier than the mightiest weapon of destruction devised by the ingenuity of man."   —Mahatma Gandhi

Conference Organizing and Our Cat

Keith Akers

Most of my experiences with Jay revolved around his organization of conferences. Besides numerous conferences of his in the 1980s and 1990s which I attended, I also worked with Jay helping organize conferences. My wife Kate and I were significantly involved with the Vegetarian Frontiers conference in Denver, Colorado, in 1991 and the International Vegan Festival in San Diego, California, in 1995. Jay's advice for me on holding a conference was, "Don't organize a conference unless it's a sure thing." We tried to follow that advice.

I was an early believer in conferences as a way to further the vegetarian-vegan cause. In those days, vegans didn't think very much in terms of vegan groups, except Jay and a few others. We saw vegetarianism as the necessary first step. I didn't make it to the celebrated 1975 World Vegetarian Congress. I wasn't even vegetarian at that point. But in 1984, I did attend my first conference, the World Vegetarian Congress in Baltimore. It was a life-changing experience; I made countless contacts some of which I still have today. Coming away from it, I also saw the tremendous effect such conferences had on others as well as on me. It seemed that an obvious way to further the cause was to hold conferences. Personal contact with other vegetarians really was the gift that kept on giving for an activist because it led to other contacts and to further action. Conferences were a breeding ground for activists.

In the 1980s, North American Vegetarian Society (NAVS) owed its success primarily to the conferences it held in the northeastern United States. Why not have conferences elsewhere as well? I talked about this with Jay and some other vegan activists, and we decided to band together with a new organization under the aegis of the International Vegetarian Union (IVU). We started the Vegetarian Union of North America (VUNA) and helped put on a number of conferences.

The first VUNA regional vegetarian congress was in Toronto, Ontario, Canada in 1987. Neither Jay nor I had anything to do with putting it on; that was entirely done by the Toronto Vegetarian Association (TVA). We all attended the conference; and TVA, out of loyalty to VUNA, allowed us to call it a regional congress and have our meetings. Jay was the most well known of us, so we elected him the first president of VUNA.

My biggest organizational contribution was publishing the *Guide for Local Vegetarian Groups*, which gave ideas as to how to start a local group and keep it going, including how to incorporate, do a potluck, and recruit members. It went through three editions, in 1988, 1991, and 1995 but is now out of print. This was, of course, long before Facebook and Meetup groups.

Jay's contribution was in spearheading several conferences in the western United States throughout the next decade. Beginning in 1989 Jay organized conferences representing AVS and VUNA. They were biannual conferences typically in the west. These led to conferences in Arcata, California (1989), Denver, Colorado (1991), and Portland, Oregon (1993).

Jay came out to Denver in 1990 to prepare for the 1991 conference and look at potential conference sites. He stayed at our house. He arrived at our house shortly after the most damaging hailstorm in history on July 11 1990, when hail in Denver broke windows and destroyed roofs, including ours. On July 15, he gave a talk to the local vegetarian group on "Reverence for Life: How Far Can We Go?" An inveterate punster, he declared that when he had first been approached about coming to Denver, he stated that he wasn't going to come until hail freezes over.

He developed an attachment to our cat, Furrus Extremis, and some months later in another moment of humor wrote the cat a letter. The message of the letter: "Meow" repeated 100 times.

After 1993, I had left active participation in VUNA, but Jay continued with the idea of having vegan conferences in the West including most notably the 1995 International Vegan Festival in San Diego with AVS and VUNA. Kate and I were heavily involved in helping out with registration for this conference. It drew about 400 people; at that time, this was the largest vegan festival ever held. This was the last conference that we actively helped with although we always helped publicize Jay's events.

In 1997, Jay put on another vegan festival in Olympia, Washington without VUNA. In 1999, we went to his last conference, the vegan conference in Boulder, Colorado, which helped establish a vegan presence in Boulder. We thank him for the work he did, sharing with local groups across America.

*   *   *

Keith Akers is the author of several books including *A Vegetarian Sourcebook: The Nutrition, Ecology, and Ethics of a Natural Foods Diet* and two books on vegetarianism in early Christianity *The Lost Religion of Jesus* and *Disciples.* He is currently the organizer of Denver Vegans (DenverVegans.org). Keith is an AVS life member.

*   *   *

Perhaps you will start a local group or help put on a vegan conference. Or you could write a letter to a friend's cat, which may spark the friend to get the connection between companion animals and animals commonly eaten.

Vote for the Plant-Based Hero

Jim Oswald

Jay Dinshah was a very polite man, my friend for many years. I looked to him for leadership. Many did. He never let us down.

I could list many attributes, but Jay was ultramodest and would not encourage this. Rather, he would change the attention to someone else, or a principle, or a story exemplifying good works. But, Jay our vegan exemplar had qualities he will forgive me for mentioning because doing so will benefit others. Jay is still a great teacher and among us in spirit. Perhaps my recollection will remind others who knew him and cause them to smile, and any description of his many strengths can enliven his memory for those newly learning about our vegan hero.

Jay was a good citizen. I cannot imagine that Jay ever missed a vote. He could not, would not, ever forget or allow himself to be in a position preventing dutiful voting in every election. His impersonations of world-famous political leaders were charmingly inoffensive, delightful every one—now on YouTube on the Powerful Vegan Messages channel "Impersonations by H. Jay Dinshah."

I figured Jay knew everything that was going on, all the time, had absolutely clear assessments, and acted on them every time the secret ballot box was available. In no conversation, at no meeting, in no conference did Jay ever attempt to persuade me that his political views were right and I should adopt them. I have no idea how Jay voted. He kept political and personal views private.

In public he taught ethics, principles, and practical applications of veganism. He demonstrated how to live the ahimsa philosophy and won my heart.

Jay wrote, edited, published, unpacked, inventoried, packed, boxed, wrapped, and mailed many, many books. Sometimes he would slip in a surprise free pamphlet or small book. No one who ever dealt with Jay could say he was other than generous and fair. He was a book lover, and this attracted me. In one workshop, he explained his simple, efficient procedural steps for getting books from ideas to markets. I remember them all. Many successful vegan book authors have benefitted from Jay's examples, editing, and good counsel.

Our dear friend Jay had a splendid sense of humor. As he put it, when vegan pioneer Scott Nearing* finally died at 100 in Helen Nearing's arms, Jay reminded that he'd told Scott this veganism would finally finish him off, and it did. Oh, Scott would have laughed, and Helen did. Scott and Helen, Jay and Freya provided the best vegan footsteps in which we walk.

Jay Dinshah was full of love for all people and animals and gave his wisdom to others. He turned every opportunity into a blessing. He lived what he believed and was an example to all the world. He made it a better place, and his influence is still with us making things better today. Count the vegans before Jay and since Jay. Consider veganism in the United States before and since Jay. Count the vegan books.

His light still shines; more and more are carrying his torch, the torch of ahimsa. Jay Dinshah was an American hero we love.

---

*In 1975 Jim and Dorothy met Scott and Helen Nearing through a teacher-training project at Dartmouth College, just after the Nearings helped put on the 1975 World Vegetarian Congress. The Nearings introduced the Oswalds to veganism. At dinner, Jim asked, "Why don't you eat meat?" He was searching for what made them attractively peculiar.

Helen retorted, "Why would we want to eat our fellow creatures?" The Nearings became mentors and great friends to the Oswalds.

*   *   *

Jim Oswald, EdD is a vegan missionary born in the middle of the panhandle of Texas; Jim loved food from the start. He got sick from the use of DDT on farms after World War II. A smart doctor told him not to eat any animal products. He became predominantly vegan in 1947 at age twelve. He was a saladaholic and a vegetable-soup eater, but his family still ate traditional foods. Jim occasionally ate animal products and became sick every time.

Jim first met Jay and Freya at one of the Vegetarian Summerfests in Allentown, Pennsylvania, where Jim lectured on nonanimal footwear, probably in 1985. Jim and his wife Dorothy are AVS life members.

Jim has been living in Pennsylvania for forty years where night and day he thinks about gardens—planting, tending, and harvesting—year in and year out. In 1997 Jim and Dorothy founded the Institute for Plant-Based Nutrition (IPBN) at PlantBased.org committed to plant-based nutrition education. IPBN demonstrates food growing, food storing, and food preparation. They work with farmers, distributors, packagers, wholesalers, food designers, retailers, restaurateurs, hospitals, schools, senior homes, and anyone else interested in learning.

Jim and Dorothy have chosen to be less accessible by computer, returning to the gardens and personal activism as their main focuses. For the next thirty years, these healthy seventy-eight-year-olds plan to encourage people to be vegan, to utilize veganic gardening methods, and to enjoy the bounty of plants. Veganic is an organic method that uses no animal products in preparation and maintenance of soil and plants.

*   *   *

Maybe you will become an organic, preferably veganic, gardener or farmer.

Abolitionist Vegans

H. Jay Dinshah

Vegans aim for much more than just animal welfare with a bit more feed for the slaves, cleaner cages for the vivisected, or another box of bandages to plaster over the terminal cancer that is animal slavery and exploitation. In short, we are abolitionists—though nonviolent ones—for how we accomplish something is every bit as important as that it is done and often more so.

There are some parallels and some differences between modern vegans and the uncompromising human-slavery abolitionists of the nineteenth century. Those human-rights pioneers were not content to press for reforming the institution of slavery that they perceived as unjust, rotten, and corrupt from the roots up. They did not just petition for lighter chains during whipping or anesthetic during maiming, campaign for a minimum age for separation of the young from their parents, press for greater quantities of feed for the human beasts of burden, or demand a more humane maximum twelve-hour workday.

Though presumably aware of varying conditions and side issues of slavery, they were not content with merely crying for more humane servitude, more compassionate slavery, or other contradictions in terms. They were not turned from the only logical goal by rationalizations that this cotton was supposedly picked by slaves whose kindly owner gave them enough to eat or that tobacco was grown by slaves whose God-fearing master had scruples about whipping on Sundays.

Of course, there are important differences too. A few of those zealous reformers of bygone years were all too willing to resort to vicious violence—including murder—in aid of their just cause and to fight fire with fire. Unfortunately, fighting fire with fire usually results in homes and humans being turned into heaps of ashes or dust. This certainly was the case with the American Civil War, that most uncivil of wars, which left a legacy of bitter hatred, injustice, and grudgingly ceded civil rights.

Most modern vegans are too ethical, compassionate, pacific, and wise to hate everyone and burn everything in sight, all in the name of a good cause. Vegans are concerned with far more than the moment of slaughter or the manner in which an animal dies. If we find fault with animal slavery—with all the suffering, exploitation and injustice—we will attempt to educate and patiently work to eradicate this terrible institution. All the while we refrain from creating the demand for its products that keep the whole engine of destruction going.

Sometimes the plight of the animals gets frustrating, especially for new vegans who now "get it," that the rest of the world does not understand the plight of animals. I have a lifetime of patience in this arena, but the stress of the animals' suffering gets to me too. Just because I—and Gandhi, Schweitzer, and many others—advocate nonviolence doesn't mean that is the path everyone chooses.

Some radical "vegans" seek to end the property status of nonhuman animals through violent methods. Although liberating animals may be analogous to saving a child from abuse, it is not yet accepted rationale in the eyes of society and its laws. It is admirable to want to save animals from places of abuse and place them in good homes and reveal atrocities committed against them. However, it often comes with the goal of inflicting economic damage through destruction of property. Despite precautions not to harm any animal whether human or nonhuman, the method known as "direct action" does not fit the true definition and intent of nonviolence.

My lifetime goal is to close all the slaughterhouses. Could it be done more quickly by going on an arson rampage? Through direct action violence, one slaughterhouse gets closed for a few months, maybe permanently. The slaughterhouse's insurance premiums go up; the slaughterhouse might be rebuilt; maybe its slim profit is countered by economic sabotage.

The use of arson and other violence is a sensational way to gain publicity, but it perpetuates a myth that vegans are radical and dangerous. These radical abolitionists are not practicing veganism, although some claim to be vegan. Sometimes they seek recognition by the media only to find their actions judged by humans, many of whom see only the violence in trespassing, theft, and destruction. The action is not commonly equated with an underlying noble cause.

It is again the law of supply and demand. We could temporarily reduce the supply by attacking the slaughterhouses. But because the demand for animal products still exists, people will build and use slaughterhouses to meet the demand as long as there is profit to be made.

* * *

How do you feel knowing the truth about slaughterhouses? Are you compelled to think about your purchase power? Think of all the fear, anger, and suffering at a slaughterhouse and the subsequent ingesting of that material, bound to have an effect on the unaware consumer. Why do consumers choose to be unaware as they make their purchases?

Have you ever felt so frustrated that you consider doing something unlawful? Challenge yourself to think of ten more-beneficial nonviolent actions to take.

For Butter or Worse

Anne Dinshah

For over one hundred years, each Iowa State Fair has enjoyed its traditional icon of a life-sized cow carved out of butter. One night during the 2013 fair, the hallowed butter cow was doused in red paint. Iowans for Animal Liberation took credit for the action. They wrote "Freedom for All" on the glass case containing the cow. Their email stated, "The paint represents the blood of eleven billion animals murdered each year in slaughterhouses, egg farms, and dairies." Some fairgoers were outraged; media punsters capitalized on the event. Marcus McIntosh of KCCI-TV Des Moines called American Vegan Society for comments and vegan reaction to the incident. I responded:

"Vegan is a lifestyle of compassion and respect for all living beings. American Vegan Society opposes acts of violence or destruction. We understand the frustrations of Iowans for Animal Liberation; as vegans they are the minority in a region heavy with tradition in animal agriculture. We all want respect for our views. Vandalism is not going to encourage people to become vegan. True vegans oppose violence to all cows—even those carved in butter.

"Iowans for Animal Liberation might want to generate a discussion of how cows are treated, bred, and slaughtered. We should be talking about whether we should eat meat, drink milk, and eat butter. But this discussion is about vandalism and it put vegans in a poor light.

"Sensational acts not only get attention, but they also perpetuate a stereotype that vegans are radical. Everyone should maximize harmlessness and positive actions towards animals and people.

"There are better ways to educate people about the suffering of animals. Host a showing of a film, have a vegan food booth, and give leaflets to interested people. Attacking people's values and heritage at a fair that celebrates the tradition of animal agriculture just makes people defensive, not open to new ideas."

American Vegan Society serves as a voice of reason in the world.

*   *   *

How do you feel after reading that story? Can you understand both sides of the issues? Can you think of five additional ideas that could have been done to positively promote animal liberation in Iowa?

"Nonviolence is not inaction. It is not discussion. It is not for the timid or weak…Nonviolence is hard work. It is the willingness to sacrifice. It is the patience to win."   —Cesar Chavez

Helping the Next Generation Go Vegan

Andy Mars

While not knowing that the vegan word existed, I was already on that path from an early age. When I was six years old, my dad took me to visit a laboratory at Rutgers University. When no one was looking, I released the lab mice from their cages. When I was seven, I made the connection that the food on my plate had been a living, breathing animal. As an innocent, questioning child, I asked, "Why do we eat dead animals?" The overpowering physical response I received unfortunately suppressed my thinking until I was in college and had my own kitchen. As I entered my new place, I allowed what had been festering subconsciously to surface and declared, "This place is never going to see any meat."

I then came to be conscious of and concerned about how I might have been using animals in other parts of my life as well. I contacted People for the Ethical Treatment of Animals (PETA.org) to find out where to get nonanimal-tested cosmetics. I received a listing from them of a few mail-order companies that specialized in this area. I wrote to each of them to receive their catalogs. One was Vegan Street, a mail-order store in Baltimore in the 1980s, which is not around anymore. When the catalog arrived in the post, I opened it and saw big and bold on the inside cover the question, "What is a vegan?" My first response to myself was, "Heck if I know, I thought it was the name of the street of your store." While quickly reading the paragraph that followed, I muttered to myself, "Wow, there's a word for me! That means I must not be the only one who believes as I do."

The very next day, I went to the library to research this fascinating new word. I came across a listing for AVS. Upon returning home, I called AVS. Freya answered the telephone and informed me that they were holding a vegan cooking class at SunCrest that coming weekend. While I did not have a car at that time, I booked a rental and made plans to trek to Malaga.

Upon arrival, I met Freya and Jay. Instant friendships were formed. Jay and I were quickly engaged in conversation and basically remained so throughout the weekend. Even as Freya taught the cooking class, my new mentor Jay and I seldom broke away from our deep discussions in the living room. Jay remarked how impressed he was with meeting a young man who had come to such realizations and conclusions without any external influence. I remarked how enthralled I was to meet someone who had shared and embodied such an array of values.

Jay gave me a copy of *Out of the Jungle*, which I read especially enthusiastically that evening. Later during that special weekend, Jay asked me to consider serving on the AVS council of trustees, which I have quite gladly done since 1986. Jay's friendship, moral support, and inspiration helped me move forward on my path of reaching out and helping so many others.

*   *   *

Andy Mars, PhD (in education) is committed to raising a more conscious generation—helping today's children and helping the world. Based in the Los Angeles area, since 1993 he has been running the Kids Make a Difference Foundation, actively engaging kids in a vast array of hands-on community service and social action projects. He runs the Veg Kids organization that helps veg kids connect with other veg kids. Children come from across the country and around the world to attend his totally vegan camp programs during summer and winter vacations. He also directs a totally-vegan licensed elementary school. Additionally, he provides a wide array of vegan programs for the community as a whole. Andy is in the AVS speakers bureau and an AVS life member. Jay's passion lives on through Andy and through the children Andy serves.

*   *   *

Do you know vegan kids who would enjoy attending vegan camp and connecting with other vegan kids? Do you know nonvegan kids who would benefit from the opportunity to learn and grow more consciously? Do you know parents who need/ want help in raising more conscious kids? Check out Dr. Mars's websites for a wealth of information: KidsMakeADifference.org, VeganDay.info, VegKids.org, and VeganCamp.org.

PETA continues to educate about compassionate living. Their youth division at PETA2.com empowers young people to make animal-friendly changes in their schools and communities. Changes include campaigning for dissection alternatives, for vegan dining halls at colleges, against marine park entertainment, for offering veggieburgers at school cafeterias, and other ways to help the animals. They also do outreach at festivals and music events to increase public awareness of veganism and animal rights issues.

The Mad Cowboy's Advisor

Howard Lyman

I met Jay at an animal-rights conference in 1987 or 1988 at a high school in Maryland. I didn't know anybody. I don't even remember why I was there. It was my first veggie event. I had never been to one and never spoken to a group of vegetarians. I was out of my element.

Jay came up to me. He asked me where I was from and what I had done. I said, "I'm an old cattle rancher who ate meat."

Jay said, "Tell them where you came from and why you are here." It was the best advice I got from anyone.

This was after my medical difficulties and I was no longer a cattle rancher. I was a closet vegetarian working in DC as a lobbyist for National Farmers Union. When I became vegetarian, my cholesterol went down and so did my blood pressure, so I wondered what would happen if I became vegan. I became a closet vegan and lost 100 pounds. My cholesterol went from 300 to 135. My blood pressure went down from sky-high to normal.

I never met a person who was more faithful to what he believed than Jay. Some people love an animal or think vegan is cool to do. Jay was a rare person who every day in every way did what he believed. I will never forget what he said, "You know, it's all about the animals. What we are doing to the animals is wrong, totally wrong." I asked what can we do.

He said, "All I can do is what I can do. I can do it every day. I will never take a day off."

How many people have you met who have such a commitment? Knowing him and spending time with him made me a better person. If I ever wanted advice, he was one person I would go to. I know he was totally committed to what he said. Jay was the most exceptional person I have known. He was my role model. He was one of a kind.

*   *   *

Howard Lyman was a fourth-generation cattle rancher in Montana for almost forty years. He followed all the modern advice and turned a small organic family farm into a large corporate chemical farm with a thousand range cows, five thousand cattle in a factory feedlot, thousands of acres of crops, and as many as thirty employees.

In 1979 a tumor on his spinal cord caused him to be paralyzed from the waist down. Howard promised himself that, whatever the outcome of the surgery, he would dedicate the rest of his life to doing what he believed is right—no matter what changes that necessitated. Howard regained the ability to walk. In 1983 he sold most of his farm and became a lobbyist for America's family farmers.

Now Howard works toward shaking up the meat industry and pesticide industry in hopes of shutting down the feedlots and factory farms. He is full of energy and happier being part of the vegan movement where he is loved. He wrote *The Mad Cowboy: Plain Truth from the Cattle Rancher Who Won't Eat Meat* (1998) and *No More Bull! The Mad Cowboy Targets America's Worst Enemy: Our Diet* (2005).

He is well known for appearing on *The Oprah Winfrey Show* in 1996 when he made remarks which led to Oprah renouncing hamburgers. A group of Texas cattlemen sued Lyman and Winfrey, but both were found not guilty of any wrongdoing. Howard has served as president of the International Vegetarian Union, EarthSave, and Voice for a Viable Future. He is the 2002 inductee into the Vegetarian Hall of Fame and an AVS life member.

*　　*　　*

Anne: Howard first told me his story many years ago at a Summerfest—perhaps in 2002. Somewhere in the back of my mind I thought, "Wow. Someday someone should write down these stories about Dad. It would make a cool book." I never thought it would be me. When I contacted Howard in 2013, I didn't remember what his story was, but I knew it was special.

I also remember how excited Dad was after first meeting Howard because "The vegan movement now has an ex-cattle rancher on our side!" The admiration between Dad and Howard was definitely mutual. Dad truly respected how hard it must have been for Howard to turn against what he had done and see the light.

*　　*　　*

Have you recently become vegan? Are you afraid to speak in public? Remember to just tell your personal story—where you came from and why you are here. You too have a powerful vegan message.

"If you visit the killing floor of a slaughterhouse, it will brand your soul for life."　　　　　　　　　　　—Howard Lyman

Awakening a Vegan Hart

Victoria Hart

As a young child, I had natural curiosity and compassion for animals, but this wasn't valued or nurtured by my environment. Struggling alone with my keen sensitivities, my compassion for animals went dormant until I exercised some teenage rebellion in high school, turning to ovo-lacto vegetarianism. I knew no vegetarians. This alienation and ensuing self-doubt I experienced—especially in the face of peer pressure—tempted me to conform. I felt my half-hearted vegetarian efforts weren't enough, sensing something was not at all right about the way other animal species were viewed and treated. I either had to go deeper and look at some hard facts or ignore my questions.

I stayed in this confused mode until my late twenties, when I came across a magazine that had shocking scenes of animal exploitation and misery that alarmed my conscience: a calf confined in a veal crate, a fox caught in a leghold trap. Then an influx of eye-opening literature fell into my path from PETA, Tom Regan, *The Animals' Voice* magazine, and books such as *Animal Factories*, *Animal Liberation*, and *Silent Spring*. All these captured my full attention and went straight to my heart, piercing it like no other pain I'd known.

Up to that point, I'd seen vegetarianism in terms of diet only; I hadn't been aware of the injustice of animal exploitation nor had I heard of the philosophy and practice of veganism. It quickly became clear that I had to cast aside my half-hearted vegetarianism and head immediately into veganism. I could revive my innate love for animals, fully respecting them while learning reverence for life. It was time to wake up.

With my recent transition to veganism, I knew no other vegans

226

and had lots of questions. With no Internet in the early 1990s, I found only a small collection of vegan books of which I took full advantage. Yet I craved a more personal experience. When I saw AVS listed as a vegan resource in Keith Akers' *The Vegetarian Sourcebook*, I hurriedly wrote a letter to Jay. He responded with a warm greeting. I needed to lean on someone supportive, patient, reliable—and who could be both gentle and resolute. Jay was a perfect fit. Plus I discovered AVS had a goldmine of helpful educative offerings.

After the initial contact, Jay and I had telephone conversations. My most pressing question was, "What can I do to help the animals and promote veganism without having much, if any, spare cash to contribute?" He responded by asking me what my favorite talents and strongest passions were. I told him I was an animal lover who made a living as a freelance artist; my specialty was whimsical animal art. I also was in love with the written word, especially when it shined with wisdom. I confessed my dream that I'd write and illustrate an endearing children's book someday. Jay liked art very much and was an artist himself. In discussing these topics, we came to an agreement that I'd write and provide art for a fun kids' page in *Ahimsa* magazine. I would also cheerfully supply cover art for *Ahimsa*. Jay issued me a life membership to AVS which sealed the deal.

Our relationship continued to develop. I am proud to say that Jay was the person responsible for teaching me not only the tenets of veganism but also how to put those foundational nuggets from The Golden Rule into action by means of dynamic harmlessness. I learned about ahimsa—the compassionate way—and memorized the six pillars as treasures to carry with me through life. These foundational elements, coupled with following Jay's shining examples of integrity and continuous cheerleading, built my strong ethical backbone needed for proudly walking the talk of authentic veganism.

I own several copies of Jay's *Out of the Jungle*; one is lovingly autographed by Jay. *Out of the Jungle* proved that Jay's writing style was as powerful as his speaking style. It is spiced with wit and wisdom that support the urgency of his messages. His words aren't candy coated, and that's admirable. Jay was a bold, intelligent man who did much for advancing veganism, tirelessly exposing the ugly truths of animal exploitation and irreverence for life. Yet he managed to keep a healthy measure of childlike enthusiasm, envisioning a world void of such atrocities. This is what I admire most about Jay; I strive to exemplify the same in my own vegan journey.

It is my hope that Jay's words nudge and gently awaken what may be lying dormant within you. Let them inspire and guide you just as they do me.

*   *   *

Victoria Hart is an ethical vegan, animal advocate, fine artist, and toy designer. She contributed to the cover design for this book and creates art for use in *American Vegan*. She provided illustrations used in the thirteenth edition of Freya Dinshah's *The Vegan Kitchen*. Victoria puts her excellent cooking skills to good use, preparing and donating vegan meals to several people regularly. She has volunteered at a vegan farm-animal sanctuary, an enriching experience she highly recommends. She cares for two rescued cats, feeding them a plant-only cruelty-free diet, on which they thrive.

Ten percent of her income is given to vegan animal-rescue sanctuaries or ethical vegan education. She donates films and books to individuals, businesses, and libraries, helping adults and children alike to learn more about vegan compassion in action.

*   *   *

What are your favorite talents and strongest passions? How will you use them to help the animals and extend the circle of compassion?

Ethical Dilemmas

H. Jay Dinshah

Now let's discuss dilemmas—the positive and negative sides of action and how we live our lives. Let us say you have been a strict vegan as I am and have been since 1957. Just how strict are you going to be? How far can you take it?

I had a discussion with a couple about the bone charcoal that's used, recycled, and reused in the process of filtering to make white sugar, although sometimes nonanimal methods are used. That wasn't even the dilemma. The question was whether it is ethical for vegans to use the molasses that is separated from the cane syrup in the refining of white sugar.

Raw sugar hasn't gone through the refinery; it's cane juice boiled down to remove the water. Commercial brown sugar is white sugar with caramel or molasses added back for coloring, and it's practically as nutritionally impoverished as the white sugar. Sugar isn't the biggest worry; if you have health interests, white sugar is a priority item to eliminate as a worthless food.

Let's imagine that we'll make the jump right up to being 100 percent vegan. Then we learn about some of these peripheral problem areas. We come down out of cloud nine or down from our wooden—not ivory—tower and have to get back to living in the real world or the world as it is at present.

If we say we're going to eliminate all animal products—all animal-source things from our diet, our clothes, cosmetics, and such. Fine. That we can do.

What about the leather belt on the machinery somewhere in Hong Kong that made this all-manmade-material pair of shoes? Do you have the means of tracing this all the way back or finding out where K-Mart bought this batch of shoes in Taiwan? Or exactly which producer even made the shoes? Can you find this out when you see a pair of shoes that seems acceptable?

If you go so far, there is still another dilemma. You go to the supermarket and buy something in the produce department. With your support of the supermarket, you're helping to pay the checkout clerk who buys some meat. Is that your fault, your exploitation and killing of animals? Should you avoid that? Can you avoid that? You would have to buy everything—not just food but everything—from people who are vegans themselves. Then they would have to use your money to buy things only from vegans and so on ad infinitum.

This is the problem: When do you give up on humanity? When do you fancy yourself so superior and become so smugly self-satisfied that you resign from the human race and go live in a cave? And grow all your own food—maybe some mushrooms in that dark, damp cave. You can't really claim to be 100 percent negatively harmless if you aren't willing to do that. We certainly don't approve of giving up on the human race. We haven't cancelled our membership in it, and we don't advocate that anyone should.

You might then be practicing to the limit—or even to excess in effect—the negative, passive side of ahimsa as only applied to the concept of "thou shalt not kill animals." Wouldn't you be completely giving up on what may be an even more important positive side? "Thou shalt help thy fellow human beings" to learn the ways of ahimsa and to do the best they can.

Not all decisions vegans make are ethical dilemmas. For example, if a person is on a shooting rampage in a school and a decision is made to shoot to kill the attacker, that may be a sound decision, not an ethical dilemma. Even on this, some readers may want to debate other solutions and put it into the ethical dilemmas category. What makes it a dilemma is that there is a question in one's own mind about the course of action to take.

Ethical Dilemmas Discussion
with Jay, Anne, and Friends

This chapter has been collected from various ethical dilemma discussions at home and at conferences. Fictitious names are used for participants other than Jay and Anne. We serve as catalysts for thoughts; we never proclaim to have all the answers.

Janice: I think we have to be ethical in investing. While buying our hybrid car recently, we had a friendly conversation with our local car dealer who told us he invests in genetic engineering and factory farming. So it seems an endless struggle trying to be ethical at every level.

Jay: Well, that's certainly somewhat removed from your making such an investment yourself. You gave your money and he gave you a car; now it's your car and his money. He can't tell you where to drive, and you have no control over where he puts his profits. If you have a choice, you can prefer to deal with a vegan car dealer. I don't know of any in my part of the country.

There are some people of certain religious persuasions who print directories of merchants of the same faith. One is supposed to deal with those people as if people of one faith or another would be more honest or deserving. We think sectarian communalism has been the curse of many parts of the world, and that kind of attitude serves to divide humanity, not bring it closer together. So we might agree in principle on avoiding transactions that would be known to put money into investing in harmful practices. But I'm not sure it would be good, right, or productive to withhold trade from someone simply because that person happens to be a meat eater and therefore should be obliged to be forcibly converted or starve.

Is it fair, good, or constructive for someone to proclaim a boycott of anyone solely on the basis of the outsider's faith or diet any more than race, gender, or sexual orientation? We can feel sorry for one afflicted with such an attitude, though we are much sorrier for their victims.

The world has seen far too much of separatist communal bigotry. In India at the time of independence, it claimed a million human lives and still stalks the land today. Also in the past century, bigotry has claimed lives in Germany, Northern Ireland, the Middle East, and the former Soviet Union, and the list goes on and on. Is there any place on Earth free from the antisocial disease, the plague of separatism and egomania?

Where can we be without hearing statements this foolish: "I am better than you are because you were raised to worship Allah and I was born into a family that prays to Yahweh"— largely a matter of linguistics that could say Krishna, Christ, Osiris, Baal, Mithras, my ancestors, or the sun and moon. "My hair is lighter than yours." Therefore insulates better? or "My eyes are a different color." This makes them see more clearly? Is that any different from "You eat pork and I eat mutton. Let's start a fight." or "I eat cow and you eat goat. Let's have a nice little holy war."

We have no intention of adding to this folly "You eat cattle and I eat cabbage. I have to hate you, deny you a livelihood, or throw a brick through your window."

Anne: However, with investments such as where to put our retirement savings, we have the right and responsibility to choose to invest in things we believe. We want our money to grow and while it is growing, it can be furthering the more ethical businesses. Sustainable responsible investing (SRI) considers both financial return and social good. They take into account environmental, social justice, and corporate governance criteria. Maybe someday there will be investing to enable an array of vegan businesses; for now that is done on a very individual level.

I know friends and organizations who intentionally invest in offending companies to create positive change through shareholder advocacy. They can do this by purchasing as little as $2000 in the offending company's stock. Unless one is investing in SRI funds, when vegan or animal rights organizations or individuals propose resolutions, chances are the mutual funds are voting against these recommendations. (For more information and a simple explanation of the main types of investment options see the "Humane Investing" article by Brenda Morris in *American Vegan*, winter 2014, or visit HumaneInvesting.com.)

We can also choose to support vegan businesses because we want them to thrive. I have a favorite local vegan café that I visit weekly when I'm in Jersey. I could eat at some other restaurant and may be satisfied, but I know how hard it is to be a small-business owner. I want my friend to succeed. I want to support vegan businesses even if I have to pay more and drive further, and I recruit others to bring their dollars to spend too.

This is elevating the positive harmlessness side of things, whereas withholding business from a nonvegan would be the negative harmlessness. When possible I choose to support businesses I know are based on positive harmlessness values.

Sarah: I didn't become a vegan until I got into the animal-rights movement and learned about the horrors of the dairy and veal industry. My problem is in going to restaurants. As a lacto-vegetarian, I could always find something. As a vegan sometimes I can't find anything.

Mel: Eating out hasn't been too much of a problem for us as vegans. Whenever we go out, we tell them exactly what we want. We used to call ahead and say we're coming there and we don't eat meat, dairy, and eggs. They would try to prepare something special, and it was usually horrible.

We found it better to just show up and tell them what we want. We select things from different dinners on the menu that they can put together just to feed us, as opposed to sending us out of the restaurant unfed.

Jay: If you like living on the cheap, cafeterias can be pretty good. You can usually pick and choose with no embarrassment if you're shy about making your wants known.

At a good restaurant you can usually ask for a baked potato with absolutely nothing on it, some salad also with nothing objectionable on it, and some plain steamed vegetables.

Places with salad bars may offer a wide variety of salad items as well as various things to dress up the spud and salad, if you like. Beware that salad bar items may be doctored or embalmed somewhat to keep them looking fresh.

Anne: I would not order a plain potato or a salad. If I want a potato, I throw one in the oven myself, not go out for it at ten times the price. If I'm going out and eat a potato, they have to at least slice it and fry it or something that I might not bother to do at home.

Salad is the stereotypical thing that everyone thinks vegans eat, and I do eat my salads. However, when I'm out, it's the last thing I'll order. I don't want to perpetuate the stereotype that vegans eat only salads. Salads are too often based on iceberg lettuce and boring. I want real greens plus beans, raisins, poached pear, toasted walnuts, or other exciting things on salads.

Nowadays I feel confident enough to speak up about being vegan, not apologize for it. It's our obligation to inform restaurant owners of the need for vegan entreés. When going to an unfamiliar city, it helps to do a couple minutes of research on HappyCow.net and have an idea where to go, if it is my choice. I've enjoyed many delicious meals and exposed a variety of people to the bounty of vegan restaurant fare.

It's been many years since I've had to go to a steak joint and settle for a potato and salad for lack of any better options, although many regions of the country lag behind in offering vegan meals. When that's the case, I get through the experience gracefully and look for opportunities to gently educate people about the increasing demand for vegan food. I can be well fed at the next meal.

Mel: We've been out with friends. They'll get fish or something like that, and we'll get a fine platter of steamed vegetables. They'll pay about twenty dollars, and we'll pay seven.

Jay: You may even have embarrassed the chef with the prospect of sending you out unfed. He'll take everything from the vegetable bin and cook it up for you, not to shame the place.

Gina: And it looks so good that the people with you who ordered the meat will even be envious. They would never have thought of ordering such vegetables.

Anne: Linda Long told me that when she asked famous chefs to contribute to her book, *Great Chefs Cook Vegan*, the chefs were ecstatic that they could choose from such a vast array of plant foods. They told her that they get tired of cooking such a limited menu since there are only a few ways to cook animal products. One chef threw his hands up in glee realizing he suddenly could start creating from such a huge array of plant foods. She advises to call ahead, especially for high-end restaurants because the chef will enjoy the challenge.

These days, vegan is common enough that there is often a vegan in every group choosing a restaurant, and the place is often chosen with this in mind. Many restaurants are learning to put at least one vegan dish on the menu. A good vegan dish is a completely plant-based dish that becomes popular not just for vegans.

Encourage restaurants in your area—impress upon them that people enjoy flavorful dishes, perhaps from seasonal vegetables with grains and beans. They will sell many, not only to vegans but also to other people interested in healthier choices. They will increase customers by gaining vegan clients, friends of vegans, and people who appreciate the bounty of plant foods.

Jay: I used to find I could do better at a regular restaurant than at some vegetarian places where they were scared silly about protein; they dumped the mayo, egg, or cheese into and over everything. Many catered to the lowest common denominator of taste, and they threw in spices and herbs by the bucketful to assure that steam would come billowing out of your ears or that you couldn't possibly discern the actual taste of the food itself.

Anne: Happily that has evolved considerably. Most vegetarian restaurants offer much of their menu with a simple switch of ingredients to vegan mayo or vegan cheese or are happy to leave it off. With so many people having allergies and sensitivities, there are more plainer-fare options on many menus, or chefs are more willing to leave out ingredients.

Some chain restaurants have difficulty adapting menu items for vegans because they really just unwrap and reheat things. Many chain restaurants do have vegan options, and it's nice to know there is something at multiple locations. One friend did humane investing and actually bought stock in a particular chain with the sole purpose of getting them to add vegan options. Another suggestion is to go to places that prepare the food on site, allowing more flexibility.

How far do you go to ask questions? If the ingredients for your dinner are verified to be all vegan, do you then ask if it is cooked on the same grill as they use for meat? Deep-fried in the same grease? Steamed in a pot sometimes used for cooking meat? I think when we choose to be social with nonvegans it is important to uphold our values, yet not appear too "out there." If nonvegans see vegan as an unreachable goal, they will not want to try. If you have the opportunity, frequent the vegan establishments where none of this is an issue. Impress nonvegan friends with how delicious and normal vegan food can be. If that is not an option, then avoid the deep fryer and hope they washed the pot before steaming your veggies.

Jay: Years ago when I was traveling a lot by air, it was possible to advance-order a special vegetarian plate. They poured dairy glop over it and threw in a generous wedge of cheese. Or often it would miss getting put on the flight at all, and you might be asked if you would mind taking either chicken or beef. Some choice. I was actually told that I could just shovel the dead stuff aside and pick at the salad as if that would somehow, miraculously, bring the poor critter back to life.

Anne: Now the airlines enhance their profits by doing away with meals on flights in many cases. You can choose to purchase a ten-dollar leaf of lettuce or a cookie. Most airlines now have a vegan option when a meal is included. Be sure to ask for it ahead of time. Don't be shy; the airlines deserve to know there is a demand for vegan food and they will supply it. Sometimes it's delicious; sometimes it merely keeps your stomach from grumbling until the next stop. You can write the airlines with your feedback.

Mary: May I switch the topic to killing for a purpose? How does one decide whether to kill a rat, mouse, moth, mosquito, beaver, bear, or other creature that may be causing a nuisance.

Jay: Apply reverence for life and weigh what is being done by the creature. If you are being attacked and your life is threatened, you may opt to choose yourself. This is not the same as going into the wilderness and hunting these creatures for food or sport.

Let's consider some examples: If a bear is mauling you, you will fight back. However, before you put yourself in that situation, remember that humans have moved into what was the bear's habitat—or the bear's ancestors' habitat—forcing the bear into encounters with humans. Humans often do stupid things, such as leaving their garbage out where the bear will forage in it. As the bears get more dependent on humans, they may lose their fear of humans. Some bears have been known to go into tents because they smell food. Bears need to be wild. Humans generally created the problem. A bear doesn't suddenly wake up one day and say, "Hmmm. I think I'll go hunt and eat a human." The bear was probably just as surprised by the encounter as you were.

Let's try someone smaller—how about a mouse. There's no reason to fear taking a hike because you might encounter a mouse. If you see one, you might watch him for a few minutes going about his mousey work with his little black beady eyes, tiny cute ears, and funny little tail. Marvel at how different his life is from yours, and remark how valuable his life is to him.

Now let's say you find that same mouse in your house. The mouse and spouse—for there is never just one—will soon have children. Two mice easily become thousands in a year, not calculating for predators. You can try the catch-and-release option, but they know how to get into your house and will probably beat you back to the door. Choose the least harm. As disgusting and cruel as it is, you might decide to trap-to-kill these two mice. It is better than having to get rid of a hundred mice. What do you think?

Anne: I've had this problem on multiple occasions. The first time, I faithfully did catch and release, including frequently driving many miles—and crossing a water barrier—to the state park in the middle of the night to let the mice go with a chunk of nut butter on bread as a parting gift. I think they ran back to my house more quickly than I drove. I wondered if I should buy nontoxic paint just to mark the mice and prove whether they were actually the same mice, but I didn't. We were remodeling the house, and in taking down the walls, we found hundreds of mouse skeletons, probably exterminated when the previous owner was horrified with the mouse problem.

One night I felt something on my inner thigh under the covers. At first I thought it was my man exciting me, but he was snoring. I turned on the light, threw off the covers, and saw a mouse scurry away. I couldn't be nice to mice anymore. We all have our breaking point. The next morning I called Dad who reminded me to do the least harm; I decided to kill two instead of a hundred.

I've lived other places such as when a roommate had a cat. No mice, but then there's the thought of whether the cat is keeping the mice away or killing them and other creatures such as rabbits, chipmunks, and birds. Are the cats doing the work of an exterminator or a hunter? And what do we feed the cat? Or dog? (See Veganpet.com or VegePets.info for food answers.)

Now I live in my own little cabin in the woods, but I travel frequently, so I might be gone for a month. I have arrived home to find shredded toilet paper. Toilet paper I can easily hide in a mouse-proof box. Next they decided to use my shirts for bedding; I can't walk around in shredded stained shirts. Or there's the time I found my homemade masterpiece quilted scenic curtains chewed and stinky with mouse pee and poop. There is a lengthy list of things the mice have destroyed over the years. I bought the most reliable, quick-kill traps I could find. Generally they work quite well—all things considered. I shudder and say a little prayer when I drop mice back into the woods to decompose. I won't ever like doing it, but I have come to terms with the decision, and it is now a rare occurrence. I remind myself it's two or a hundred or be violated, and I pick the least harmful.

More important than how to deal with the mice is how to prevent them from entering or make it less inviting. I employ all the suggested tricks for keeping mice away, such as stopping up potential mouse entrances with hardware cloth, tidying the kitchen after each meal, cleaning the floor daily, removing all food when I go away, spraying a vinegar solution outside, dabbing peppermint oil in corners inside, plugging in ultra-high frequency mouse-deterrent devices when I am gone. And now I am landscaping with plants such as tansy, lavender, and mint that deter mice, ants, and other invaders.

For mice I draw the line at entering my house. There seem to be significantly fewer mice crossing that line. Everyone who enters must have an invitation.

And then there's Lady Dowding's suggestion. I wish I could do that. Dad, do you want to tell her story from *Here's Harmlessness*?

Jay: When Lady Dowding was a teen, her mother had reached the realization that all life was one and that she should not harm any part of it. A very large and flourishing family of rats took up their abode on her property. Her mother took the problem to a very wise friend who gave her this simple advice:

"First you must get rid of your fear and dislike of the rats, for you can do nothing without love. I would suggest that you watch them until gradually you begin to distinguish one from the other. See that they have distinct personalities and are clever too. When you have overcome your dislike, then—and only then—can you begin to speak to them. Explain the difficulties they are causing you, and ask them to go away."

It took her mother some time to overcome her repugnance to rats. The discovery of their larder with the food neatly stored appealed to the housewife in her. At any rate, she was eventually able to talk to them, and they all left.

Anne: I've tried talking to my cabin mice to no avail. However, when I was at AVS working on this book, a mouse took up residence in the kitchen. Everyone saw him a couple times a day go into the living room and return. Being at AVS, I felt I should at least try the catch-and-release method first because there are other people's ethical dilemmas involved in a common space. I bought both kinds of traps and talked to the wall next to where I believed him to be in hiding. I set the trap there and explained that I would give him the opportunity to leave on his own accord, or I will escort him out in a live trap. Should he choose to return, I will resort to the other trap. I never caught him nor saw any sign of him after that. I even left food out overnight and it went untouched.

We've talked about mice and rats; let's move on to beavers, a much misunderstood animal. A friend used to live in a house near a swamp. A beaver moved into his neighborhood and did wonderful engineering to make a dam to form a lake. Unfortunately it caused flooding at my friend's house. This was before I met him, so I didn't have the chance to tell him about beaver bafflers that influence the water in a mutually satisfactory way. Instead he went hunting. Here the creature didn't enter his house but caused damage. I can understand his reaction. His lack of knowledge at that time meant the demise of a beaver. Next time he will contact my friends, The Beaver Defenders of Unexpected Wildlife Refuge in Newfield, New Jersey, or other experts for advice. (See UnexpectedWildlifeRefuge.org)

For all animals, try to remember that we moved into their territory in our quest for human housing. I'm sure the beaver ancestors occupied his land for generations before he bought it. And did he really buy it? Whose land is it anyway? Try to weigh all the sides of an issue. Do the least harm and make sure you can live with your decisions.

Mary: I think I have a good grasp on animal difficulties. Shall we move onto insects? What do you do?

Jay: There are some people who are so peaceful that even a mosquito will not bother them.

Anne: Or they eat so much garlic that nothing will fly close enough to bite them?

Jay: Many people opt to wear bug spray, but it is usually a combination of poisons.

Anne: Friends and I made some homemade bug spray from natural products. You could probably find a recipe online. I will admit to swatting a few mosquitoes and not just in my house. Anything else—unless it's biting me—I just leave it alone outside.

Inside, my goal is to get it to go outside: spider, moth, bee, fly, you name it. Depending on the invader, I might use a cup and paper for catch and release. However, there's also a flyswatter hanging in the corner if I really need it. Flies can be a real nuisance and a health hazard to my companion rabbit. Sometimes, such as often is the case with moths, despite turning off all indoor lights, I'll release one, and two more fly in the house. That may change my tactic. Again, do the least harm, and do what works in your home so you and your visitors can be comfortable inside. Remember that outside is the insects' home and act accordingly.

Since I mentioned my rabbit, let's return to another ethical dilemma for some vegans—companion animals. Are they not still captive like those in the zoos we protest? Or have humans created a problem with domestic creatures and now it is our responsibility to protect them and nurture them because they would no longer survive in the wild? At least try to help a rescued companion animal instead of adding to the overpopulation by breeders. Be aware that a rabbit is naturally vegan. A cat or dog should be treated as an individual in the transition to vegan food; some animals won't go completely vegan.

Luther: Shall we talk about employment?

Jay: Well, are you a butcher or a shoe salesman?

Luther: Neither, but let's pretend I'm a butcher who has been suppressing feelings for years, and now I want to be vegan. The obvious answer is to quit my job immediately, right?

Jay: Of course. However, what if you are a butcher who is the sole source of income for your family living paycheck to paycheck and often you get paid in meat. If you quit, your family might starve. Sometimes the best time to look for a new job is while you already have one.

Anne: Or quitting could free up your time to more actively seek a new job. Talk with your family. Perhaps someone else can do something to ease the financial burden.

Jay: Maybe reach out to a local, organic vegetable farmer and offer to work for vegetables until you get your next paid job.

Anne: See if there's a local Food Not Bombs nearby where you can get food. Then when you get back on better financial footing, remember to help someone else and volunteer there.

Luther: What if I were the shoe salesman?

Anne: Can you influence the company to have more nonanimal options and promote those products?

Jay: Use your position to do the most good. If shoes are equally serviceable, steer people towards the vegan option. If there is any reason why the leather shoe is actually better, acknowledge that. Then also present a nonleather shoe and the ethical points involved. Let the customer make an informed decision.

Anne: If your employer is okay with you presenting options and opinions, this is good. If your employer prefers to sell leather shoes—such as if he makes more profit from them—you may be unemployed quickly.

Jay: Maybe it's another case of looking for a new job while you have one. If you have the financial security to be able to quit, that is an option. Maybe you have another option?

Anne: How about taking all your good knowledge and some of your savings and opening your own shoe store?

Luther: What if I'm already self-employed? I own the butcher shop.

Anne: Talk with your customers about health, ethics, and an exciting new venture. Change to being a specialty vegetable shop with all sorts of cleaned and chopped veggies fresh to order. Utilize one's best skills veganized, and help others change too.

It's a unique opportunity in switching from selling cuts of animals to cuts of plants—an opportunity that wouldn't exist if you merely started up a veggie store from scratch. Where a veggie store attracts people looking for veggies, your butcher shop attracts people looking for meat, and you can provide a better option. Albeit a few people will be annoyed that they have to find a new butcher. It would be an awesome way to showcase your ethical decision, which is no longer a dilemma by then. You can also have fun with keeping a variation of your shop's name aligned with your new values.

I recommend reading a wonderful true story about a pig farmer's ethical dilemma in John Robbins' book *No Happy Cows*.

Jay: I remember the days before digital cameras when cameras used film containing an ever-so-thin one-thousandth of an inch thick smear of animal gelatin on it. A friend thanked me for turning her on to ahimsa so much that she quit the photography business.

She did not feel she should continue using her talents in commercial advertising to help further the marketing of unnecessary material items and using an animal product in the process. Her work was selling new brands of the same old stuff, pretending there's some miracle ingredient, and selling the sizzle—in their own term. She quit cold, saying, "If it came to being asked to do a little photography for a vegan magazine to help the animals, then I might consider it."

Back in those predigital days, many vegan friends refused to be photographed. I've had my own thinking to do on the topic. The old saying "a picture is worth a thousand words" had to be considered with *Ahimsa* magazine. Clearly everyone would see my choice printed on the pages. As an artist and editor, I love photos but used them sparingly, weighing the good each would do.

Anne: That's why I don't have much of a photo album from those days. I grew up on the pages of *Ahimsa*. That's also why I was so excited to find the rare photo of us that I selected for the cover of this book. I never knew it existed or expected to find such a photo, but I felt compelled to do some tidying in the office and voilà.

On the employment topic, I have a friend who is the food-service director at a major university. He was definitely not vegan. Then a student dared him to try eating vegan for thirty days in his own dining halls. He took the challenge two years ago and remains vegan to this day. Most accurately he's ninety-nine percent vegan, which is vegan as we have shown in this book. For work he is required to taste samples of dishes the university will serve. Clearly consuming animal products is not vegan, but he employs reverence for life, weighs his options, and takes responsibility for them. His tasting of animal recipes has greatly diminished as he tries to focus his team on more vegan food.

By keeping his job that includes supervising the preparation of nonvegan food, he is doing greater good by introducing vegan options to the general campus population. He is frustrated by the lack of change, but he does what he can by increasing plant-based food options and inviting vegan speakers. He understands that a university's role is to educate, not dictate. I applaud his efforts and encourage him. He hopes to someday create an all-vegan dining hall like the highly successful one at the University of North Texas that is now copied by other universities and was the cover story for *American Vegan* in fall 2013.

Jay: Whenever I had a job that I discovered wasn't aligned with my values, I continued to do what I was doing until I couldn't to do it any longer. Then I stopped. For example, I had a bookkeeping job where the boss told me to falsify billing records. I quit right away. Your conscience is your own gauge. Evaluate possibilities to take your skills and go somewhere else.

When making the conscious decision to do something that is not vegan, the harm must be weighed against the good that will come of the action. Be sure the result is overwhelmingly in favor of the greater good.

Anne: It is important to make the best decisions with all the information available at the time. People may change their stance on an ethical dilemma when introduced to new information. It's okay to change one's stance. That's what makes it a dilemma. If it were an easy answer, that stayed the same in every instance, it would cease to be a dilemma.

Dad said vegans shouldn't keep animals captive. He also initially didn't like animal sanctuaries because when you save one animal, the farmers just breed another to replace it; think of the law of supply and demand. Later in life he changed his stance on this.

When I was thirty I adopted my first companion animal, a rescued French Lop rabbit named Brando. He was an awesome bunny who would actually sit at the dining table and eat his own dish of salad at dinnertime. Dad always loved rabbits, wild ones in the yard—they're vegan. Dad loved doing the bunny hop too.

I sent Dad a photo of Brando and let them talk on the phone. The conversation consisted of Dad saying the word "meep" repeated a few times, as that's what he selected as rabbit lingo for everything—changing the tone for meaning. Brando just looked curiously at the phone. I found out after Dad's death that he had enlarged the photo and set it on his desk. He added the caption, "Eating rabbit food is a wonderful habit. Who ever heard of a tired rabbit?" He loved his furry grandchild.

Mom (Freya) said he also changed his stance on animal sanctuaries. He decided the animals in sanctuaries and some of the companion animals serve to help us make the connections. They represent all the animals who suffer every day for humans. Dad visited The Cow Sanctuary in Shiloh, New Jersey, a loving, forever home with lifelong care and rehabilitation for cows, emus, horses, goats, pigs, ducks, and geese, many rescued from cruelty and neglect. Mom recalled in *Ahimsa* October 2000:

It was time for Jay to visit up-close representatives of these animals who are exploited as milk and meat machines and for whom he had been an advocate for so many years....Willis—a really big black and white steer who makes sure he's noticed—came forward to give Jay a special thank you. He licked Jay's red knitted hat, and then they stood cheek to cheek. Just one of Willis' front legs and shoulder were bigger than all of Jay!

Then the next week, Willis' face filled the TV screen as Jay called excitedly that there was a spot on the local news about the sanctuary and the life-sized "cowches"—handmade stuffed animals shaped like cows that are great for lounging company. Helga Tacreiter makes them to support her friends. (See TheCowSanctuary.org.)

*   *   *

Visit a farm animal sanctuary to connect with the ambassadors who represent all the animals that you are no longer hurting. Check online for one of the many sanctuaries nationwide such as Farm Sanctuary in New York and California, Woodstock Farm Animal Sanctuary in New York, Chenoa Manor in Pennsylvania, Pigs Peace Sanctuary in Washington, and Animal Place in California. Perhaps you will volunteer there.

Becky's Dilemma

Anne Dinshah

Becky is a close friend who has been vegan for many years. Her name and details of this dilemma have been changed for publication, but it is based on a true story.

Becky has volunteered countless hours for her local vegan group and is a kind, levelheaded, realistic person who practices dynamic harmlessness to the best of her abilities. She went back to school to become a lawyer because she felt she could help empower people against injustice. I visited her shortly after she passed the bar exam. Becky was busily helping people—many of them pro bono. She seemed happy about her work and family, but something else was bothering her.

Becky informed me that she and her husband are no longer vegan. "We are on a plant-based diet. We don't use the vegan word anymore." I was saddened by this but tried not to belabor the subject too much, knowing she would explain in her own time. Over the course of our weekend together I learned her reasons.

The main one centered around her car. She had a reliable car that had plenty of life left in it. Her father suddenly died and Becky's mother insisted Becky take his car. Her mother would be more comfortable driving Becky's old car, so they switched to make her mother happy.

Her father's car was in terrific shape and would last much longer than her old car. It basically had low mileage in terms of around-town miles, but a few trips to Florida made the odometer display a high number. She estimated it was worth at least $23,000 in relation to what it would cost her to buy a comparable car on the market. However, she would only get about $15,000 for it if she tried to sell the car due to the high mileage and some minor damage. She was practically the original owner because she knew the car's history, but selling it would make it a third-owner car. Most importantly, the car had leather seats, which didn't sit well with her vegan values. She had much to consider.

Her vegan friends immediately chastised her for keeping the car and refused to travel with her. They even told her she couldn't call herself a vegan anymore if she drove the car.

Becky analyzed her options. A: She could sell the car, use the $15,000 from it with $10,000 she already had saved towards her next car, and purchase a potentially comparable car. That would put the leather seats back in the supply chain for someone who actually wants leather seats—thus potentially saving an equal animal. B: She could sell the car like in "A" but go into debt by applying the money to a more expensive, truly new car that would also require a loan. Or C: She could be thankful for the gift, keep a sentimental connection with her father, have a known reliable source of transportation, not incur further debt, and have $10,000 do with what she pleases. Don't forget D: Take the car to the junkyard—not much of an option on many ethical and environmental levels, but it does respond to the throw-out-nonvegan-items-immediately plan. Or E: Give the car away. How would she get to work and what would her mother think? Perhaps there is option F.

The car was exactly what she needed other than the seats. It made good sense to pick option C except that she hadn't owned anything else leather in years. Becky needed a reliable car immediately as she was beginning her new job. She decided to keep the car at least until a better option presented itself.

Becky couldn't sleep with her decision. She didn't feel connected to the plant-based-diet moniker. She wanted to be vegan. Perhaps there was a way to make atonement.

What if she donated the $10,000 that she had been saving towards a new car to vegan causes that would help more animals than the ones hurt by the leather seats? She resolved to do that and asked me to help her. I offered opinions on organizations that do good work. She suggested I use half the money towards speaking engagements at organizations that could not afford to pay a speaker's fee or even travel expenses. Some of the speaking could be in her region, and she would help set up the tour. She would save the other $5000 until she was confident at her new job and had comfortable savings again. If all went well, she would finance a lecture tour, traveling further afield with the other half of the money the following year. Becky insisted, so I agreed.

For the first group of lectures, I stayed with Becky. On the way to each lecture, she drove me in her husband's car. Although I respected her decision she knew it would be best if she didn't flaunt her leather seats under my bottom for all to see. Then a few miles from our destination, his car had a minor breakdown. It could be repaired but not quickly enough to get me to the lecture on time. Her husband came to pick us up, switch cars, and fix his.

So I—the vegan speaker—arrived at the venue in a car with leather seats. Luckily no one noticed, or at least no one said anything. Is that different from when I buy an airplane ticket, step onto the plane, and notice leather seats on the plane? I can't really get off the plane and hope the next one doesn't have leather seats. Or do I need to call every airline and keep track of which flights have leather? Even if I did, they frequently need to change the planes on the route at the last minute.

I slept okay that night despite sitting on a leather seat in her car. Two people came up to us after the lecture thanking me for the information and pledging to become vegan immediately. If we are keeping score, that already atones for keeping the car.

This story helps us think not only about an ethical dilemma but also about the hazard of being judgmental of others. People who take a holier-than-thou approach by rating others are not practicing ahimsa. Pushing others down and stepping on them, in action or words, is not the way to get to a higher level. Remember that the path of ahimsa opens new doors to creative service, altruistic and unselfish living, and devoting oneself to helping make this world a better, saner, more harmonious place in which to live.

*　　*　　*

Becky shows it is not always as simple as Plan 1, 2, or 3, and it is not right for anyone else to judge an ethical dilemma.

"The love for all living creatures is the most noble attribute of man."　　　　　　　　　　　　　　　　　—Charles Darwin

Victoria's Ethical Insights

Victoria Hart

In developing her story in this book (page 226), Victoria also shared her insights into ethical dilemmas:

Those roots of authentic veganism that Jay helped establish have grown into golden threads that are now woven into the fabric of my life. I work as a professional artist and designer. I make great efforts to find and use eco-friendly, cruelty-free art supplies, which can be challenging, depending on the project.

Over the years, I have refused jobs that conflicted with my ethical vegan values. In one such case, I turned down lucrative work from a zoo that wanted plush animal toy designs to sell in their nature gift shop. I needed the money badly but still would not accept the work offered. Nevertheless, it was a test of moral conviction for me, and it led to greater gains.

Aside from work challenges, there are personal ones I faced, too. It's a good thing that I didn't expect veganism to make me wealthy, likable, or popular. Close family connections are missing since I've spoken out against animal victimization. My family thinks I am a dissident who's extreme and self-righteous. As my ethics grew and developed from living as an authentic vegan, friends started to disappear. My beliefs conflicted with their indoctrinated pro-harm/pro-exploitation mindset from which I was able to break free. That was tough.

Once I had to move quickly from my apartment because of death threats I received from a neighbor. This was the result of coming to the rescue of a cat he and his girlfriend were torturing. More recently in a similar incident I chose to flee a different apartment temporarily because of the danger I faced after coming to the rescue of a neighbor's emaciated and severely mistreated dog. I can only confirm that the dog survived and has a loving new home now. I don't know what became of the cat, though she did escape her torturers. I have no regrets about speaking out for animals and doing the right thing, even when my own safety was at risk.

The primary principle of veganism requires us to stand up against exploitation and harm, which in turn has made me more courageous and less egocentric than I could have imagined. The rewards don't end there; they are continuous and ever surprising. I've never felt like I sacrificed anything by going vegan. It has been said that as long as there is true conviction there is no sacrifice. So it is a joy, comfort, and gain to be this in tune with my awakened core values and to embrace reverence for life, which is an equally important principle of veganism.

Because I have a natural talent for it, I have followed the call to be a "vegan buddy." I make myself available to help people achieve their own stated goals. When they need help implementing or being faithful to authentic veganism as they themselves have stated they want to do, I am there.

We all find it difficult if not impossible to walk in a straight line towards veganism. As with any goal or ideal we set, this seems to be the norm: we stray side to side and teeter-totter more often than we'd like to admit. I know I have. Some people stay stuck in places for great stretches of time. I have. This is not abnormal behavior, and no one should be shamed for it. What I've found to be true is that there are some people who—when they are in danger of falling off track or falling back asleep—need a kind and considerate wake-up call coming from another caring person. When that is the case, I nudge them back to their upright stance with LOVE in capital letters. They can regain their bearings and once again head straight for their desired goal. Maybe even with more gusto than before.

There was a time I thought I wanted to "wear a vegan police badge." I had erroneously thought they were akin to vegan buddies. But after talking with Anne and Freya about this, I saw how the term vegan police is often misconstrued, carries a negative connotation more often than not, and can be detrimental or even downright dangerous. It is, after all, an unregulated authoritative position; think of how an unscrupulous self-appointed vigilante might act. Then I realized that many people acting as vegan police pollute the vegan movement by refusing to acknowledge or embrace the foundational principles and ethics of veganism made clear in the definition and explained in this book. That is most unfortunate and saddens me.

One of the most effective things I can do as an usher to a viable vegan world is to be a good example. People do not realize how powerful their example is. When humans witness living examples of effervescent, glowing love which is what veganism spotlights and nurtures, they do lean in a little closer—like a moth to a warm bright light—and are likely to open wide their eyes and ears, and ultimately their hearts open up as well. This is powerful stuff. Veganism is not interested in opening wallets and purses or in attaining shallow human relationships. Veganism seeks out and speaks to those who are ready to discover and develop all that they can in this realm of selfless truth and beauty—the land of The Golden Rule and reverence for life.

In ethical dilemmas I do not judge others but must exercise careful discernment. I may objectively help people discover a previously unconsidered solution. I believe we should strive to uncover—or create—a nonviolent/nonharming alternative to every obstacle or ethical dilemma we face. There is always at least one to be found. We need not ever cause harm.

If, for example, vegans feel they must take a prescribed medicine that has been tested on animals and is made with animal sourced ingredients, then they could at the very same time they are swallowing pills use the other hand to urgently write or otherwise contact the pharmaceutical companies, helping create public demand for 100 percent cruelty-free medicines that harm no creature in the making and testing. As a result of their activism in the direct correspondence with drug manufacturers, perhaps they may discover that there already is another medicine for their ailment that fits their demand. In any given instance, we can be a part of the solution rather than opting to be a part of the problem. Believe it and make it happen.

I remember the first time I faced an ethical dilemma in the work world after becoming vegan. I made a desperate phone call to Jay and explained my situation. Jay listened attentively and then gave me the answer I needed. I have never forgotten it because it is so simple and useful for every ethical dilemma I've faced since. Jay told me about the time he worked at a gas station where one of his duties was to sell cigarettes.* If you know anything about Jay's beliefs about personal health responsibilities, you understand how repugnant this must have been to him. He went on to explain, "I did it until I couldn't do it anymore. Then I stopped." What he meant—and said so succinctly—is that his conscience wouldn't allow him to continue the disharmony. Whatever it takes, however long it takes, actively pursue the correction to what the conscience says needs to be aligned. It may happen sooner than you think.

Heroes, mentors, leaders, and vegan buddies have their place as inspirational guides and helpers, but in the end we are each responsible for our own failures, success stories, and walking our talk. Here's what I've learned over time and wish to pass on to the reader as a final thought worth sharing: Believe in and be scrupulously committed to moving towards the goal of veganism in its true ethical meaning with the pillars of ahimsa. There is no requirement that your beliefs and actions be met with acceptance by anyone else. It's only important that they align within yourself.

*This was in New Jersey where gas station attendants actually do pump gas as their primary responsibility, then and now. It should be noted that Jay had everyday needs, including a family to feed, but actively pursued work more aligned with his values and found it. Ethical dilemmas test values, and there are multiple factors to consider, not all of which are disclosed in recounting a story.

*   *   *

Authors' reminder: Please remember that individual medical and/or dietary advice should be given from qualified professionals, preferably vegan themselves. This book and all opinions contained within are for general educational information. Often the most powerful tool to enable change is to have a friend who shares your values; that is the beautiful role of a vegan buddy.

*   *   *

Victoria has developed new friends, including the authors, who love her. True friends understand and accept you. Have you experienced negativity in becoming vegan? Maybe your family and friends are not yet ready or willing to be awakened to their role in perpetuating violence in the world. Family and friends are the hardest to convince that you are doing the right thing. Consider joining your local vegan Meetup group; they may become like a chosen family. If there isn't an existing group, then start one.

Convinced Canadian

Dennis Bayomi

I first met Jay at the joint conference of the American Vegan Society (AVS) and the Vegetarian Union of North America in Portland, Oregon, in the summer of 1993. Initially I was somewhat surprised that the president of AVS was so serious and businesslike, but as the days progressed, the lighthearted, indeed playful side of Jay Dinshah became quite apparent. Jay's veg-oriented imitations of notable historic figures at the evening sessions were hilarious!

The most substantial impact Jay had on me was his and Freya's dedication to the vegan movement, organizing an event bringing together the leading North American vegan activists. I'd been lacto-vegetarian for two years when I arrived at my first-ever veg event. With so many convincing presenters and sessions at the conference—and such a well-stocked book room—I became vegan during the first night!

*　　*　　*

Dennis Bayomi started the Winnipeg Vegetarian Association (WVA) shortly after returning home from the 1993 conference. WVA fosters vegetarianism and veganism in his region of central Canada. In 1999 he launched VegDining.com to expand his vegetarian outreach beyond the local community. Both the WVA and VegDining still run today continuing the common mission of promoting vegetarianism and veganism far and wide.

*　　*　　*

Watch "Impersonations by H. Jay Dinshah" and other videos on YouTube on the *Powerful Vegan Messages* channel.

257

Vegan Advocacy: A Global Imperative and Personal Declarative

Saurabh Dalal

As followers of the Jain religion and placing great importance on the principle and practice of ahimsa (nonviolence), my parents instilled in me early on the fundamental idea that animals have the capacity to think and feel and therefore have a moral right to existence just like humans. I've been vegetarian since before my entrance into this world, and I've been vegan since 1991.

Becoming vegan was one of the most important decisions I've made for myself and a result of learning how animals are exploited, abused, and killed for food in our world today. Because animals are denied the right to live for their own purposes, I wanted to end my involvement in their oppression—a personal choice but also part of a greater movement to make the world a more just and peaceful place for all.

In 1990 I became involved in veg advocacy. I knew of People for the Ethical Treatment of Animals (PETA) and Vegetarian Resource Group (VRG), and then I found the Vegetarian Society of the District of Columbia (VSDC) as a group working in the local community. Within a year, I was asked to be on the board. Then I was asked by Madge Darneille (page 89) to be on the board of the Vegetarian Union of North America (VUNA) and soon after became the North American regional secretary for the International Vegetarian Union (IVU).

The 1993 Portland, Oregon, conference was my first veg conference where I met Jay and Freya. Although I was raised vegetarian, at the conference I was amazed by the commitment of so many people in promoting the vegan message, and I made many personal connections. Planning began for the 1995

International Vegan Festival (IVF) in San Diego, and I got involved. Regular contact with Jay and Freya was motivating and memorable. VUNA and AVS were co-organizers.

A direct result of the IVF in 1995 was the genesis of the DC VegFest. I wanted to have an event in the DC area and devised the idea of a miniconference organized by VSDC that was free, open to the public, and easy to access for the people of Washington DC. We had speakers, food booths, videos, and information. From the first DC VegFest in 1997, it has grown to an annual event now organized through Compassion Over Killing and attended by 10,000 people.

Founded in 1927, VSDC is the oldest veg group in North America before the word vegan was coined in 1944. Since I was named president in 1996 everything VSDC plans is always vegan including the VegFest. Being an all-volunteer group presents many challenges so one ongoing focus area for a group like VSDC is to keep meeting many people and then find and nurture interest in those who have the greatest organizer potential. We are always looking for people to be involved and keep the view that any skill or talent a person has can be utilized by VSDC. We also manage the DC Area Vegan Meetup group. With five to seven events per month that we organize there's always something happening in DC.

I spent a weekend with the Dinshahs in Malaga when we were organizing the 1995 conference. It was completely inspiring. I remember staying up late into the night with Jay and Maynard Clark discussing the philosophy of ahimsa and what we should do with our lives. It congealed the notion that each of us should play our part in building a better society. It broadened my thinking to see the potential of my involvement in the promotion of ahimsa as one small part of a large and broad-based movement for change—a global imperative.

Jay's dedication, conviction, leadership, and passion have helped me to see the importance of each of us working to make a difference in our world that desperately needs this important message. It's not just the words but what people do with every ounce of their being. It's important for all of us, to whatever extent we can, to do what we can.

More recently, we're learning about resources, inefficiency, and the waste associated with food production that exploits and kills animals. There's an increasing understanding of climate change and the enormous connection with animal agriculture. This connection has the potential to move many people towards veganism.

Global organizations are starting to get it: if you really want to make the world a better place in so many ways, eliminate animal products. This type of information has to reach the masses again and again and become part of the vernacular. And once people go vegan for one reason, they start to understand its importance for other reasons. I feel that people who go vegan for a reason other than respect and compassion will appreciate the ethical reasons in time too.

A lot of people think being vegan is a sacrifice, that it takes a lot of effort to do it. Actually I've found that it's something that makes us feel more alive and really good about who we are, putting into perspective our place in the world, and challenged to build the world we really want to live in. What we gain from even small accomplishments far outweighs any sacrifice. Helping empower people to make positive changes in their lives—there's no better feeling!

*　　*　　*

Saurabh Dalal enjoys being involved in outreach, education, and greater advocacy of sustainable veganism and ahimsa as compelling solutions to many global problems. Saurabh serves as deputy chairperson of the International Vegetarian Union (IVU.org) and has been president of VSDC (VSDC.org) since

1996. He was VUNA president from 2005 to 2011. He works in various capacities with many other like-minded nonprofit groups and has been active in the Jain community on the local and international levels. He holds graduate degrees in physics and engineering, takes part in several professional and technical societies, and explores ways of integrating sound science into related areas. Saurabh is an AVS life member.

*   *   *

Check out all the great vegan events being offered in Washington DC. Attend the events or be inspired to create similar events in your area. Attend the DC VegFest or a VegFest near you.

Volunteer for your local group. You don't have to volunteer to do everything; just start with one thing and do it well. Encourage others to do likewise.

"I have from an early age abjured the use of meat, and the time will come when men such as I will look upon the murder of animals as they now look upon the murder of men."

—Leonardo daVinci

Becoming Vegan

Vesanto Melina, RD

The plight of egg-laying chickens and veal calves hit me hard, and vegan seeds were sown when I attended the 1993 AVS conference in Portland, Oregon. It was my first vegan conference, although I had been vegetarian for fifteen years and just mailed off to the publisher the manuscript for my first nutrition book, *Becoming Vegetarian*. Jay and the other Dinshahs provided rich soil to support growth of those vegan seeds into a strong vegan plant. At that vegan convention I had access to tasty vegan meals, a range of presentations that were informative, scientific, and inspirational, and of course wonderful people who had chosen with body, heart, and soul to be vegan—a new community.

I now have a series of vegan nutrition books in seven languages, most coauthored with dietitian Brenda Davis. When our book *Becoming Vegan* was first published in 2000, the dedication read "To those who inspire us with lives guided by conscience and compassion" and then named Jay and Freya Dinshah.

* * *

Vesanto Melina, MS, RD does consultations on vegan nutrition. (Nutrispeak.com) and is on the AVS speakers bureau. The entirely updated *Becoming Vegan Express Edition* received star rating by American Library Association as the "go-to book" on vegan nutrition and received a 2014 Canada Book Award. The more-detailed, fully-referenced *Becoming Vegan Comprehensive Edition* (2014) is for health professionals, college courses, and those fascinated by nutritional science.

* * *

Do you have nutritional questions? Are you *Becoming Vegan*?

Of Figs and Thistles

Anne and Jay Dinshah

We begin with an item that has been covered in the news in the past few years: pink slime. Also known as lean finely textured beef (LFTB), this is a main ingredient in hamburgers fed to school children. Many children don't have another option for lunch, nor do they really understand that it is parts of a cow.

Pink slime is comprised of scraps left after making cuts of meat from cows: connective tissue, blood vessels, nerves, and cartilage. To treat bacteria the industry treats it with ammonia. What a treat! Even representatives of the United States Department of Agriculture (USDA) have called it pink slime, although one producer of pink slime actually sued ABC News for defamation in covering the story.

The real issue is why do people eat hamburgers? Is it just tradition to put burgers on the grill? Why do people eat cows when there are so many compassionate food options? Isn't it really the seasonings and texture that attracts consumers, not the actual source of the burger?

According to many people who eat them, the best meat hamburgers are made from cows. Pink slime caused an outcry that LFTB may be worse for people's health than what was assumed to be "better" parts of cows. The meat industry continues using LFTB, but sued because the product was given a derogatory name. Let's call it correctly: "the last parts of dead cows with chemicals."

Given a true informed option, I believe most children don't want to eat animals. The inherent kindness and compassion born in most children has been suppressed by societal norms and big business marketing. If burgers are desired, let's give kids the option of veggie burgers, bean burgers, or nut burgers at every school in the country. It's vital to educate children about their food choices and give them true informed options. The next generation must ask, "Why?"

*   *   *

Twenty centuries ago, a wise teacher asked in an allegory whether we could gather any grapes from thorn bushes or pluck figs from thistles. He noted that a good tree cannot bring forth evil fruit nor a corrupt tree yield good fruit. (*Matthew* 7:16-18)

Here we are a couple of millennia later still taking away the freedom, the natural form and shape, and the very lives of billions of sentient and sensitive creatures each year, sacrificing them on the altar of our taste buds. We are still trying to find decent nourishment for our human bodies in the pathological animal matter that should be given a decent funeral and buried in a toxic-waste dump, not promoted with a government stamp of wholesomeness.

Such is the eternal optimism of the American consumer. We will accept this stuff as food even if it has a little label on it warning that it can make us very sick or past our expiration date if we don't keep our carrion deep frozen before we cook it to a cinder. Or a rubber-stamp on it certifies that a government expert has carefully watched as so many thousand chickens were dunked in the same septic tank of fecal-contaminated water. It seems the USDA wants us to think it's all right to carefully wash our family's food in the toilet if we sprinkle a little cleanser over it to make it pure and clean.

The problem is not just the manner with which the filth is handled or the technology used to process the garbage. When we start shopping among the products of the animal kingdom, which are capable of passing dozens upon dozens of diseases directly to humans, we are looking for our food in the refuse pile.

Truly we are attempting to gather grapes from thorns and

pluck figs from thistles. All the USDA directives attempting to whitewash the failure to produce wholesome offal will not conceal this fact.

There is a vast difference between a rutabaga and roadkill; and—like a rose—each will still smell the same by any other name. Heaven help the unwary or the gullible who confuse the two. Personally I prefer to eat my food ripe, not after rigor mortis has set in. I have yet to see a head of cabbage with a caution that you can wind up horribly sick or slightly dead if you cut it up and then use the same knife to slice your cucumber.

The vegan movement is not a political party, although some noted politicians are vegan. We will not win at all costs. We're not afraid of truth, even if your truth according to your conscience happens to differ a bit from mine at this point in time. We don't have to get elected to make a difference. What each of us eats, does, and says, helps change the world.

What we say about politics is equally true for religion. We can certainly learn what great world teachers have said about how good it is to be good and how much better it is to be kind, gentle, sincere, truthful, honest, and vegan than to be cruel, violent, devious, untruthful, dishonest, and meat eating. I am not suggesting these virtues or failings necessarily go together in the same individual. In examining and discussing various concepts and values as specifically applied to veganism, we need not come to blows over cultural, mythical, or theological points and beliefs.

Most of all, we should understand that in working to help animals—including humans—we cannot abandon our own humanity. My friends, have we not all seen fellow vegans embarrassing the movement in their well-intended but ill-advised efforts to further it? Some vegans think that our choosing foods with compassion gives us license to be rude, obnoxious, self-righteous, boorish, or downright threatening. Remember that one can love thy neighbor and disagree with his or her decisions.

A normal cat or dog will sense the kindness you express when you approach him or her and may lick your hand; if you brandish a stick at the same creature you will see a different reaction. Why should we expect a meat-eating human—or any human—to react to love or hatred in a less predictable manner? How can we hate creatures of habit who don't know any better, who do what we ourselves may have done last week, last month, or last year? Mahatma Gandhi said that "Means and ends are convertible terms in my philosophy of life."

The end does not justify the means. Dr. Rajendra Prasad said that "Gandhi was a firm believer in the maxim that the righteousness of the end does not and cannot justify the use of unrighteous means in attaining it. If wrong means are employed, and in the process the end itself becomes distorted, what is ultimately attained is not the righteous end as originally conceived but something akin to the unrighteous means applied."

In sixty-six years as a vegetarian—some two-thirds of this time as an active educator—I (Jay) have helped thousands toward this better way of life. I do not believe I have ever won an argument nor have I been able to help someone who felt threatened or antagonized by me or just didn't want to be educated about veganism. If we could wave a magic wand to hurt and punish all the meat eaters for their ignorance, we would still be left bearing our own burden of hatred, violence, and ignorance that we had made so heavy and ugly.

You build a skyscraper with steel and stone, not mud and muck. I've never been clever enough to understand the rationale of using thoughts and methods of hatred, belligerence, injustice, and exaggeration to build a better world of love, peace, fairness, and truth. I do know the animals appreciate you not eating them.

*   *   *

The New York Coalition for Healthy School Food teaches kids about food choices in schools and works with schools to provide options. Learn what you can do in New York, or get ideas to do likewise in your state at HealthySchoolFood.org.

Berry Inspirational

Rynn Berry

Jay was a tremendous inspiration to me because he was wholly dedicated to the cause of advancing veganism and animal rights. One day when he was toiling in the bookroom at the Vegetarian Summerfest conference, I vividly remember asking him if he ever took vacations. He said that he couldn't take a vacation until humans stopped abusing animals. He had a sense of urgency and mission that made him an indefatigable worker in their cause. Every act he performed was in the service of saving animal lives.

It is important to remember that, in addition to being an educator, Jay was also a great communicator in his own right. He was a writer of limpid, highly-readable prose that was on display in his quarterly journal, *Ahimsa*. He was also a compelling speaker who regaled his audiences at Summerfest and at the AVS conferences that he and Freya organized.

I am indebted to Jay for inviting me to be a speaker at the AVS conferences in Portland, Oregon; Seattle, Washington; and Boulder, Colorado; and the International Vegan Festival in San Diego, California. Not only did they provide a venue for me to influence and educate others, but also they gave me an opportunity to learn from other speakers. In fact, the germ of my book *Food for the Gods: Vegetarianism and the World's Religions* grew out of a series of talks on comparative religion and veganism that I was invited to give under AVS auspices at Lewis and Clark University in Portland, Oregon, back in 1993. Jay's brother Roshan filmed my presentations, copies of which are among my most precious possessions.

*　　*　　*

Rynn Berry (1945-2014) was the historical advisor for NAVS and a passionate speaker on the history of vegetarianism and veganism. He was the author of numerous books, including: *Famous Vegetarians and Their Favorite Recipes*, *The New Vegetarians*, and *Vegan Guide to New York City* with annual editions until 2014, and coauthor of *Becoming Raw* with Vesanto Melina and Brenda Davis. Rynn was on the AVS speakers bureau.

*　　*　　*

Watch Rynn's 1993 videos on the American Vegan Society YouTube channel.

Do you know vegan history so you know how to best further the work begun by others?

"As long as man continues to be the ruthless destroyer of lower living beings he will never know health or peace. For as long as men massacre animals, they will kill each other."　—Pythagoras

Strong Vegan Pillars

John Pierre

I owe a tremendous debt of gratitude to Jay Dinshah for his profound role in my introduction to ahimsa. I first met him in 1994 at Vegetarian Summerfest; I was making presentations on fitness.

After that initial meeting I looked forward to seeing him at more conferences. Although I enjoyed Jay's lectures what I cherished most was spending individual time with him. I chose not to go to other presenters' lectures, so instead I could be with Jay during the quieter times he worked at the Summerfest bookstore. He invested numerable hours in me every year with unwavering enthusiasm as I quizzed him on everything from the pillars of ahimsa to the Jain religion.

Between personal interactions, I reread his illuminating books, *Out of the Jungle, Health Can Be Harmless*, and *Here's Harmlessness*. They have served as a guiding light to me and countless others who continue to spread his message.

Jay's profound words persevere in fueling my desire to carry on his mission of love and care for all living beings. His messages of compassion and peace were the instrumental catalysts that inspired me to write *The Pillars of Health* especially the chapter on compassion and love.

*   *   *

John Pierre is a nutrition and fitness consultant, famous as a personal trainer to celebrities, rock stars, and Fortune 500 CEOs. For over a quarter century he has been improving the lives of others through his expertise in the areas of geriatrics, nutrition, fitness, women's empowerment, green living, and cognitive retainment and improvement. He teaches group classes and individual sessions and is a popular motivational speaker. John's book *The Pillars of Health* explains four solid principles that provide a strong foundation for vibrant and lasting health: nourishment from real food, creative stimulation for the mind, joyous physical movement for the body, and a spiritual philosophy focused on compassion, love, and peace. John is a member of the AVS speakers bureau.

*   *   *

As Jay aged, sometimes he preferred the quieter times in the bookstore over the role of conference coordinator or speaker. Perhaps he was grooming John and others to carry the torch of ahimsa.

*   *   *

You don't have to have met Jay for the illuminating message of ahimsa to reach you. Use books such as *The Pillars of Health* and *Powerful Vegan Messages* to illuminate the way. Catch a lecture by John Pierre when he travels through your part of the country. Also be sure to exercise to keep your body as strong as your mind.

Professional Vegan Cooking

Ken Bergeron

At my first Vegetarian Summerfest in 1994, Jay greeted me before anyone else and made me feel good by knowing who I was. I was very impressed when I realized who he was. Jay set the foundation for me to work in the vegetarian-vegan movement.

At the time I never could have imagined that my work would entail teaching vegan cooking workshops for dining services at many colleges and universities, and sometimes workshops for students too. I became the Summerfest directing chef the next year where I relished educating dining staff at the University of Pittsburgh at Johnstown (UPJ) about vegan foods. About dulse, one of the UPJ staff said, "I ain't eatin' no tobacky!" And several years later she admitted that she tried it in the Manhattan Sea Vegetable Chowder and liked it very much. Another cook said he would never eat tofu. A fellow cook said to try the Tofu Cutlets with Mushroom Sauce. He did and had two portions!

In 1999 I published a cookbook titled *Professional Vegetarian Cooking*. When it first came out I wished to offer it at Summerfest, and Jay was in charge of the bookstore at that time. Jay asked me how many of the recipes were vegan. When I replied, "All of them," his smile told me that he was pleased.

Jay also became my culinary adviser for curry dishes on the menu at Summerfest. I would go to the bookstore and ask Jay if he had a moment to check my seasoning. He always made time for me, and we had some time to chat together as he became my curry master!

*　　*　　*

Ken Bergeron is an executive chef certified by the American Culinary Federation. Ken was the directing chef for sixteen Vegetarian Summerfests from 1995 to 2011. His children enjoyed accompanying him to the conference.

Ken won the first-ever gold medal for a vegan table at the Culinary Olympics in Frankfurt, Germany in 1992. Competing against nonvegan entries, he showcased a complete meal which included appetizer, entrée, side, and dessert with a theme of vegetables around the world. In 1990 he achieved the first vegan gold medal for a seven-course meal in the United States at the Connecticut Chef's Association in the American Culinary Federation. Ken attained the first gold medal for a vegan pastry table in the United States at the Connecticut Chef's Association on April 1 1993, fooling everyone who couldn't believe he used no cream, dairy, or sugar. They were also surprised with his creativity in presentation such as a lentil dish that turned out to be chocolate, and a soup made with oatmeal cookies.

*　　*　　*

Do you have a passion for cooking? Cultivate that passion and share vegan food on a big scale. Maybe you will also be a Culinary Olympian.

"Be the change you want to see in the world."
—Mahatma Gandhi

To Tell the Truth

H. Jay Dinshah

To tell the truth we must live it. Only when our every thought, word, and deed can stand the strong light of conscience's scrutiny can we really be called truthful. Every sincere and earnest seeker comes upon many moments of truth in a lifetime.

When one's attention has been drawn to injustice, cruelty, exploitation, suffering, and pain, does one greet the revelation with a head-in-the-sand attitude? Or does one meet it in the forthright manner, searching one's soul to learn what can be done to remedy—not merely alleviate—the situation?

You have to live with your own conscience. Let me be more specific. How pleasing would that stylish fur wrap be if the wearer realizes the suffering of the little creatures dying in the snow with their feet caught between relentless jaws of steel? How tasty would that steak be if the consumer could hear the shrieks and groans of the helpless animal dying to give him that meat?

How warm would a person sleep under those woolen blankets, with an understanding of the callous cruelties of the world's wool-and-mutton industry. Would one's heart perhaps melt a bit, were she to suffer as the hapless sheep so often do, including in many cases freezing to death with the all-or-nothing shearing practices? How much cow juice could a child swallow if the awful cries of grief were ringing in his ears—cries of mother and baby separated so he could have the stolen moo-milk?

How long would a woman wear that lovely silk scarf if she could feel one tenth part of the ordeal that each of those tiny silkworms had to undergo in being roasted or boiled to death—a process known in the trade by the quaint name of stifling? What value would thoughtful, sensitive people place upon a strand of natural or cultured pearls were they to be apprised of the terrible slaughter of harmless creatures for each and every pearl?

How thrilling would that rodeo be to any but the most callous and sadistic person were the general public to be made aware of the fiendish pressure put by a leather strap on the bucking bronco's most sensitive glands to make him buck and appear ferocious? How many parents would want their children to see the pitiful trained animal acts at circuses, if they had to endure the countless prods, electric shocks, and other tricks used to train animals to remember their cues and stunts?

How differently we react to everyday materials when faced with the truth about them. Note the totally different reaction to "pâté de fois gras" as compared to "enlarged liver of diseased goose." How easily we accept pig flesh or backside of swine when proffered as bacon or ham or some other euphemism.

How many intelligent and devoted human beings would call their loved ones honey if they ever understood the simplest facts about this material that is mixed with the bee's bodily fluids for digestion and then spit up to be re-eaten by other bees? How many could bring themselves to eat an egg if they bothered to learn the most rudimentary points of anatomy and biology?

If modern people were obliged to forage for their food or grow it themselves—instead of buying it neatly wrapped in plastic— how different might the picture be? It is easy to envisage highly developed, intelligent, and humane men, women, and children plucking a dinner from the bountiful boughs of trees and the plants of the garden.

Have you ever visited the places where poultry and eggs are "grown" or the factory where steak is "produced"? To a person of even average sensitivity, every single sense cries out to flee such a place via the nearest exit with all possible haste, as I wanted to do in the introduction to this book.

One of my favorite quotes is from Victoria Moran. "The most beautiful thing about ahimsa is that its rightness defies doubt.

When one is in a quandary of all the mystical aspects of what spiritual leaders have taught, the only point that's beyond criticism totally is doing the most good and the least harm one can."

When this truth is known to us—really understood at last—are we ready for it? To tell the truth and to live up to it may at times seem to be the most difficult thing on Earth. It is also the one really worthwhile thing there is in this life.

May you be blessed with such truth.

*   *   *

Throughout this book we mention many individuals and organizations. Check out their websites and also those of the following organizations promoting a vegan lifestyle:

Circle of Compassion, CircleofCompassion.org

Compassion Over Killing, COK.net

Friends of Animals, FriendsofAnimals.org

In Defense of Animals, IDAUSA.org

Physicians Committee for Responsible Medicine, PCRM.org

The Vegan Society (U.K.), VeganSociety.com

United Poultry Concerns, UPC-online.org

Vegan Action, VeganAction.org

A Side We Didn't See or Hear

Maynard Clark

Both Jay and Freya charmed me, but watching and hearing Jay play the piano, though he often denied it, delighted me most. I attended one Vegetarian Summerfest alone as a graduate student. After the first dinner, since I hadn't yet made friends and didn't want to miss anything, I wandered into the evening meeting. I was early for the 7:00 pm meeting, around 6:20, and Jay was preparing the stage and moving things around.

When Jay had readied everything for the evening program, he sat down at an old piano and began playing—sometimes energetically, sometimes with relaxation—Christian hymns and other songs. His versatility and repertoire were impressive. Jay's emotional warmth with the piano reassured me in my very first vegetarian conference. Most of the other conference attendees missed seeing a side of Jay Dinshah I will never forget—something truly special and endearing though seldom mentioned about him.

At an AVS conference on the west coast in 1994, Jay pulled me aside to ask my opinion about collaborating with Vegans International, a new European group that wanted to visit America in the form of a vegan conference. They wanted AVS to organize the event for them, and Jay asked me if VUNA might want to partner, sharing the work and the profits. For a decade I had organized the Boston Vegetarian Society's expert speakers' series and had worked with Jay and Freya in their west coast program. If VUNA signed on, I would become the program coordinator for the five-day International Vegan Festival in San Diego, August 6-13 1995. The VUNA Council agreed, so we met several times in Portland, Oregon, then later at the SunCrest AVS headquarters.

Saurabh Dalal and I represented VUNA in the planning meetings, Jay and Freya represented AVS, and Julia Hope Jacquel represented Vegans International.

An effective and meticulous worker, Jay seemed to squeeze results from each moment. He physically walked us through the AVS production building with its book storage, magazine archives, and the production materials and equipment for *Ahimsa*, which he was then trying to modernize. I stayed in one of their gracious upstairs guest rooms, which Jay had nearly finished renovating.

Over several months, Jay mentored me, coaching the details of booking and negotiating with speakers, setting up the program budget, and not conceding to speakers more than our budget could handle. He also taught me the mechanics of organizing and running three to five concurrent and balanced program tracks and crafting catchy lecture titles accompanied by succinct descriptions of their content.

Because Jay had walked me through how to organize the larger conferences, I learned to do larger events with confidence. Within weeks after the festival ended, I brought together a group of Massachusetts Institute of Technology students—mostly graduate students—and traveled in two or three cars from Boston to Canada see the Toronto Vegetarian Food Festival in mid-September. We imagined the Boston Vegetarian Food Festival, first held on May 5 1995. We consulted with the Toronto organizers and customized for our own use their protocol handbook. Later we organized for VUNA an online "How to Organize a Vegetarian Food Festival" manual using a graduate student in creative writing who distilled these instructions and experiences for general use by vegetarian and vegan community organizers.

*   *   *

Maynard Clark became vegan while he was a Harvard graduate student because of Freya Dinshah's friendly, nondirective influence at an NAVS vegetarian conference. He has been vegan most of his life.

Maynard founded the Boston Vegetarian Society in 1984 and led it for many years. He was national education coordinator for FARM's annual Great American Meatout campaign before the Internet had become general reality. Using the telephone, he grew the "meatout" outreach event from about 150 United States events to over a thousand events in the United States, Canada, and Mexico. In 1993, he founded and guided the Vegetarian Resource Center in the greater Boston area. Around the year 2000, Maynard urged vegetarians onto the Internet and into special interest groups and focused online discussion and networking groups.

Maynard has served as vice president and council member of VUNA. Currently, he hosts and sponsors several active vegan Meetups in the greater Boston area and remains active with the Boston Vegetarian Society. He works for the Harvard School of Public Health in global health. He is an AVS life member.

Maynard is a vegan buddy mentor for new vegans as listed online in the Animal Rights Zone's global mentor program at: ARZone.ning.com/group/vegan-buddies.

*   *   *

Are you new to vegan advocacy and want to do bigger things? Have you found a mentor? Mentorships can be created through vegan organizations both at the professional and personal levels. You might opt for an online mentor or a local one. Sometimes great mentors don't realize they have something to offer until you ask them.

Remember to Relax

Anne Dinshah

Now that you have been inspired by many people and have begun brainstorming all the many ways to be a vegan advocate, I would be remiss if I didn't remind you that Dad died of a heart attack. He internalized all the suffering of animals and was typically under great stress.

Unfortunately his idea of good exercise was swinging a hammer. His real exercise rarely went beyond a little nature walk. He did enjoy a bit of boating, music, and dancing, but usually he was too busy. Remember to save some quality time for yourself—more than Jay did.

Also remember to earn enough money that you can take care of your basic needs before serving others and the animals. We never felt poor—we were rich in so many more beneficial ways than money. I remember too often Dad having to humbly ask the local bank for another loan, using his good name to keep the heat on in the winter while we prepared for a conference and to purchase books. He repaid them after the event. He took long-term loans from members for AVS general operating expenses. Once he sold a donated sofa and our TV to buy food. Sometimes Mom did seasonal sales or factory jobs. We were fortunate to also have family around for support.

Generally Dad worked nine-to-five jobs in bookkeeping or sales and then worked at AVS at night and weekends. Then he worried about how many hours he was wasting making money that he should be campaigning for solving the animals' plight. There was often not enough time left for fun and relaxation.

Carole Baral reminisced, "I would be up very early in the morning to get ready to teach my yoga classes at Vegetarian

Summerfest, and when I got to the room at six in the morning with my mat, there was Jay playing beautifully on the piano not even aware of my presence. It was a private side of Jay."

Dad's work bore no commitment to the clock. He might work until two in the morning and be up again at five. Sneaking that piece—or peace—of relaxation for a moment at random hours of the day helped him focus on all he needed to do the rest of the time.

Every time Dad returned home from scouting college campuses to host future conferences, he reported on all the important things, such as how many Bösendorfers and Steinways he could access and if there were a chance to play a pipe organ in an auditorium. He loved to play and sing the oldies for an empty room. At home, providing light evening entertainment got him out of doing dinner dishes.

Whether it's a sport, music, or social endeavor, people need ways to free their minds, even if only for a little while and without admitting its importance, but it's healthier to admit to being a well-rounded person. Dad internalized the suffering of the animals to the point that it hurt his health and, I believe, ultimately led to his death. Yet, he believed he was invincible.

Once he drove to Austin, Texas, to visit me there and switch cars because mine was giving me trouble. I convinced him to stay and relax for a couple days by allowing him to work at driving the motorboat for me while I coached rowers. He loved saying he was working, so he volunteered to drive for another coach; Dad loved boating.

One evening I invited our vegan friend Gabriel Figueroa over for dinner. After dinner, we played *The Book of Questions*. Dad was asked, "If you have to die of your own choosing, when and how would it be?" He answered, "Age 348 by the bullet from a jealous husband." Then he remembered I am his daughter and said, "Don't tell your mother I said that." I have every confidence that he was faithful to Mom, but his answer revealed his belief in his own immortality, vitality, and virility. It also exposed the knowledge that it will take many more years than an average lifespan to accomplish his goal of closing all the slaughterhouses before he takes a day off.

Carole said, "Another memory: Jay and his daughter Anne would do bunny shows to entertain the group. He would hop around and wriggle his nose like a child with innocence and abandon....A man who could also play."

When Dad was required to go to a social function that involved a dance, he resigned himself to have optimal fun. Many people couldn't believe it was Jay on the dance floor hopping around like a rabbit. He was one of the most energetic people when he was on the dance floor. He actually took dancing classes when he was a young man, hoping it would be a good way to meet his mate. As it turned out, he wooed his love Freya by writing, not dancing.

I hope this book is inspiring you to take an active role in helping end the suffering of animals, encourage better human health, and make a stand for plant-sourced foods to save the environment. Activists tend to be some of the most hardworking, passionate people on the planet. Many are new to veganism and expect everyone to get it quickly and right away. Be patient, yet keep the sense of urgency. The world is counting on our success. Occasionally one must break from the burdens and enjoy a different melody to lighten the load.

*   *   *

Have you been working really hard to further your career, your life goals, and/or veganism? Remember to take time to relax occasionally for your health and well-being. You will be happier and able to do more good in the long run. Keep fired up to do good work instead of falling victim to activist burnout.

Vegan and Sharing

Jackie and Jay Steinberg

Jackie recalls: Ilse from Ulm Germany was visiting this country for the first time, and I wanted to serve her a delicious American meal when she came to my apartment. I had prepared a fried-chicken dinner with all the trimmings. When she came to the table she said, "Oh, I don't eat that!"

I said, "You don't eat what?" She went on to explain that she didn't eat any flesh foods and that she loves animals too much to require anyone to kill them for her lifestyle pleasure. I love animals too, and so it made a lot of sense to me to live a lifestyle free of animal violence. Hence, I learned to choose delicious vegan foods, and Ilse learned to tell her host before a meal was served that she didn't eat any flesh foods.

My husband, also named Jay, and I attended our first of many AVS conferences back in the late 1990s to be with like-minded individuals and to learn from them. We were struck by this new concept of consideration for all life and to seriously look at the choices we were making. It was obvious how compassionate and dedicated Jay Dinshah was when he gave a seminar or talked to you one on one.

When one has love and compassion for all life, the ahimsa concept for living makes sense. Jay talked about The Golden Rule and that we cannot only look at "What's in it for me?" but to have a much broader vision to include all life. His example gave us the foundation to live more of the ahimsa concept and sometimes to share it with others.

However, we usually find that most people are only interested in making dietary changes if it will enhance their health rather than to make changes based on compassion. And, interestingly, they require others to do the dirty work in order to satisfy their dietary requirements. If they had to do the killing themselves, they would be vegans today!

My husband goes to business luncheons and always orders a vegan meal. Most people at the table are very impressed by what he is served and often decide to order a vegan meal next time themselves. Over the years, he has noticed many more businessmen and women choosing the delicious vegan entrée over the meat offering. Our family and friends are very cooperative in accepting and accommodating our dietary preferences. Progress is slow but coming.

*　　*　　*

Jackie and Jay Steinberg live in a suburb west of St. Louis, Missouri. Jay is a commercial real estate agent and teaches continuing education classes for the Missouri Real Estate Commission. Jackie is retired from a career as a music education instructor for kindergarten through eighth grade general music and fourth through eighth grade chorale and instrumental music. They both like to read. Jay loves to grow vegetables in his veganic garden. They are AVS life members.

*　　*　　*

You don't have to be an author, doctor, or dynamic speaker to teach others. Be a positive glowing example of the vegan way of life. People are naturally inquisitive and attracted to your actions. Be the neighbor, the coworker, the friend who touches people one -on-one by being yourself. Sometimes those closest to you such as family and friends are the hardest to reach with vegan messages. Actions aligned with your values may speak volumes to those who do not hear the buzz of information from louder sources.

Shine the Light on the Environment

Dr. Michael Klaper

If the ethical reasons for not eating the animals are not enough to convince you, let's discuss the basic environmental problems with our human greed for meat. Protecting the environment is another ethical responsibility we all share as temporary inhabitants of the Earth.

In 1967 H. Jay Dinshah wrote a book entitled *Out of the Jungle* that has become a classic on the theory and practice of veganism and ahimsa—dynamic harmlessness. Most of us who grew up in the northern hemisphere were raised with a biased awareness of the jungle—the darkest parts of deepest Africa, the mosquito-ridden overgrowth of the Amazon, and the dense and ominous jungles of Borneo.

The very word jungle conjures up images of poisonous snakes, deadly diseases, fearsome spiders, man-eating cats, and perhaps most frightening of all—man-eating humans. So Jay used this term as a metaphor for the ethical jungle of our behavior toward our fellow humans, fellow animals, and the planet we all share. He knew that the jungle we hold in our fears is the darkest reality of ourselves.

We gaze at our planet through orbiting satellite photos and discover more about the belt of tropical green that girdles the Earth at the equator. We learn that these are not the loathsome jungles of our imagination but actually the richest concentrations of life on Earth. These are what we have now learned to call rainforests.

Life-giving waters pour from tropical skies daily in South America, Africa, and Asia, and the forests respond—lush, verdant, and powerful. Cradles of life on land, these towering cathedrals of green are massive storehouses of millions of life forms and most of the DNA on Earth. Each rainforest tree is a Noah's Ark for multitudes of species of plants and animals living together in patterns of unimaginable complexity and interdependence.

Untouched by the Ice Ages that buried and gouged the northern continents, these ancient tropical forests are integral to forces essential for all life on the planet—the cycling of oxygen and carbon, the maintenance of normal weather and rainfall patterns, and the stability of global temperature. The rainforests are the sources for the longest and most vital rivers on Earth, the Amazon and the Nile.

Yet daily, the massive disruption of this intricate, life-sustaining system occurs in rainforests around the world. The astronauts have reported that, on some days from two hundred miles above Earth, they haven't been able to see the Amazon basin and most of South America at all due to the smoke from the fires of the burning rainforests. The reasons for rainforest destruction are many—exploding human populations, poverty, greed, economic desperation—but the main driving force is the rapacious appetite for land on which to produce beef cattle and soybeans to feed them.

When forests are burned, the charred remains are usually used for soy monocropping to produce livestock feed. Otherwise, the land can be stocked with only one hungry bovine per acre, on average, as that's all that the resulting vegetation can sustain. Even then, the land typically becomes unusable for grazing cattle after only a few years. So it's nonsensical for "experts" to call for intensifying cattle-grazing on this land, as they often do.

Where the Earth-aware person sees rainforests as abundant life, the industrialist, politician, or cattle rancher sees cash. The smoke from these tragic infernos not only contains the ashes of trees and the animals who lived in them but the secrets of plants that some researchers believe might have held potential botanical treatments for cancer, HIV/AIDS, or other dreaded diseases.

A final tragedy of rainforest beef is that most of it is not even destined to feed the hungry South American and African people upon whose land it is produced, but is exported to the restaurants and meat markets of North America and Europe. Soy feed and beef are a cash crops, as are sugar, coffee, and bananas. In the tropics, land that once supported lush rainforests and could today support carefully limited numbers of people living harmoniously on it—growing their own grains, potatoes, fruits, and vegetables—is held in bondage to soy monocropping and millions of bovine four-legged locusts that devour the now-sparse vegetation and erode the exposed and dried-out soil.

Fortunately, our destructive past need not be our future. There is a way out of the deadly circle of deforestation, eco-desecration, and health degeneration. We do not have to treat the Earth, the animals, or ourselves cruelly or in an exploitative manner. We can live harmoniously and nourish everyone—the Earth and all who live upon it.

Jay's words are a road map that leads us "out of the jungle" of our violent past into a future of health, harmony, and peace with the Earth and all who dwell upon it. His book should be considered required reading for all who aspire to reach the higher aspects of humanity.

*   *   *

Dr. Klaper's preceding passage was originally written in 1993 for *Here's Harmlessness*, more than twenty years prior to the writing of *Powerful Vegan Messages*. The urgency of the situation has escalated. With the Internet reaching more areas, more people are aware of what they don't have. They want to be more like Americans because they think we have achieved a measure of success. One main yardstick is the ability to obtain and consume animal-based foods—namely meats, dairy products, and eggs. It should be our patriotic duty to go vegan for the benefit of our country and the world.

"Livestock's Long Shadow" is the often-cited 2006 study from the Food and Agricultural Organization of the United Nations (FAO). According to that report, eighteen percent of the world's human-induced greenhouse gas was attributable to animal agriculture. The International Livestock Research Institute—which normally promotes expansion of the livestock sector—estimates that livestock systems already occupy forty-five percent of all land on earth.

Robert Goodland and Jeff Anhang, environmental specialists employed at the World Bank Group, wrote an article "Livestock and Climate Change" for the Worldwatch Institute in 2009, which estimated that the lifecycle and supply of animal agriculture is responsible for at least fifty-one percent of human-induced greenhouse gas emissions. There are other grave environmental impacts of livestock, but climate change presents the highest risk uniquely imperiling human civilization as we know it.

Dr. Klaper and others who also have focused on the environmental impacts of animal agriculture look forward to seeing vast tracts of lands freed for more fruitful uses than feed-grain production and cattle grazing. Farmers can grow organic produce and grains instead of fields of fodder oats. Former forest lands liberated from cattle production can again support tall stands of healthy trees, yielding wood and fresh water and providing habitat for abundant wildlife. Farmers and ranchers can be assisted in making the essential transition to sustainable food production. The hundreds of billions of dollars now channeled in government subsidies worldwide toward meat, egg, and dairy producers should be re-routed. Those subsidies would be better channeled toward supporting alternatives to animal agriculture, including education promoting truly health-supporting nutrition and encouraging people to buy the healthful grains, legumes, fruits, and vegetables from sustainable organic farms.

Powerful Vegan Messages

As the evolution towards a more life-affirming diet progresses, the health of the Earth will reflect these changes. The forests will return, the topsoils will stabilize, the waters will run pure again and teem with fish. The children will grow strong and healthy. One can only surmise that animals will rejoice as their habitat returns and the animal world is freed from breeding in bondage to the factory farm and the specter of the slaughterhouse.

*   *   *

Are you interested in learning more about the environment? Read the two reports mentioned in this story at FAO.org and WorldWatch.org.

Also check out TheFoodRevolution.org, Greenvegans.org, and ChompingClimateChange.org for environmental information.

"Never doubt that a small group of thoughtful, committed citizens can change the world. Indeed it is the only thing that ever has."
— Margaret Mead

Buy the Books

Robert Cohen

I quit dairy products after learning that every sip of milk naturally contains powerful steroids and protein-growth hormones. I met Jay in 1999 at a three-day Florida vegetarian conference after I'd given up all dairy products yet was still not a vegetarian. During that conference, I spoke many hours with Jay and was so inspired by his arguments that I left Florida after investing $300 in vegan books, which I consider my first step in adopting a plant-based diet.

By 2000 Jay had become my hero. My inspiration. My mentor. Jay's spirit will forever be a part of mine.

In recalling the spirit of Jay, and the direction that my own life has taken after researching, writing, and distributing nearly 5,000 Notmilk blog columns during the past fourteen years, I am reminded of the words of one of history's great scientists regarding those who influenced his life. Sir Isaac Newton wrote, "If I have seen further, it is only by standing on the shoulders of giants."

Before I became the Notmilkman, I had been a real-estate syndicator and developer with one yuppyish goal: make lots of money! This change put meaning into my life, and I've never regretted my decision.

Four years ago, I spent a year in a wheelchair after having undergone a spinal fusion operation. The surgery failed. Three surgeons agreed that if I did not have a second operation, I might not walk again. I passed on the second procedure, which would have required the implantation of cow bone. Instead, I spent the year eating and juicing the color green. Two years ago, I completed my first triathlon, which involved swimming one mile, biking twenty-five miles, and running six miles. My current good health spirit is due to something more than just being vegan. It is due to the fact I stood upon the shoulders of a giant named Jay Dinshah.

*　　*　　*

Robert Cohen's new mission is to continue his activism while inspiring others to understand that the key to good health and longevity is SECS: Sleep, Exercise, Clean food, and Study. One must be vegan to perform at one's best. He has spoken at numerous conferences and written the books *Milk A to Z* and *Milk: The Deadly Poison.* Read his daily blogs at Notmilk.com.

*　　*　　*

What beverage did you drink this morning? Are you understanding that happiness can be found joining with others for a noble purpose?

Nourishing Wildflower

Eric Nyman

I never met Jay Dinshah, but I have been deeply inspired by his legacy of accomplishment.

Since becoming vegan in 2006, I have wanted to merge my livelihood more fully with my values. In 2009 I read *Out of the Jungle*, and its candor and directness hit home as a total affirmation of the ethical argument for veganism. That same year I attended Vegetarian Summerfest on AVS scholarship; the message I took home from the conference was "feed people."

In 2010, I had a newborn son and no job. The pipe organ construction company which had prompted me to move to South Jersey had gone under. More than ever, I felt it imperative to do something meaningful with my life instead of merely working for money. While collecting unemployment and with no restaurant experience, I purchased a lunch truck which sold sausage and peppers, pulled pork, and Italian meatballs. Renaming it "Wildflower—earthly vegan fare," I offered a 100 percent vegan menu to the route's customers who largely embraced it.

The gas-guzzling '77 Chevy never turned a profit. It was plagued by mechanical issues and restricted in sales options by lack of a certified kitchen. (In the early days, we illegally cooked everything at home.) I knew the only way the business could grow was with the acquisition of a legitimate commercial kitchen so I could expand the availability of our food beyond the small under-the-table route.

We opened a takeout-only café in the not-so-thriving Millville Arts District in the beginning of 2011, expecting the majority of our business to be catering and wholesale to local health-food stores. We kept limited open hours just in case anyone actually wanted to come in and order something. Amazingly, the local newspaper ran an article about us on the front page, and we got very busy, very fast.

Nine months later the beloved break-even-at-best Wildflower van was sacrificed to fund expansion into the adjacent unit to have indoor seating. The demand for a true all-vegan eatery was and certainly is there.

Feeding people is wonderful. We serve fresh, local, and organic vitality entirely from plants, and it has been incredibly rewarding to hear regulars who have eaten here for years proclaim without prompting "So… I'm vegan now."

Through the efforts of Jay and others, vegan fare has gone from fringe occurrence to commonly accepted option. The next step is to make it the standard.

*   *   *

Eric Nyman is a lifelong vegetarian and vegan since 2006. His mother and son are also vegan. He has a BA in philosophy from Montclair State University. Wildflower is open seven days a week in Millville, New Jersey. WildflowerVegan.com

*   *   *

We can all demonstrate that vegan is possible, and we have the power to affect many. Do what you believe, don't accept failure as an option, and the impact will be profound.

If Jay were here, he would definitely eat at Wildflower.

Priorities

H. Jay Dinshah

You can put down this book any time. You can opt to do nothing differently.

If your eyes have been opened, will you take a step on the path? Do you see a different light in your future?

Do you go to your nine-to-five job and find yourself occasionally dreaming of a better occupation? Do you spend your leisure time devouring sources of vegan information?

*   *   *

I'd like to share a couple of jokes with you. One of them I first heard as a youngster, many years ago.

A little girl was given two nickels and was sent walking to Sunday school. One nickel was to be given to the church as a contribution, and the other was for her to buy herself a candy bar afterwards. (Yes, candy bars were five cents.) She went skipping merrily along, clutching the coins in hand, 'til she dropped one of them, which proceeded to roll right to a grating and down into a storm drain. "Oh, oh!" she said, without missing a step. "There goes the Lord's nickel!"

There is a world of human psychology in that little story.

The other joke I heard more recently.

A hen and a pig were walking along the road one fine morning when they happened to see a big billboard bearing the religious message: "What are you giving to God?"

They continued walking for a while, thinking about this

question, and eventually the hen said, "Let's give God bacon and eggs for breakfast."

"That's all very well for you to say," replied the pig. "For you that represents only a token sacrifice. But for me, it means a lifelong commitment!"

Of course, vegans know that the use of eggs demands far more than a token sacrifice from the hen, but we can appreciate the story anyway. It is easier to suggest some good work to another, particularly if it entails a considerable measure of difficulty or self-sacrifice than to take the plunge and do it oneself.

Many are those of this world who yearn for peace and harmony on Earth but will not really work very hard for it. They truly desire to have a better world but not at the cost of their own comfort and convenience.

*   *   *

Some time ago, a vegan friend complained that there wasn't enough time to do the good work for the cause. This is certainly a problem with which I can identify and sympathize. I advised that it is often a matter of priorities.

If we permit ourselves to be bogged down in the pursuit of material things, there will probably be very little time and energy left for doing the truly important things in life. However, we must have food, water, shelter, clothing, and some other necessities, and there's no harm in having some fun too.

Personally, I believe that the cause in which we struggle is worthy of—and badly needs—the very best and most unselfish efforts of which we are capable. This is not to imply that tangible things in our personal lives are of no consequence at all, only that we must keep them in proper perspective and not let them crowd out of our lives the more important values and goals.

Thomas à Kempis, a Dutch clergyman, said it much better,

half a millennium ago: "Food, water, clothing, and other necessities are burdensome to a devout spirit. Now, it is not lawful to cast these things aside because nature must be supported. But to seek excess, and very delightful worldly things, this the holy law forbids. Why is this? Because then the flesh becomes haughty against the spirit." And he said: "The perfect victory is to triumph over one's self. Your love for yourself is more hurtful to you than anything else in this world. What can be more free than he who desires nothing on Earth? Forsake all and you will find all. Vanquish your desires, and you will find peace."

Roman philosopher Seneca said 2000 years ago, "It is not the man who has too little, but the man who craves more, who is poor."

Some twenty-five centuries ago, it was similarly taught by the Buddha: "Pleasures of men are extravagant and luxurious. Hugging those pleasures, men hanker after them....Slaves to their own desires, men pursue the torrent of craving, just as the spider follows the thread of the web which he has made himself. When wise persons cut these shackles at last, they go onward—free from sorrow—leaving all pain behind."

Look around you in this materially wealthy country and see how much mischief, misery, and misfortune can really be traced to a lack of this simple wisdom that has been around for at least twenty-five centuries. It seems to be part of the very nature of so many humans to think that every luxury or new gadget is now a necessity of life. This is not to say there is anything inherently dignified or glorious about abject poverty. That is not what I am advocating. Simply that enough is enough and more than enough is probably too much.

When I see what seems to me to be a conspicuous and extravagant waste, I may be tempted to think it a great pity, "We could print another book with that amount." Then a little reflection with a bit of humility thrown in tells us that the knife is held to the grindstone for the purpose of sharpening the knife.

This big old world is like a huge and heavy grindstone. While you and I are sidling up to the grindstone, we are surely changing its shape some—and it is right that we should do this—but it is sharpening us as well.

*   *   *

If we think of our lives as our own and isolated from the rest of all humanity, we may make some rationalizations about the need to look out for number one. We are likely to concoct some clever little sophistries with which to convince ourselves that we did not create all the misery and suffering in this world. We can hardly be expected to clean it up all by ourselves. We will surely see the common sense in just seeing to our own lives, our educations, our careers, families, recreation, and so on. Yet some crumbs will fall from the table of our plentitude, and we will call this our contribution to the cause.

One of the most encouraging and gratifying aspects of this great vegan movement is to have met over the years so many who look at life from another point of view. Whatever knowledge or wisdom we may have acquired, whatever material possessions are needed to sustain our lives and even the very breath of life itself—all of these are lent to us, given in a conditional loan or stewardship. If we have been fortunate to be entrusted with a little more, then so much the greater is our responsibility.

*   *   *

There comes a time in the life of every caring, sensitive person—a time to realize that fame is as ashes, massed fortune mere dust. It may be the last thought you think in this life. If at such a time you can truly say, "I have done my best," and your only regret is that you could not have done more, then you will have done very well indeed.

296

*   *   *

There is an old saying among charitable organizations, "Give 'til it hurts!" This I am not saying for there is already too much hurting and suffering in this world. I say, "Give 'til it helps."

That is usually said of monetary contributions that are always needed. I do not say it just of cash. I ask a far more precious sacrifice. I ask you to give of yourself—your time, your effort, your lifestyle. I ask that you get involved. I ask that you rearrange your priorities of life. You become determined that you will do the good work that needs to be done. This needs precedence over the mere struggle to get ahead in your job or standard of living.

Some express the view that we don't have to help in this life because there will be a better life to come. I cannot ignore the clear cries of anguish from the victims of injustice and exploitation in this life. I promise you nothing except that you can make a difference to many lives in this life in this world. You can do your share and then some to make this world a little less like the hell for animals—and for humans also in many respects—that we thoughtless and selfish humans have made it.

*   *   *

In my humble view, life is far too short and the call to service too loud and clear to waste time and energy in the pursuit of a fat wallet and a fatter paunch. Making no vain pretenses to sainthood, I freely admit that I am well aware of many siren songs this world can sing to distract us from what we perceive as our duty to help. But these cannot be permitted to drown out the desperate cries for succor.

*   *   *

We are standing on a pier at the seaside, and someone has fallen into the deep and turbulent water. Who is so crass as to call to the one in such distress, "Keep splashing and thrashing while I go and have my lunch. I will come back in a while, and then I'll throw you this life preserver. But I'm hungry right now."

Indeed it can be argued that you did not push him in. The ungrateful wretch should be glad that you even plan to eventually come to his rescue at all.

*   *   *

We are standing on the curb and see a car with its driver under the influence, speeding toward a little child crossing the street. We can probably save the child with perhaps little risk to ourselves. But we are wearing a new pair of loafers, and the street is rather muddy. Would we pause to consider our new shoes and their cleanliness? After all, we are talking about the value of life, and one may find all sorts of loafers in this world.

*   *   *

We are passengers on a huge ocean liner that has been badly holed below the waterline—doubtless a mortal wound—and the ship is rapidly sinking. What can you do? Get to the lifeboats and help in an orderly manner. Fine.

Now supposing you are still below, and you notice an important watertight door has failed to close automatically. You realize that if it could be closed the ship would stay afloat longer with more lives saved—many more, though not all.

Then you realize that there is an emergency hand-crank system for closing the door. The water is now rising fast around you. There is great risk, but you know that you may be able to close that door in time to save many lives. It is fun to daydream and play the hero—is it not? So you stay and crank the door shut, and then go up and have a nice happy ending.

But life is not always so neat. Did I forget to mention? Due to some human error in design, the only passage to safety is now on *that* side of the door while the cranking mechanism is on *this* side of the door. A small detail but it does modify the price of heroism somewhat. Is our answer still the same? Honestly?

* * *

One of the greatest teachers of unselfishness said that no one has any greater love than to lay one's life down for one's friends. Surely no less is the love that impels one to lay one's life down for complete strangers—those one does not know personally and whom one will never even meet. There are many ways of laying one's life down for others. It can mean the ending of only the egocentricity—the selfishness. It can mean the bringing of one's life to lay it at the service of life itself. It can mean devoting one's life to righting the wrongs done to animals who have no choice in where they lay.

* * *

I wrote earlier in jest about giving God something for breakfast. I think it would be presumptuous to really speculate about what such a divine repast should be. However, I am convinced that it wouldn't be bacon and eggs.

If instead of meddling and muddling about such matters, we can substitute the term good for God. Do what good works we can in this life. Act exactly as we should if such a one were constantly looking over our shoulder. We will not go far wrong in this life. We certainly should have less difficulty perceiving our duty to help the cause of life in this life.

*   *   *

Get involved. Volunteer to work—full time or part time depending on what you are able to commit—for any of the groups who are currently doing great vegan work. Learn more about veganism and animal rights while already beginning your journey on the path. It doesn't matter if you are shy or outgoing, old or young, or any of a multitude of opposites I can name. If your heart is inclined to seek where to put your efforts, you will soon be doing good work.

Make a list of all your terrific abilities and interests. Do you like writing, editing, organizing events, selling books, video production, speaking, cooking, showing documentaries, caring for animals, leafleting, or other activities? Where will you put your talents to the greatest good? You will be fixing the leak instead of rearranging the deck chairs on the *Titanic*.

*   *   *

On a typical day in the United States, according to 2010 statistics from the United States Department of Agriculture (USDA), the death toll of animals killed for food is estimated at roughly one-hundred-thousand cattle, three-hundred-thousand pigs, eight-thousand sheep and goats, six-thousand rabbits, twenty -four million chickens, six-hundred-thousand turkeys, fifty-thousand ducks, and—uncalculated by USDA yet relevant—millions of assorted aquatic animals.

That is the incredible slaughter required for just one day's breakfast, lunch, and dinner on the American table not including the animals who perish before they can be brought to slaughter. This is the total commitment imposed upon the "food animals" by their human masters. Such statistics cannot begin to really convey a true picture of the agony suffered by the creatures, borne at the very personal, painful, individual level.

*   *   *

Now, what else did you think you had to do with your life that seemed so important?

Let's All Be Bright Luminaries

Rae Sikora

Please read this page; then close your eyes and reflect on what you read.

It is thirty years in the future. The earth has gone through a remarkable healing. Humans were able to widen their circle of compassion and include all species and the earth herself in their caring. Everyone has been surprised at how quickly the healing of the environment and all species, including humans, occurred once everyone woke up to a culture of compassion.

You are sitting under a tree relaxing, and a young neighbor girl comes and sits next to you. She asks you how old you are. When you tell her your age, she says, "Oh, you were here during the scary time, the time when most people did not care for themselves or other species or the air or the water. I heard that most of you thought you were all going to die and that the earth was too poisoned to support most life. That must have been so scary."

Then she asks you, "Can you tell me what it was like? Were you afraid or sad or angry during that time? What did you do to not be scared during that time? How did you stay positive? What did you do to make a difference? What was your part in helping to turn things around?"

*　　*　　*

Rae Sikora has been a full-time spokesperson for other species for over thirty-five years. Rae is cofounder of Plant Peace Daily, Vegfund, and the Institute for Humane Education. She leads compassionate living and ethical consumerism programs for diverse audiences from schools and prisons to businesses and universities. Her work takes her from the United States to the Middle East and Central America.

She lives in Santa Fe, New Mexico, with her partner, J.C. Corcoran and their ever-growing pack of rescued dogs. Rae and J.C. coauthored the book *Plant Peace Daily: Everyday Outreach for People Who Care*. The book and her life are part of a lifelong global effort to invite humans to the possibility of compassion for all life. Rae is a member of the AVS speakers bureau.

Jay and Freya Dinshah were the first inductees into the Vegetarian Hall of Fame in 1993. Twenty years later Rae Sikora was inducted as the 2013 honoree.

*   *   *

Do you have a great idea for a vegan activity that will inspire people to choose a vegan lifestyle? VegFund.org funds activities such as food sampling or movie screenings.

If you are interested in learning how to turn your compassion and convictions into action through education consider a masters or doctorate degree with Institute for Humane Education. HumaneEducation.org

Vegan work continues, and when you share Rae's optimism and ethics for work, play, and compassion, there is a bright future for everyone. What are you doing today?

Closing Words

Anne Dinshah

Dad won many arguments, and if he didn't, he at least got the other person to think. Eventually, upon further reflection they may conclude, "He was right." Today many individuals have learned veganism, but the world collectively has yet to come "out of the jungle."

Once, Dad was invited onto the *Morton Downey Jr. Show* with its purpose of ridiculing vegans, unbeknownst to him. He had driven to New York City on a very hot day in a car without air conditioning, and he looked tired. He gallantly explained why he didn't look as suave as Morton or as glamorous as the other guest—a model in a fur coat—was because he was working long hard hours towards his goal of closing the slaughterhouses. He was devoted to trying to help people understand how much suffering goes into the things people wrongly believe are beautiful or needed, such as furs and animal foods. Dad used the opportunity to deliver his message to a large audience; he encouraged them "out of the jungle." We cannot accurately count how many people were influenced by the show, but people have told me that he made an impression on them that evening.

Dad loved to read books for pleasure. The brilliant nineteenth-century engineer famous for designing the Brooklyn Bridge, John A. Roebling, was one of his heroes. Sometimes I shared this fascination with bridges. When I went to Notre Dame, I planned to be a civil engineer; I wanted to build bridges. Then I learned I wasn't suited for the heavy math and physics; I preferred arts and writing. I graduated with an American studies degree. The closest I came to bridges were the ones I rowed under every morning on the Saint Joseph River. Now I finally am a civil engineer of sorts.

I build bridges for people to come to veganism. Ahimsa provides the construction materials.

Many of us spend our lives looking for our purpose. Dad knew his since 1957. Regardless of your background, education, orientation, career, age, family status, and finances, I hope this book will help you find your mission in life. It has already helped me more than I can express here.

I'm nothing like Dad yet everything like him. When giving lectures based on my book *Dating Vegans*, I often remind vegans to interact patiently and compassionately with people who are not vegan. "Remember who you were before being vegan; you were worthy of being loved and treated with kindness." Recently I was reviewing the old VHS tapes of Dad speaking, which I had not previously viewed; I was working on the videos for *Powerful Vegan Messages*. Dad said basically the same thing about being patient and compassionate to all people who are not yet vegan.

Dad and I both like to give speeches, although in other venues we both could be shy. Once I told a rowing conference organizer that I'd like to see more about mental training at the next conference. The organizer made me promise to come the next year and present it. I was like Lorene Cox in her story with Dad.

Positive mental training is essential to accomplishment of most physical goals. Visualize the goal. Talk about it. Write it down. Build the team committed to the goal. Make a plan. Take steps in the right direction. Practice daily. Develop confidence. Reinforce with visualization the ability to accomplish the goal. Remind each other of the importance. Believe it can be achieved.

I re-read this manuscript many times before I realized that actually I'm more like Dad than I am Lorene. Dad's biggest gift to the vegan movement wasn't his writing or speaking, as I had thought, but rather his coaching of others. Perhaps my rowing coaching career was really training for my role promoting veganism. I need not be afraid of furthering his message; I am well prepared for where that river flows. I have come to realize

I'm strong. I have good technique. I'm determined, and I work well with others—qualities good for rowing and veganism.

I'm a coach. I didn't row in a national championship, but twice I coached collegiate teams that won national championships. Similarly perhaps people will take the information we provide and win a national championship for veganism.

For the sake of the animals, I have to encourage people to try veganism. I know now that I will always be on this team, and we are headed for success. My favorite thing to do is to accomplish a goal together.

I believe the slaughterhouses will close in my lifetime. Society is approaching a turning point. Believe with me in the power of veganism and ahimsa. Imagine the world where all animals are happy, free, and in natural proportion and settings. All the world's people are fed. Violence has ended. The earth returns to environmental balance.

Let's build bridges with all the people who have yet to live The Golden Rule, share reverence for life, and understand ahimsa. Let this book be your new strong tool. Tools are created to help make our work doable. If you now understand ethical reasons for veganism, or even if you still have a few questions, please join our family.

We can all be united on a common mission that is more important than being blood relatives. We are united with the blood of animals, the blood that is on everyone's hands if we sit idly by or do anything less than everything we can. It is blood we can never wash clean until all the animals are freed from human harm. Today embark on a mission with me to create a different world.

*   *   *

Please join our family; become a member of AVS. Give gifts of *Powerful Vegan Messages* to everyone, act on the lessons, write the next chapter, and the animals will thank you.

Afterword with the Campbell, Dinshah, Esselstyn, and Robbins Families

We welcome readers to join Anne at the dinner party with all the people from the foreword: LeAnne and Tom Campbell; Freya and Clint Dinshah; Jane and Rip Esselstyn; and John, Deo, and Ocean Robbins. The afterword captures the sentiments of this group and is based on quotes from actual interviews. The involved parties edited and approved the liberties taken in creating the flow of conversation for publication.

Anne: John, would you like to share a blessing?

John: Holding in our hands a piece of bread,
May we be touched
By the clouds and the rain
That enable the grain to grow;
May we be moved by the fertile Earth
In which the great waving fields are rooted;
And reminded of the radiant Sun
Whose warmth and light are converted by plant life
Into the energy on which we all are sustained.

Holding a piece of fruit, may we be grateful
To the women and men who dug the wells,
Planted the seeds and seedlings, tended the plants,
Harvested the fruit, and in countless other ways
Brought forth the bounty of the Earth.
May we live with respect for those who
Build and maintain the roads, trucks, markets, and delivery systems
That bring this fruit to our hands.

In eating, may we remember and give thanks
To all the innumerable people
Each with his or her own name and spirit,
Who have labored that we might eat.

May all be fed.
May all be healed.
May all be loved.

Anne: Thank you, John.

Rip, shall we pass around the appetizers?

Rip: I made Ripped Kale. Clint was a big help washing all the kale. It's raw dinosaur kale that's been massaged. We ripped it in half to make appetizer-sized portions and rolled it around a stuffing of ripe mashed avocado, steamed broccoli, and my personal blend of pleasantly roaring spices. I love kale; it's angry lettuce with an attitude. (Rip and Clint make friendly dinosaur growls they must have practiced in the kitchen.)

Clint: I like washing kale. More people should let kids help in the kitchen. I'm only three, and I help every day! (More growls and laughter.)

Rip: Everyone helped make dinner. This is going to be quite the celebration. It's all about collaboration.

Anne: Let's give a name to the bigger collaborative efforts among us. We can invite all the readers of *Powerful Vegan Messages* and everyone in the world to become the Vegan Generation[3] with the "3" indicating the ripple effect of our actions. There is so much good information available to guide people to becoming vegan. Let's figure out how to help them on the journey.

LeAnne: A toast to collaboration! The power of coming together to achieve common goals—of seeing the world in win-win terms, where synergy replaces competition. (All clink glasses of organic sparkling white grape juice.)

I hope everyone enjoys this book as much as I did. My favorites stories are about the 1975 World Vegetarian Congress, a solid example of Jay's grassroots strategy and outcomes. Look at what has been accomplished through the efforts of the Graffs, Alex Hershaft, and 1,500 other people.

Jane: Meanwhile, I liked the stories of remembering about being children by Dr. Tosca Haag and Heidi Fox. We have such a responsibility to educate.

Rip: Those were great, but as a motivational speaker I liked what Howard Lyman shared. There were many stories inspiring both reflection and action. Can I reflect on the appetizers or would anyone like action on them?

Anne: Go ahead, Rip. Let's pass around Freya's homemade bread and Jane's salad.

Jane: I made the salad because I love so many vegetables. Tom's favorite veggies inspired this green and bean salad of steamed and chilled green beans and cranberry beans, diced red peppers and homegrown tomatoes, all tossed with a spring mix of dark green lettuces.

Clint: I shelled the cranberry beans and added my favorite— raisins! Then I got to shake the dressing.

Jane: The dressing is minced fresh basil and mint, lemon juice, and a drop of maple syrup. No oil, of course.

Anne: Any vegan meal can showcase the variety; it's especially fun to share it with friends. Options using only plants are impressively abundant and infinitely delicious. There are so many great vegan cookbooks available that there aren't any recipes in *Powerful Vegan Messages*, except the recipe for why and how to do good in the world.

Deo: How did you come up with the menu for tonight?

Anne: I asked everyone's three favorite vegetables and anything they dislike or allergies. I love to play this game of puzzling together a great menu that pleases everyone. I've even done whole lectures based on audience preferences.

Deo: Your lectures sound fun.

Anne: They are, and my dinner parties are always fun, especially when people come early and help cook. I just gather the ingredients and let the fun begin.

Tom: This food is wonderful. Are you sure you assembled us to contribute thoughts on activism, or was it to share good food?

Anne: I like to be creative. Here's a quick anecdote to explain why I needed to invite all of you to the dinner party, albeit an unconventional way to do a foreword and afterword:

Years ago I took three years off from my main career to try all the other career paths of potential interest. I was taking flying lessons with an instructor who looked like Tom Cruise. He had my attention. I was a star student learning all the lessons efficiently. I could almost hear the *Top Gun* soundtrack playing in my mind as we practiced stalls high above Madison ,Wisconsin. I had one more skill to learn before solo piloting the plane. I needed to safely land, but I kept bouncing the landings. I practiced flying around the airport traffic pattern—wasting precious money and fuel—getting more frustrated with each attempt. Finally I quit.

The next week I was at my job pumping fuel into one of the Cessna 152s for another instructor. He asked how my lessons were going and if I soloed yet. I told him about the landings and quitting. He invited me to fly with him. He gave the same goal as the first instructor—to land the plane safely, but said it in a slightly different way. He showed confidence in me, and I responded with a perfect landing on the first try.

The world is rapidly spinning out of control. Pick your topic: health, environment, ethics. It will take all of us—those at the table, readers of this book, and people who have yet to hear of veganism—to land the world safely.

Ocean: Let's do this! One thing in common our generation brings to this table is strong, well-known fathers. I'd like to know more about them. LeAnne, tell me about your dad (T. Colin Campbell).

LeAnne: Dad was single-minded; work and research were important. I grew up hearing the evolution of his thoughts. Wherever we lived, we were out in the country on a gentlemen's farm because he's a farmer at heart.

When he got the evidence about animal protein, he wasn't expecting it. He had first gone to college to study how to produce animals better for human consumption, but he's a man of integrity. He put aside his farmer bias to follow the evidence where it led him. He's curious. Dad found animal foods are not good for our health. He had been all about animal-based farming, but he learned and changed.

Tom: Dad presided over the mammoth epidemiological study known as "The China Study" in the early 1980s. From data on 367 variables across 65 countries and 6,500 adults, he concluded, "People who ate the most animal-based foods got the most chronic disease...People who ate the most plant-based foods were the healthiest and tended to avoid chronic disease."

LeAnne: Mom (Karen Campbell) was fully supportive. She is a great cook who saw it as an opportunity to explore. His story would have been different if not for Mom.

Dad struggled through the years because of the stance he was taking as the only scientist promoting what he had to say. Our family talked about his discoveries at the dining table. We all understood why we were steadily transitioning the animal products out of our diet.

I have been motivated and inspired by Dad's humanitarian focus. He always wanted to know what's really happening and find the highest ethical solutions such as when he worked with malnourished children. From an early age, I have been drawn to the work he did.

Tom: Dad's accomplishments are so remarkable because he reached a high level within the scientific establishment. He interpreted findings with honesty and integrity, communicating the findings to the public even though it might threaten his professional status. He advocated for what he believed to be true without regard to popularity of the message. His work was featured in the film *Forks Over Knives* with Rip's dad as the two main interviewees. Rip, what is your dad like?

Rip: He's garnered a lot a lot of awards for his work summed up as his book title *Prevent and Reverse Heart Disease,* but personally he is a terrific father. Dad set a fantastic example of someone I'd like to emulate. He has an amazing work ethic, integrity, and credibility; he never compromises that. He has unwavering commitment to doing the right thing, going against the grain with research, following his heart, and doing the truth.

Jane: Mom (Ann Crile Esselstyn) was where the rubber hit the road; she made this happen. Mom and I are now doing our own cookbook together. It was great working with Rip too, most recently doing the recipes for his book *My Beef With Meat.* Now the whole family has got the momentum going.

And we have Ocean's parents right here, so he ought to have a good answer. What has been your Dad's greatest accomplishment?

Ocean: For me, my dad's personal accomplishment is the greatest, personified in the kind of dad he is and the kind of dad he had. When he was growing up, dinner was formal, children were to be seen and not heard. They didn't speak unless spoken to. There was no dialogue, and his home was a deeply lonely place.

In contrast, my dad encouraged me to speak my mind at the dinner table. Our family dinner table had real conversations; we learned together about what excited us. As I was growing up, we talked about dreams, how we care about animals, people we love, the horrors of factory farms, the state of the world, and what we wanted to contribute to the world.

My dad has always supported me in living my dreams. His dad wanted him to follow him in running the Baskin-Robbins ice-cream empire from which he walked away. I have a dad who is unconditionally loving, and that is part of why I feel so full and also blessed to have the opportunity to work with him in The Food Revolution.

My parents are total partners. My mom loves feeding people; she is the first sounding board for my dad and his top advisor. She has perspective, unconditional love, and tremendous wisdom.

Anne: The Robbins have come to the right place for dinner tonight! We're serving a big helping of meaningful conversation. When Dad and I took long car rides, just the two of us, those are the conversations I remember best.

Ocean: Where did you go? You're not far from the ocean here?

Anne: I don't remember going to the ocean with him. Long drives were to conferences or lectures, especially in the summers; everything he did was work related. I enjoyed it at the time, but as I grew up I had to do my own thing. One of my first jobs was as an ocean lifeguard. Dad didn't like to swim or get sand between his toes.

Freya: Fortunately, Jay allowed himself some half days off! He liked walking on the boardwalk, probably more after Anne went off to college.

Rip: Three of us have coauthored books with our fathers: Tom, Anne, and Ocean. That takes a special bond and a lot of patience. Anne, tell us about how you came to work with your parents again, something I can't read for myself, the long version while I eat more of this amazing salad and bread.

Anne: After growing up with AVS, I resided in nine different states for education and work. I've always been a rowing coach, friend to many, and good vegan cook for a lucky few people who came to dinner.

Dad convinced me to compile my recipes as *Healthy Hearty Helpings* for which my parents did the editing. That was in 1999, and Dad died the next year before teaching me how to market it. I wasn't planning on doing more writing. Mom (Freya) became president of AVS. The workload is enormous; she slowly drew me in with a bit of writing for the magazine and an invitation to be on the council of trustees.

My book *Dating Vegans* started as a series of articles in *American Vegan* magazine, based on helpful, real-life experiences as a vegan in the nonvegan world. Radio hosts loved the book, and I could talk all day about it, but I wasn't ready for them calling me vegan royalty or part of a vegan dynasty like I had something important to share with the world. I was content to be "the girl next door" who happens to be vegan.

Freya had a grant to write *Apples, Bean Dip, and Carrot Cake: Kids! Teach Yourself to Cook* but no time. I needed a third job, so we talked by phone at about ten o'clock in the evenings. She would lie on the sofa and tell me her thoughts. I typed as fast as I could until I heard snoring and we were done for the session. It was all her vision. I tested the recipes individually with twenty-six kids. Writing, photography, and layout are only the first half; there's also the marketing and promotion.

Now I'm doing a book "with Dad." I've become confident in expressing my values and embracing my heritage. Like everyone here, I understand the urgency of conveying our knowledge in ways people will receive and utilize. I'm glad you guys are giving me ideas for promoting *Powerful Vegan Messages*.

Rip: I'm happy to help promote it through our robust social media.

Ocean: And I also always look for natural allies for projects and doing things we can share on social media.

Anne: I appreciate everyone's help. Now someone who wanted to eat more plants for his heart health has a good opportunity to learn to use his heart to guide him along a path of ahimsa.

Someone who only had a concern about factory farms will learn about veganism. This is the start of collaboration among us. We will achieve the common goal to get people to eat plants instead of animals.

Tom: A lot of individuals promote optimal nutrition. The more interconnected we are, the more support we give each other, the better it will be. Mutual cooperation will be the most important. We need to remind ourselves that we are a small band trying to change the world and offer collaboration.

Anne: Collaboration takes hard work because it may mean some compromise, but it doesn't mean compromising one's ethics. Dad knew it takes ingenuity to remain true to oneself while he acknowledged that a lone voice doesn't do any good if no one hears it.

Freya: When Jay was working with the natural hygienists, he worked within the organization that was mostly aligned with his values, the American Natural Hygiene Society, now National Health Association. He did what was for the greater good. On one occasion that included having to pick up the cheese for the banquet, he certainly was not going to eat it.

When we put on the 1975 IVU World Vegetarian Congress, we vegans were working with the lacto-ovo vegetarians to form the new organization, North American Vegetarian Society (NAVS). It was customary to include milk and eggs in the congress menu. I was able to keep our integrity by insisting all recipes were completely vegan. Milk and eggs were optional side items only for the first few NAVS conferences. Recipes remain vegan at all NAVS conferences to this day. All IVU world events are now catered completely vegan too.

Jane: Hats off to you, Freya. Integrity is such a vital theme here. I wish I could have met Jay.

Freya: He would have enjoyed this dinner with all of you. There were not a lot of vegan professionals thirty years ago. For the

AVS conference in 1985, we invited a prominent doctor to speak because of her health knowledge. Her diet was without animal products except honey. She wrote books on nutrition and near-vegan cookbooks promoting oil-free recipes even before the Esselstyns. She gave a great lecture on the advantages of a wholesome plant diet. Afterwards she thanked us, saying we had been a positive influence, and she was becoming vegan replacing leather and wool.

J. N. Mankar (1895-1977) was cofounder of the Bombay Humanitarian League in 1910, which hosted the IVU congresses held in India starting in 1957 and every ten years thereafter. Mankar was a survivor of throat cancer, but as a consequence he was only able to swallow milk. When he visited us, we offered vegetable juices and homemade soymilk, seed milk, and nut milk strained smooth, but they proved unsuitable. Jay purchased cow milk for him. Mankar dearly wished he could be vegan. He was artful in involving people to further the cause.

We are part of communities. We do better work by acting in community than retreating.

Ocean: Thanks for sharing inspirational examples. May I inquire about the inspiration for the intriguing dish in front of me?

Anne: Inspired by Clint's favorite peas, we made rustic—not peeled—mashed potatoes with peas.

Clint: I scrubbed two potatoes for each person here, so there are twenty potatoes in our dinner.

Anne: John and Ocean's favorites combine in the mushroom-onion gravy to go on the potatoes. It's the first of three dishes that can be mains but might be a side dish, depending on serving size and location on your plate.

LeAnne: I love how there's no need to chase peas around the plate; they are already integrated.

Deo: Great work, Clint! One of the best things to do is spend time with kids preparing real food. LeAnne, I understand you had a great experience cooking with your kids recently.

LeAnne: Yes, for years people had been asking Dad for a cookbook consistent with the health message in *The China Study*, but it hadn't happened. I was between jobs and took it on as a family project with my teenage sons, Steven and Nelson. Steven took all the photos and they both helped create and test all the recipes. Mom helped too. It's 100 percent plant-based and as close to natural as possible, no oil, limited processed food. I call it the garden approach—eating a variety of the plant parts: fruits, grains, leaves, roots, legumes, flowers, and nuts. Then mushrooms are their own category.

Freya: I like the garden approach. When I do outreach with kids, I use Vesanto Melina's game. Kids enjoy this quiz about what parts of plants we eat. I hold up various fruits, vegetables, grains, and beans—one item at a time—and ask kids what part of the plant it is. They call out, "root" or "flower," etc.

Clint: Deo, do you play with kids, too?

Deo: Yes, I work with our grandchildren, using a wonderful program for people with autism called SonRise.

Tom: What do your grandkids think about The Food Revolution?

Deo: My grandkids are pretty passionate about healthy, plant-based living, and they don't really understand why anyone would want to eat junk food.

Rip: I'm looking forward to trying Freya's Cauliflower Casserole. This looks awesome—a big, round centerpiece with its lightly-browned sauce.

Freya: Thank you. It's a steamed cauliflower topped with a sauce of corn and celery made in the blender; then bake it. The Dinshahs carve the cauliflower at holidays, a focal point guests appreciate since they often miss the traditions more than the actual dead bird. Sometimes people think vegans only eat vegetables, so I'm serving it on a bed of quinoa tonight to encourage whole grains.

Deo: Freya, what was it like writing *The Vegan Kitchen*? I can't believe you wrote that in 1965, the first cookbook in this country with the word vegan in the title. Now there are so many more options.

Freya: Jay was an idealist; I was practical. He never told exactly what he ate in case people didn't like it, whereas I made a cookbook with sample menus.

I know LeAnne likes corn, and I thought Cauliflower Casserole would go well with your lovely dish.

Deo: I do love cauliflower! I also love any kind of roasted veggies, so my dish includes lots of Rip's favorite beets, Clint's favorite sweet potatoes, Ocean's favorite carrots, plus turnips and parsnips. I washed and chopped the root vegetables, tossed them with balsamic vinegar, soy sauce, maple syrup, and pepper. It's baked at 400 degrees for at least an hour. I make roasted veggies often but tried something new today. I added LeAnne's other favorite asparagus and made it without oil in honor of the Esselstyns. I stirred it a couple of times.

Freya: I took a taste test. I was curious how Deo's Veggies would turn out without the oil. They are soft, moist, and sweet. Lovely!

LeAnne: We will be well fed here. We definitely work well together making a meal. I want to know where everyone is with their work so we can develop how we are going to work together promoting veganism. Ocean, where do you flow?

Ocean: I'm pointing people in a direction. Vegan may or may not be their desired destination. I would rather 100 people move 50 percent of the way than 5 people move 100 percent. My interest is in fewer factory farms, less pesticide use, less junk food, less corporate control of our food systems, more humane, organic, natural, sustainable foods that contribute to thriving communities and a more compassionate and sustainable world.

Anne: What would you say is your ultimate goal?

Ocean: I'd love to see a world in which humanity completely outgrows the use of toxic pesticides and cruelty towards animals, the earth, and other humans. And I appreciate every step we can take in that direction.

Anne: I agree with you that we must get more people going in the right direction. When people begin to open their eyes to some of the issues, they desire more knowledge. Then they are more likely to turn to veganism instead of being afraid of it as a term they don't understand. AVS gives the vegan goal because many people want to do all they can do to create a world free of animal exploitation. We don't fault anyone for where they are along their journey; we encourage people.

I'd rather have dinner with ten nonvegan friends than one vegan one—no offense to any of my vegan friends. Most of my nonvegan friends love eating vegan food but haven't learned enough about it yet. With an open mind and respect, the journey to veganism can be fun for people. I keep in the back of my mind that it's never fun for the animals who people choose to consume.

Ocean: Yes, if we only talk with those who agree with us, our impact will probably be small.

LeAnne: The Robbins family is having a big impact on many. Deo, who went vegan first?

Deo: John and I went vegan together in Berkeley in the 1960s. It was a crash course that began the day we realized that living on ice cream and pies was probably not the best idea for long-term health and what we put into our bodies could actually affect our well-being and experience of life. We were also discovering yoga and meditation and were introduced to the concept of ahimsa.

Jane: Ocean, how did you get involved in the family business?

Ocean: When I was ten, my dad began researching *Diet for a New America* for three years. He was learning about factory farms and sharing his knowledge with me. To my eyes, factory farms are an affront to our basic humanity. We have a moral responsibility to manifest compassion. The tragic reality and enormous cruelty it unleashes on animals was extremely painful. This knowledge galvanized me to the cause in my preteen years.

I worked for twenty years with leaders throughout the world in the nonprofit organization Youth for Environmental Sanity (YES!), which I founded when I was sixteen. I worked with leaders in over sixty-five nations, and I kept seeing that one thing we have in common is that we all eat. And wherever in the world we are, what we eat has an impact on our health, our community, and our planet. Food may be the single most potent point of leverage we have. It turns out cows may impact our planet more than cars. What you eat can determine whether you live in health or die in disease. What you eat helps shape the economy, our ecosystem, the well-being of our kids, and the future of our elders. From global warming and deforestation to water pollution and from factory farms to social justice in low-income communities, the impact of food is everywhere.

Jane: Now you are bonded with your dad in that food revolution! What's it like working together?

Ocean: I'm good at Internet organizing, building an enterprise, the business side of social change, and mobilizing a team. My dad is a brilliant speaker and writer who likes independence and thrives with a certain degree of peace and privacy. I thrive on social media, building a platform, and creating a structure that can help our work reach more people.

I realized a few years ago that my dad's books sold a total of two million copies, and he'd been on national talk shows, but he had an email list of only 6,000 people. He could do so much more with a bigger platform. I sought to build a social-profit enterprise. I wanted to combine big hearts with business smarts. So now we fund our efforts through revenue by offering resources instead of depending on grants and donations. If we develop an enterprise whose scale is tied to its success, then the more good we do, the more we can grow.

LeAnne: How is it going?

Ocean: It's going great! We went from 6,000 to 124,000 people in the first two years. We sponsor The Food Revolution summits online, which have reached over 200,000 people. Our tagline is "How you can heal your body and your world with food." We've been honored to have Rip, Dr. Esselstyn, and Dr. T. Colin Campbell all appear among the speakers in our online summits.

Anne: You're casting a big net, Ocean. Rip, with your books and working for Whole Foods Market, you are angling for a lot of people too. Whole Foods Market sells other products you wouldn't buy, but they are a strong ally to promote a flood of good information. Where are you currently going?

Rip: I guess puns are irresistible with an Ocean and a Rip here. And Ocean has twin sons, one named River. Jane can be the Hurricane. Maybe Tom changes to Tide, or do you prefer Tsunami?

Tom: Either can create massive change. LeAnne is more like a serene Lake, found anywhere in the world in connecting with the main Stream, while Anne gets to be a beautiful powerful Waterfall. Our generation is poised to change the world. Shall we wash the world's problems away?

Rip: My goal is to have a big impact. People need to make the connection between food and food's ability to restore health. No big master plan, just connecting the dots. It's amazing how, if you are passionate about something, doors open.

Anne: You are certainly doing your part to destroy any misconceptions about vegans being wimpy with your physique and choice of terminology.

Rip: I love the term plant-strong™ as a good description and introduction. In my circles, the word vegan is polarizing with judgments that are not necessarily accurate. I want them to go to a 100 percent plant-based diet. Plant-strong is a great double entendre. Eat plants, be strong, and eating plants you're plant-strong and as certainly people should be. My problem with the word vegan is one can eat vegan but choose to eat unhealthy foods—white sugar, white flour, oils, soda, and fries.

Anne: Veganism with its ethical component for animals certainly doesn't absolve one of being ethically kind to one's own body. Vegan junk food may be part of a transition to healthier eating as part of the long-term journey.

There are inherent difficulties with any term once it's gained popularity. People give a word their own meaning without knowing the history. The word vegan has been around since 1944 when Donald Watson and friends coined the term and started The Vegan Society in England. One can read about it in their first newsletter, now available online. They developed the shorter word from vegetarian to reflect their unique humanitarian reasons for refusing all animal products. Donald acknowledged they were pioneers and the path would be difficult.

Freya: At that time, people thought veganism would be worse for health. Donald and his friends experienced individual improved health, but the research didn't exist. Trying to get countries back together after the war, governments were touting animal products as first-class protein.

As a vegetarian child in the 1940s and '50s, I thought it was good to eat eggs and cheese. I suffered terrible asthma. I began a transition to being vegan in 1959, completed in 1960. I understood the ethical side but was unsure about health implications. I became vegan, not knowing whether my health would suffer but convinced I would not be responsible for animal suffering. To my surprise, the asthma disappeared. It only returns if I indulge in vegan junk food.

Anne: Dad started promoting veganism in the 1950s and infused it with the pillars of ahimsa. Many people today throw the term vegan around as if it's only a diet. That's a big reason why "he" had to write *Powerful Vegan Messages*.

Rip: Toast to Jay! (Glasses clink.)

LeAnne: And Anne! (Clinks.)

Anne: Thank you. I feel like Dad and I are on a great adventure, but now I get to drive! We're driving to a destination of a vegan world despite all the detours. Important road signs point people in the right direction with issues such as America's health-care crisis, genetically modified organisms (GMOs), and environmental destruction. Sometimes we are in a blinding snowstorm with all the marketing and distribution of products for the traditional Standard American Diet, but I enjoy the scenic overlooks too. Shall we discuss some of those issues on the signs and what to do?

Tom: America's worsening health crisis is my biggest concern. Every day I see patients suffering from diet-related illnesses, and they have no idea they have diet-related illnesses. They have no concept of the power of diet or how to implement dietary change.

The elephant in the room—diet and lifestyle as a fundamental approach to disease prevention and treatment—is draped in a very effective invisibility cloak for everyone involved. We must uncover the basic truth that to improve personal health and the economics of medical care we must heed the cause of our illnesses. A combination of personal counseling, financial-system reimbursement, and public-health initiatives can bring to bear the same kind of changes that were implemented to lower the smoking rate.

Freya: Those are great points, Tom. I think happy social occasions are also important ways to uncloak the elephant. Potluck groups are important for learning how to eat better and in good company to share recipes and taste results. Have a speaker or a film to bring in the health information.

Social-action groups are important too, but it's good to make it easy to start simply; join a group as the first step in a big journey. We can each help society in different ways. For example, some people are good at cooking food; others are good at publicity that brings people in to try it.

Tom: To promote plant-based nutrition we must promote the basic medical information, but to affect societal change, we have to make healthy choices be thoughtless and effortless. It may sound cynical, but most people don't think about their food or how they eat and they don't want to. Choice is more a function of emotions, convenience, price, and ease. If we make healthy choices conform to those requirements, we will do great things on a societal level.

Jane: Information is what arms us and protects us. Availability of grains, vegetables, fruit, and beans to everyone is a whole other issue.

Freya: Or it's an adjunct necessity. Some communities only have the corner store with a limited selection of packaged foods. Packaged food is worse because it contains sugar and salt to make it taste like anything. People in these "food deserts" often don't have reliable transportation which enables going somewhere for fresh produce. People eat poorly for many reasons: lack of access to good quality food, lack of knowledge, lack of ability to prepare food, lack of time and inclination.

Anne: It's not just people in this or that community or economic class eating poorly; it's everywhere. Poor choices lead to poor finances and poor health. Good choices can make people rich in ways more valuable than money and possessions.

Tom: For our personal health and the associated economic difficulties, look at how so much of the population is diabetic or obese. It's like wearing cement shoes and walking deeper and deeper into the pool.

LeAnne: Based on his findings in *The China Study*, Dad says, "If everyone in America consumed a whole-food, plant-based diet, over seventy percent of all health care costs would go away."

Freya: Part of the problem is that the cost of things has gone up, such as housing and food. Tom, how do you think we will reach all of these different people in our country?

Tom: It's useful to start with professional groups to begin to recommend healthful diets. Ultimately that will have to translate to public health. A plant-based diet has to be tasty, easy, convenient, and cheap. For a lot of people with all they have to think about in life, food falls lower on their list of things they do thoughtfully. We have to make healthy food thoughtless so the masses can do it easily. We need to start with the leaders for America.

Deo: LeAnne, do you have a different opinion?

LeAnne: Tom and I both hope to create change. Tom is doing a wonderful job in his leadership of the nonprofit foundation. He is the one in our family who will most help to carry forward what my father started.

I work more with empowering individuals—students and teachers—creating learning experiences and curriculum for global change. I focus on poverty, schooling, and issues such as gender, class, and race.

Anne: Please tell us your story about how this relates to your becoming vegan. Many people would think you changed for health reasons, your father's influence.

LeAnne: I was still eating animal products when I joined the Peace Corps after college. I was in a rural area of the Dominican Republic working directly with impoverished families and their malnourished children. Near our village was a thousand-acre cattle farm that occupied much of the neighborhood, but only fed a small portion—those who could afford meat. The cattle had an abundant supply of water, but most of the locals had to walk a long way to the river and carry water—often contaminated—home in gallon jugs. I looked at this paradox from a humanitarian perspective and took a step toward reducing my consumption of animal-based foods.

Anne: Your work is so important to helping people understand this connection. People come to veganism for a number of reasons, and the personal stories each contain a powerful message. I understand you also came to veganism from an animal-rights perspective?

LeAnne: Yes, during that time another experience impacted my food choices. Next to my house was a neighbor's pasture where a goat lived. He often came to the fence to visit me. When I returned from work each day, the goat heard my motorcycle, ran to the fence, and waited for me. Then one day I came home and saw him dangling from the fence. His throat had been cut, and his blood was splattered across my yard. His eyes seemed to be following me. Those eyes were no longer smiling; they were pleading in deep pain, almost begging me to help. But I could not do anything.

Later that evening, my neighbors brought me a plate of goat meat, but I could not eat it. It was the meat of my friend the goat, and I kept recalling his pleading eyes. I stopped eating meat altogether.

Clint: Everyone should hear your story. People need to meet animals, not eat animals!

John: The single most important key to living joyfully with children is communication. Be clear about values. Even young kids can understand how to choose foods that make their bodies strong and healthy.

Clint: I'm eating all my veggies so I can grow strong and healthy!

John: A fine example, thank you, Clint. Many kids actually appreciate parents choosing to spend less money on things, so they can have more time to spend with their children. Some older children can benefit greatly when they are included in family deliberations about how to spend time and money.

Ocean: My parents valuing my ideas had a huge effect on the good choices I make today.

Freya: Kids can learn and be active by connecting with the earth and having a small vegetable garden. In the city, it can be on roofs, vertically up walls, on windowsills, or in pots on balconies. Growing plants is a magical experience for children. They need to see and understand their food options and from where food comes.

Clint: I want to grow my own vegetables.

Rip: You will enjoy it, Clint. Community gardens are great too. Many urban areas are finding ways to change abandoned lots into bountiful plant foods.

Clint: I also like picking out food at stores or farmers' fields.

Ocean: Community-supported agriculture (CSA) encourages farmers to grow organic food by having local people commit to purchasing the produce. We need to reconnect with our food from the farm to the table.

Clint: And enjoy time with kids in the kitchen making food!

Anne: That's a terrific idea. We don't all have to cook. People who like to cook should invite others to share in the fun or to teach neighborhood kids. It's not just "what's in it for me." Giving and sharing has a way of coming back to you.

Clint: I can help make muffins, green smoothies, oatmeal, pumpkin pies, and wraps. Things I make all by myself include cold herb tea and trail mix.

John: That's great! Most children have a natural desire to help others. Knowing they are making a positive contribution creates a sense of their worth that doesn't depend on consumerism. Some families volunteer at soup kitchens, food banks, or river or beach cleanups. Giving kids an option of forgoing a birthday present in order to donate to a nonprofit of their choice can be a good way to strengthen kids' self-esteem and generosity.

Freya: I volunteer at the local afterschool program in a community that has a lot of people who haven't experienced the bounty of wholesome plant foods. Kids clamor for their opportunity to work in the kitchen. Most Tuesday evenings we make a snack or meal for thirty people of all ages.

Anne: People who cook professionally also need to offer better options in restaurants and catering. Healthy, vegan, fast-food joints will be key because people balk at the time it takes to make something versus driving to a window. Sit-down meals are much better for our digestion and should also be encouraged.

Freya: AVS helps make culinary students aware of the need to cater to a growing vegan clientele. We host vegan dinners at the Academy of Culinary Arts at the Atlantic Cape Community College. It becomes part of their curriculum. AVS consults with the culinary school chef-educators, markets the event, and takes reservations for sixty-five people eight nights a year that are typically sold out. Vegans and nonvegans together enjoy vegan fare: appetizer, soup, salad, main dish, and dessert. The template for these events is being used increasingly throughout America. Sometimes we show a documentary film too.

Anne: Big films and little videos all help, right Clint?

Clint: My friends and I make videos. We help kids make good choices even when their parents don't like to cook. Our YouTube channel is *Kids! Teach Yourself to Cook.*

Ocean: Films and videos are ways to use technology for good purposes.

Anne: Communication is going to be key. Rip, how did you get involved with this work?

Rip: It started slowly with a gradual build up like getting water to boil. In 1987 I began eating this way after my parents got into it. By 2004 I was in completely when the guys at the fire station were all in, and we got media attention. I wrote my first book in 2006, and I've been at a rapid boil ever since.

Anne: I read part of your book while on a date for my third book. Now we are sitting here discussing how to work together.

Rip: What we all are doing is meaningful; it is real. The deeper we dive into this lifestyle, the more reasons we learn, including our health and kindness to animals. I'm getting more interested in the connection between diet and environment.

Ocean: The impact of what we eat doesn't just affect you or me. It impacts our food systems and our whole world. The science behind this is basic. I bet I can explain it so Clint can understand. It takes at least seven pounds of grain or soybeans to produce one pound of feedlot beef. Cows eat the grain, and some of it turns into meat, but some of it turns into the energy the cow burns to move and stay warm; some of it turns into manure, and some of it turns into hoof and hide and bones. So feeding grain or soy to cows is not very efficient. A lot of the earth's land used to be forest, and those forests have been cut down to create land on which to graze cattle or to grow food that is fed to cattle. Forests absorb carbon dioxide, whereas cows emit large amounts of methane, a powerful gas that has a huge impact on climate. Factory farms also cause water pollution and are linked to deforestation, species extinction, and many of our other leading environmental problems.

Clint: I get it. When we don't eat animals, we are kind to them and to the planet. We have more trees, pure water, more species of animals, and better weather.

Anne: Cows don't care whether people choose not to eat them for compassionate reasons or environmental reasons. All animals have a will to live.

Someone may travel a parallel highway to get to the vegan destination. I'm compelled by the compassionate path, but I also want good environment and health. Every part of the puzzle is important.

Clint: I like puzzles!

Anne: Yes, you are part of the puzzle of the United States and the world. If people feel small and insignificant, we have to empower them.

Rip: In five years there may be no recourse for the damage people have done: floods, droughts, polar ice-cap melt, methane gasses. We also read in this book that, according to Goodland and Anhang in "Livestock and Climate Change," in 2009, at least fifty-one percent of human-induced greenhouse gas comes from animals' lifecycle or the supply chain of getting them onto our plate. In 2006, it was said to be eighteen percent in "Livestock's Long Shadow." Goodland and Anhang reevaluated the information, adding in uncounted, overlooked, and misallocated emissions. It's become more imperative we don't consume all the precious resources: water, land, fossil fuels.

Ocean: If people want to think globally and act locally...well, you can't get a lot more local than the food on your plate. Reducing or eliminating meat consumption is one of the most powerful steps you can take. Food is one place where the same choices that are good for our bodies turn out to be good for our planet.

Anne: Some people, especially some vegans, are critical when you suggest reducing meat consumption as an option, as if it's okay to just reduce. They must keep the big picture in mind and keep the words in context. You don't say both options of reducing or eliminating meat are equally good, you say start with steps.

Most people reduce meat consumption before they eliminate it. This is a transition as people learn to select and prepare healthier vegan options. We have to help them continue on that path so they don't think it's enough to just reduce.

If someone thinks about the environment and its connection with animal exploitation, they may be open to learning the ethical points, which may help them become vegan. I generally require information from many reliable sources before being convinced of anything.

I'm sure I don't have to convince anyone to eat dessert.

Jane: May I help clear away the dinner plates?

Anne: Thank you, Jane. For dessert, we have my dad's favorite, a banana-split bar, prepared tonight by the Campbells.

Tom: Start with a banana that's been split lengthwise. Add a scoop or two of nondairy ice cream—here we use peeled frozen bananas whizzed in a food processor. Then add whatever you want on top. Ocean and Clint picked the fresh strawberries and blueberries this afternoon.

LeAnne: We also have toppings of maple syrup, slivered roasted nuts, minced fresh ginger—the hot ginger satisfies those who like to live dangerously. And Clint's favorite...

Clint: Raisins!

Tom: And we made Anne's favorite—crumbled Oatmeal Raisin Cookies from *Dating Vegans*.

Anne: Wow! This looks wonderful! The banana split should chill us out before I get Ocean heated up with the topic of GMOs. I was able to find all organic, mostly local ingredients for dinner. We aren't eating GMOs.

Most people don't realize that GMOs bring up an ethical question in addition to health and environmental issues.

Ocean, you have good ways of explaining GMOs.

Ocean: Unlike traditional crossbreeding or plant hybridization, in genetic-engineering, scientists splice together strands of DNA across species barriers. They may splice the genes from a virus or a bacteria or a fish into corn or soybeans or a tomato. The resultant creation is actually a new life form. Because it's alive, it will reproduce and impact life on this planet in perpetuity.

Anne: That raises ethical questions. It may become difficult to decipher what is from the animal kingdom versus the plant kingdom. Also it uses animal testing. Then there's a lack of labeling the GMO products, combined with big corporations deceiving the people.

Ocean: Monsanto and the biotechnology industry told the world—and a lot of people believed it—that their genetically engineered seeds are an answer to world hunger. They said their seeds would lead to crops that would produce bigger yields, be more resistant to drought, have higher nutritional content, and use fewer pesticides. So far, nothing Monsanto has brought to commercial scale has any of those attributes.

Mainly, we have received two things. First, many genetically engineered crops produce a toxin called *Bacillus thuringiensis* (Bt.) This means farmers don't have to spray insecticides any more because the plant is a living insecticide factory. If a susceptible bug eats any part of a Bt.-containing plant, its stomach splits open, and it dies. Bt. is considered relatively harmless to humans. It's been used in organic agriculture for a long time. But I don't know anybody who wants to sit down and drink the stuff. Putting something on the outside of a plant in judicious amounts is completely different from embedding it in every cell of the plant. Bt. crops contain an insecticide you can never wash off.

Now we're consuming massive amounts of this toxin. It's true that the farmers who grow Bt. crops don't have to spray insecticides on their fields any more. These crops are now literally registered with the EPA as insecticides.

Secondly, we have another class of genetically engineered crops that are resistant to specific herbicides—most commonly Roundup®, which is Monsanto's proprietary herbicide. The active ingredient in Roundup is glyphosate. Farmers who plant Roundup Ready crops can spray Roundup over their entire field. The weeds die, and the genetically engineered crops remain standing. But we're starting to see a new crop of superweeds develop that are resistant to Roundup. Chemical companies are coming up with new ideas for even worse weapons. Don't get me started talking about the concept of "agent-orange corn."

We're spraying massive amounts of toxic herbicides on our fields. These chemicals are ending up polluting our rivers and groundwater. Roundup is now believed to be found in the body of every human being on Earth. We don't know conclusively what the health impacts of all this Bt. and Roundup really are. There have been no long-term studies conducted on humans. The reality is that we are human experimental tests, and no one is monitoring the experiment.

Anne: It doesn't matter which reason one uses to object to GMOs, they are wrong for personal health, for the broader environmental concerns as these companies poison the land and destroy heirloom plants, or for the human and nonhuman animals involved in the experiment. The more we work together, the more people will know, and the reasons back each other up.

Jane: Again, information is what arms us and protects us!

LeAnne: We can best address the GMO problem by encouraging people to buy local, organic food. Promoting these whole plant foods is an important part of our families' work.

Now let's talk more about another aspect that all of us do with our families' missions. John, what's your perspective on working cross-generationally?

John: The opportunity to work with people of differing ages keeps teaching me that each of our varying viewpoints is needed. Our different skill sets are important and have a role to play. Our society tends to segregate people according to their ages. It starts early, in schools where students are placed in classes with children the same age and deprived of the opportunity to learn from those who are older and younger. The same kind of segregation is in retirement communities, which are only open to those past a certain age. This is a great loss. We need each other; we need to interact and engage with others who are at different stages of life, who have their own distinct cultural experiences and perspectives. It can be challenging, but what experience worth having isn't? That's how we grow. That's how we remain open-minded.

Anne: We must work cross-generationally to find better ways to communicate with everyone. Although we are in an age of instant information, we are also bombarded by corporate greed marketing, status quo, neighbor envy, hot dog heritage, grandma's meatloaf, and societal norms. If a slaughterhouse video comes by, it isn't taken to be the real thing. Maybe it's akin to a video game or another channel of movie violence; it's too easy to change channels and turn it off. People buy plastic-wrapped pieces of meat at the supermarket as if it grew there. They ignore the ingredient list in packaged goods, or may I call them packaged bads.

When people understand the issues, some get angry at others who do not know. I frequently ask, "Remember who you were before you became vegan? Were you not a kind, compassionate person deserving of being loved?" I remind people to give someone else that chance to learn. Most people need to hear a message from multiple sources before embracing change. That's also the beauty of working cross-generationally to reach everyone.

John, what hope do you have for the next generation in the general population to become vegan or travel towards it?

John: When I wrote *Diet for a New America* in the late 1980s, the word vegan was unfamiliar to most Americans. Now we have an increasing number of cultural icons—including Bill Clinton and Al Gore and many famous entertainers and world class athletes—becoming vegan. Vegan is becoming cool. It's becoming sexy. It's becoming more and more attractive to young people.

Rip: Some athletes know eating this way can actually give you the edge—and it's legal. We have a strong collection of athletes at this table. We have numerous marathon accomplishers: John, Ocean, Tom, Anne, Jane, and me. Ocean ran his first marathon at age ten. Jane swam at the Olympic trials. Anne was a national champion in beach wrestling. John, Deo, and Freya are fitter than many people half their age, and they enjoy pursuits from dancing to hiking.

Anne: And Rip was a world-class triathlete, and his dad was an Olympic gold medalist in rowing. I love that Howard Lyman called your dad "the greatest upstream rower there has ever been" in an interview with Joe Connelly of *VegNews*. His accomplishments are impressive. I'm also impressed by John's personal story about the important things in life.

John: I grew up in a wealthy family. We lived in an expensive home with an ice-cream-cone-shaped swimming pool. At twenty-one, I left behind that way of life and the money it represented, making it clear in both my words and actions that I did not want to depend on my father's financial achievements nor follow in his footsteps.

Deo and I built our cabin in 1969 on a Canadian island. Our simple and rustic dwelling of 320 square feet was located deep in a cedar forest. When I remember the ten years we lived there, I feel fondness and gratitude, for it was the first time in my life I ever felt truly at home.

During those years, I sometimes visited my parents. My father said something to me that I will always remember. "What bothers me the most about you is that you are the only person I've met who can't be bought. Everyone else has their price, except you." I took this as a compliment, although I'm not at all sure he intended it that way.

LeAnne: Definitely a compliment.

John: Smaller homes free up our time and energy. With lower housing costs and less house to clean and maintain, we can spend more time with our children, our friends, and our partners. We have more time to write poems, paint pictures, plant gardens, bake bread, play tennis, make love, or volunteer. Anne, I understand you are into cabin life?

Anne: I had a tough section of my personal history after which I decided to only rely on myself for shelter and happiness. Since 2005 I've had my little piece of paradise, a ten-by-twelve-foot board-and-batten cabin with a ten-by-six loft. I'm on ten acres of wooded hillside in western New York on the first big elevation south of Lake Erie—distant lake-view property.

LeAnne: It sounds beautiful. Where do guests stay? A tent on your land or a motel in town?

Anne: Guests are why I'm building a second cabin. The big cabin is a lesson in sociology, budgeting, pain, and patience. I'm building it out of what I can afford—thus no mortgage. Most of the work I do myself or with the help of friends. I pay people to do things such as plumbing and electrical. I'm decent at masonry and carpentry. I've learned from mentors or trial-and-error. The cabin is timber-frame, board-and-batten, saltbox-shape, shotgun-style on a stone walkout basement with concrete poured by hand, a 768-square-foot cabin on a sixteen-by-twenty-four footprint. It's more than I need, but there's a local ordinance requiring a 760-square-foot minimum. The little cabin is really the outhouse: a shed with composting toilet.

Clint: We live in Clint's cabin while we build Mom's cabin.

Anne: The cabin gives me the freedom to choose what I want to do in life. It's a glorified storage shed, luxury camping, and a springboard for adventures.

Our next party will be at my writer's cabin. For this dinner party, I wanted everyone to come to the AVS headquarters so you could appreciate what Dad built, which may help us figure out how to work together.

Rip: You seem to be at AVS more than your cabin. How is that?

Anne: People started to tell me that my inheritance—like it or not—would be AVS. I'm a creative type more than an office person. I like working for AVS—inspiring, educating, and promoting positive change—but there are days it's overwhelming. I wrestle with understanding what fuels me, creating a sense of balance in my life, and how to further the vegan message to best reach everyone. I treasure my father's words and wisdom. Occasionally I yell into the wind for his guidance or get lost in thought among the AVS archives. Sometimes I pray for the day we can go out of business because everyone becomes vegan and we are no longer needed to do this work.

Freya is a terrific resource, and we love working together. Yet sometimes I feel alone like a unique burden was put on me by my ancestors. Maybe that feeling helps me understand how alone people say they feel when they first become vegan opposing their animal-based heritage. That's why I reached out to those of you who can cherish the years of truly working together with your parents on our mission. You re-energize me.

Clint: Mom, I will help you.

Anne: Thank you, Clint. (Hug.) He reminds me that innocence and compassion are inherent in children. Clint at age two ran around saying, "Don't hurt cows." and "Pigs are my friends."

Clint: I tell people to be kind to cows and pigs. Don't forget chickens and rabbits and ducks and goats and turkeys and frogs and fish and everybody!

Ocean: My boys remind me of the future of the world too. So Clint, in the future will people put animals in factory farms, and then kill and eat them?

Clint: No! They should stop being mean to animals. Animals get hurt and die when people want to eat them, and kids learn to hurt animals too. People don't know what they are doing. Animals want to live and play.

Ocean: We must teach them about living with respect for life. Do you like writing your column for *American Vegan* ?

Clint: Yes. I'm vegan. I eat plants. People should not eat animals or drink their milk or use any animal. I want the world to be happy.

Anne: He's had help typing, but it's essentially his ideas. I find I'm more like my dad every day; I grew up on the pages of *Ahimsa* magazine.

Ocean: I remember Clint's photo eating blueberries in *American Vegan*. May we finish these blueberries?

Clint: Yes, let's eat them. Ocean, I want you to pick blueberries with me again soon.

Ocean: I'd love to. Picking organic local blueberries is high on my list of fun!

Anne: And top of my list of fun is helping people go vegan!

Clint: Me too. Along with puzzles!

Freya: Thank you all for joining us. This has been a lovely evening. We have all enjoyed this time together. Let's take a walk through the woods and watch the sun set across the field.

Anne: Envisioning a compassionate world together.

*   *   *

Have you solved the puzzle of *Powerful Vegan Messages*? How will you apply what you read to your life and your role in the world?

*   *   *

Be part of the Vegan Generation[3] campaign. The superscript "3" indicates the ripple effect of one's actions. If you are not vegan yet, learn about veganism from at least three different sources. *Powerful Vegan Messages* lists many other resources. If you are a vegan, think of at least three ways to share knowledge.

For ideas, reflect upon the stories you've read, see the Vegan Generation[3] campaign at AmericanVegan.org, or contact AVS.

About the Authors

H. Jay Dinshah (1933-2000) was a motivational speaker, lifelong vegetarian, vegan since 1957, founder of American Vegan Society in 1960, editor of *Ahimsa* magazine, and president of AVS for forty years. Jay was especially skilled at planning conferences and encouraging people to get involved.

After touring a slaughterhouse in 1957, he vowed to work every day until all the slaughterhouses are closed. Jay lived every moment in tireless service to the cause of helping animals by educating people. His tools of choice were veganism and ahimsa. He believed in the powers of cooperation, nonviolent action, and communication.

He married his pen pal Freya who worked alongside him for forty years and continues as AVS president today. Their two children are Daniel and Anne.

Organizational Leadership: In addition to leading American Vegan Society, Jay also was a cofounder of North American Vegetarian Society (NAVS) in 1974, the first NAVS president 1974-1979, and editor of *Vegetarian Voice* 1974-1980. At various times he worked for American Natural Hygiene Society (now National Health Association) including as acting executive director in 1983. He was also the first president of Vegetarian Union of North America (VUNA) 1987-1989. Jay was on the International Vegetarian Union (IVU) Executive Committee as international council member 1967-1984 and executive vice-president 1971-1984.

Speaking: Jay lectured throughout his adult life, encouraging people with his powerful vegan message. He spoke in person in two dozen countries on five continents. Videos of his talks are available on the YouTube channel *Powerful Vegan Messages*.

Books: Some of Jay's lectures from the 1960s are compiled in *Health Can Be Harmless. Song of India* chronicles four months of his lecture tour in 1967-1968. He edited *Here's Harmlessness: An Anthology of Ahimsa.* His best known book was *Out of the Jungle: The Way of Dynamic Harmlessness*, which provided much of the framework for *Powerful Vegan Messages.* Jay's books and archived issues of *Ahimsa* are available from AVS.

Awards: Jay was honored as a vice president of The Vegan Society (U.K.), inducted into the Vegetarian Hall of Fame in 1993, and awarded Vegetarian of the Year 1996 (International) from The Vegetarian Society (India). Jay received posthumously the IVU Mankar Memorial Award in 2000. *Ahimsa* #41-4 commemorates his life and work.

Anne Dinshah is the daughter of Jay and Freya Dinshah, a lifelong vegan, vice-president of American Vegan Society (AVS), managing editor of *American Vegan* magazine, and a motivational speaker. She has a BA degree in American studies from the University of Notre Dame and an MEd degree in sport administration from the University of Texas. Her career as a rowing coach takes her to a variety of locations throughout the United States where she enjoys socializing with people.

Anne credits Freya with instilling in her a love of cooking. She credits Jay for inspiring a love of speaking to large audiences. Anne and her son Clint enjoy traveling and exercising together.

Speaking: Invite Anne to speak in person by contacting the American Vegan Society. Her videos are available on YouTube at Powerful Vegan Messages and other channels.

Books: *Healthy Hearty Helpings* (1999); *The 4-Ingredient Vegan* (2010) coauthored for Maribeth Abrams; *Dating Vegans: Recipes for Relationships* (2012); and *Apples, Bean Dip, and Carrot Cake: Kids! Teach Yourself to Cook* (2012) coauthored with Freya Dinshah.

American Vegan Society

Ahimsa lights the way.

American Vegan Society (AVS) is a 501(c)(3) nonprofit organization that promotes, supports, and explores a compassionate, healthful, and sustainable lifestyle. The diet is entirely plant-sourced, varied, and abundant. For ethical, health, environmental, and other reasons, we reject all animal products in food, clothing, and commodities. We also refuse to exploit animals for sport, entertainment, and experimentation.

AVS is guided by the doctrines of reverence for life and ahimsa with taking positive action for social change. AVS provides community and friendship to those following and learning about this way of living.

Tax-deductible donations support outreach at public events with books, literature, and speaking; annual Garden Party; website; video productions; lecture tours; hosting gourmet vegan dinners; responding to inquiries via phone, email, fax, and in person; cooking classes; conferences; and book publications. AVS publishes the magazine *American Vegan* (2001 to present), formerly *Ahimsa* (1960-2000). Become a member.

Jay enjoyed freely giving away information. However, it is the memberships and contributions of both time and money from members that allow the organization to continue supplying information to help more people become vegan. Your support helps us achieve more goals.

What are your skills and assets? How can you express your love of animals? How important is the future of the world? What is the best way to demonstrate your values? Get ideas and learn about American Vegan Society at AmericanVegan.org.

Books Published by AVS

Apples, Bean Dip, and Carrot Cake: Kids! Teach Yourself to Cook by Anne and Freya Dinshah

Compassion: The Ultimate Ethic by Victoria Moran

Dating Vegans: Recipes for Relationships by Anne Dinshah

Health Can Be Harmless by H. Jay Dinshah

Healthy Hearty Helpings by Anne Dinshah

Here's Harmlessness: An Anthology of Ahimsa edited by H. Jay Dinshah

Powerful Vegan Messages: Out of the Jungle for the Next Generation by H. Jay Dinshah and Anne Dinshah

Song of India by H. Jay Dinshah

The Vegan Kitchen by Freya Dinshah

Books may be purchased individually at retail price. AVS members get twenty percent off all books sold by AVS. All AVS publications are available as a mixed case with a minimum of ten books for fifty percent off the retail price.

For more information contact:

AVS, 56 Dinshah Lane, PO Box 369, Malaga NJ 08328 USA
Phone 856-694-2887   Fax 856-694-2288
AmericanVegan.org

"Someone must speak for reason, compassion, and hope—and this book will be a powerful voice for that cause."

—Dr. Michael Klaper